The Lotus and the Pool

The Lotus and the Pool

How to Create
Your Own Career

Hilda Lee Dail

Shambhala
Boston & Shaftesbury 1989

Shambhala Publications, Inc.
Horticultural Hall
300 Massachusetts Avenue
Boston, Massachusetts 02115

Shambhala Publications, Inc.
The Old School House
The Courtyard, Bell Street
Shaftesbury, Dorset SP7 8BP

9 8 7 6 5 4 3 2 1

First Shambhala Edition
Printed in the United States of America on acid-free paper.

Distributed in the United States by Random House and in Canada by Random House of Canada Ltd. Distributed in the United Kingdom by Element Books, Ltd.

Dail, Hilda Lee, 1923 –
    The lotus and the pool : how to create your own career / Hilda Lee
Dail. — 1st ed.
        p. cm.
    Bibliography: p.
    ISBN 0-87773-478-X
    1. Vocational guidance.   2. Career development.   3. Creative
ability.   I. Title.
HF5381.D144   1989   88-35165
650.1—dc19   CIP

To Roderick,

my companion and mentor for forty-eight years,

who accepted me when I was chaotic,

celebrated me when I was creative,

and stood by me in the struggles in between;

and to our children, Jan and Rick,

who are now my partners in exciting enterprises.

To my clients

for high moments of mutual affirmation.

❀ Contents

✿ Acknowledgments

I am deeply grateful to my associate, Ottie H. Sonen, M.A., D.T.R., of Helion Counseling, P.A. in Oak Ridge, New Jersey, who referred her daughter, Linda Barton, to me as a client. Linda lives in San Francisco and came to Myrtle Beach, South Carolina, to work intensely with me for a few days. Here she shared a cabin at the Meher Spiritual Center with Kendra Crossen, an editor at Shambhala Publications. This led to Kendra's discovery of *The Lotus and the Pool*, which Linda was reading. Thus through this chain of events the second, revised edition came about. This remarkable example of networking is implicit in the principles used throughout the book. I acknowledge with gratitude my debt to Ottie, Linda, and Kendra, who know who I am and affirm me to keep my message alive.

The completion of the task could never have been accomplished without my dedicated volunteer friend, Sue Ellis, a retired school counselor from Columbus, Ohio, recently moved to Myrtle Beach. She spent many hours typing, checking, and correcting the manuscript—all without pay. A truly remarkable gift.

The new section about dreams was made possible by my recent clients in Myrtle Beach. They provided dream material in addition to the information required in the original training design in *The Lotus and the Pool*. Working with dreams has enriched the career development process and kept me growing in my concept of the relationship of symbols in dreams to the mythic self and to creativity.

Finally, I am grateful to the following publishers for permission to reprint excerpts:

Excerpt from "Little Gidding," in *Four Quartets* by T.S. Eliot, from *Collected Poems 1909–1962*, copyright 1936 by Harcourt Brace Jovanovich, Inc.; copyright © 1963, 1964 by T.S. Eliot. Reprinted by permission of Harcourt Brace Jovanovich, Inc.

Excerpt from "Two Tramps in Mud Time," by Robert Frost, in *Complete Poems of Robert Frost*, copyright 1916, 1923, 1928, 1930,

✿ Preface

A community which allows unemployed members to exist within it will perish because of them. It will be well, therefore, if every member receives a definite task to perform for the community, that he may know in hours of doubt that he, too, is not useless and unusable.
—Dietrich Bonhoeffer, *Life Together*

In my work as a development consultant, I focus the center of my being on the central core of the person sitting in front of me. Together we face the fear, chaos, inertia, conflict, confusion—whatever the state is. We embrace it, plunge into it. For here is where re-creation will begin.

Often, at the beginning of our work together, I ask the client to draw a symbol of who he or she is. One man, whom I will call Henry, said, "I can't visualize a symbol. All I see is a dark murky pool."

"All right, experience the murkiness. Dip down into the pool. What do you think it is?" I asked.

Suddenly he began to weep. "It concerns my father," he explained.

"What about your father?"

"He died when I was three years old. I don't remember him. Every time I got to this place in my therapy, I would bog down. I couldn't go on. I can't deal with it."

"So you are angry with your father. He left you," I replied. "He deserted you by dying before you were old enough to look after yourself. Experience your anger. It's OK. You deserve to have a father. You need a father. Stay with this feeling a moment. Let go."

"I feel guilty. As if I were responsible for my father's death," he murmured.

"Well, that is natural," I answered. "Children usually feel guilty when their parents are sick or in trouble, and when they die. They participate in the event but are not able to make knowledgeable decisions. Now that you are an adult, you know that as a three-year-old child you couldn't possibly be responsible for your father's death.

"Close your eyes and look again at the deep pool," I continued. "Is there anything else there that symbolizes what you *can* be now? Take even a fragment of an object that comes to you. Don't refuse it."

We were silent together for a while. Then he whispered: "I saw a half-formed flower, just for a moment."

"Henry," I said quietly, "your father left a deposit with you— strength, imagination, perseverance, all the qualities that have brought you this far. He gave them to you when you were born. This is your heritage.

"Be like that flower—a lotus. It is perfect beauty floating on top of a murky pool. Its tendrils reach down to the depths where there is food for growth."

We were silent again. After a while, Henry opened his eyes, and his face was radiant. Energy filled the room. The creativity process has begun.

Since then, Henry has accepted the fact that his job in the company where he had worked for thirty five years has been abolished. This fact, which was part of his dark pool, has been transformed into the opportunity to take a position in a university, where he can get free tuition and begin working toward a degree in a new field. Henry has created a new career.

In reflecting on the incident, I knew I had discovered something very important for creativity and career development. The lotus flower is an ancient symbol in the Hindu and Buddhist traditions. It will not grow in clear pools; its environment is always murky water with a lot of muck and gunk at the bottom. With its roots in this chaotic medium, the beautiful flower—a symbol of perfection—is formed.

Henry Brooks Adams, a nineteenth-century philosopher and historian, said, "Chaos often breeds life." In James Weldon Johnson's epic poem, "The Creation," God saw chaos and cried out, "I'll make me a world."

This book shows you how you can use the creative process to take charge of your life, create your own career, out of your own chaos, and learn the creativity "secrets" of artists, poets, and inventors.

It is a guidebook for you. Use it if your job is disappointing or disappearing. Use it if your will to win diminished or even disappeared after you walked your first hundred miles looking for work, after your so-called education was completed. If your wounded pride, battered image, blistered feet, uncertain smile, and fear that nobody wants you around push you to despair and you experience chaos, you are an excellent candidate for the creative process. In fact, you are already in the first stage of creativity. This book will help you harness your creative force, but first you must be willing to stop blaming:

The economy
The tight job market
Your boss, who boxes you in
Your company, which has few opportunities for women, or
    minorities, or white males
Your ill-chosen college major
Your lack of paid work experience (all those years of doing
    only volunteer work while you reared your family or went
    to school)
Your appearance
The "over" syndrome (overage, overexperienced,
    overpriced)
The "under" syndrome (underage, etc.)
Your sexual orientation
Your family
Your race or ancestry
Your geographic location
Your horoscope and biorhythm
The personnel people who won't let you past them to the
    president of your chosen company

You have exhausted your blame list. The time has come for you to dare to participate in the work of the gods—to create a new world for yourself! Come with me *through* chaos. You will learn to integrate your past with the present and to see the implications for the future. James Joyce expressed this idea poetically when he wrote:

Hold to the here, through which all future plunges to the past...We walk through ourselves, meeting robbers, ghosts, giants, old men, young men, wives, widows, brothers in love. But always meeting ourselves.[1]

Out of the chaos experienced by the hundreds of job seekers, career changers, underachievers, and unemployed or undirected individuals who have been my clients over the past fourteen years, a winning formula has emerged. This book tells you how to apply it to your situation.

The model for this formula emerged from a design that I first used in 1961 to train writers in India. I did not want to impose a sterile "how to" technique from which they would try to write like Americans. I wanted, instead, to expose them to the creativity process, with which they could discover their own symbols and metaphors, growing out of their own heritage and developing their individual form, style, and content, suited to their specific audience. So I wrote ten lectures that embodied the ten steps of creativity based on the symbols in the world's creation myths. The techniques these lectures described helped my Indian students learn how to write, discovering their own ways to communicate.

I redesigned these lectures in 1977 in a writing course for managers I taught at the American Management Association (AMA) in New York City. Top corporate executives and recently promoted "hard hats" from a power company, along with women struggling up the success ladder, used the same ten steps to learn to be good business writers and communicators.

I prepared the material for the AMA course at the same time I was doing career counseling. Gradually I sensed that the process I was using to train people to communicate effectively in their business environment contained the same elements that I was employing to guide my career counseling clients. I was combining the knowledge from my many years of experience in creative communications with the skills I had recently learned from my special training in psychology and career development.

○ **Why Is This a Superior Method?**

To my knowledge, no one else has written a book explicitly connecting career development with the process of creativity emerging from the symbols implicit in the creation myths, and furnishing documentation of how this holistic[2] approach can be used by individuals caught in a career crisis. Most of the literature has emphasized coping techniques. Coping, however, is a reversion of creativity. And some books offer a rather glib description of how to *survive* in the jungle of the job market.

Career development built on the principles of creativity rather than coping or survival, on the other hand, offers an in-depth existential framework in which you can flourish. Not only can you find a solution to the career problem you face, you can create an *exquisite* way of transforming your total life. You can tap into the resources of your "mythic self" that connect with the universal creation myths, and find energy for experiencing the truth about your "being" as well as your "doing." With this method you discover the transcendent dimensions in human development.

This book has come into being over a span of fourteen years. It is a distillation of material from thousands of hours of counseling people in relation to their careers. Everything in it has been observed by me personally. All the stories are true—right out of my files. (The names have been changed, and some details have been rearranged to protect the identities of my clients.) I have credited the sources and ideas I have drawn from other persons in the fields of psychology, creativity, and career development.

This book has been written with you, the individual job seeker or career changer, in mind. I speak directly as one who has felt all the pangs of early life confusion, middle-aged blurred identity, intermittent misdirected energy, anger and anxiety from losing my job in my mid-fifties, and finally a satisfying syntheses. I *know* the process I offer you works because I have proved it myself. I have seen it work for my thousands of clients. Now I give it to *you*, with confidence that it is connected with the Universal Source, where Creator and creature are one, and where career grows from this existential center.

○ **Who Influenced Me?**

In career development: I am indebted to the forerunners of the career development field (credited in the text). I was trained personally by Bernard Haldane, one of the career counseling pioneers. He was one of my consultants when I developed a national career development program for the National Board, YWCA.[3] I have taken Richard Bolles' special training for professional counselors. My special advisor and mentor during the formation of my own consulting business and during the writing of this book was Ralph Minker, a Washington, D.C., career counselor.

I was influenced by Eli Ginzberg's theories, developed in the early 1950s and significantly revised in 1972, in which he emphasized the stages of development. I have also studied John Holland's work on personality types and the process of matching environments with certain types. I then modified it through my use of the Myers-Briggs Personality Type Indicator. However, this test was developed from general concepts derived from Carl Gustav Jung, (who, I suspect, also influenced Holland). Donald Super's formulation, stressing the dynamic, flexible nature of self-development, has also influenced me. (I am aware that Super was building on Bueler's pioneer work in developmental psychology done in the 1930s.)

I have included in my considerations Abraham Brill's psychoanalytic approach, which makes use of the unconscious and sublimation, allowing for the inclusion of emotion and the integration of the pleasure principle and the reality principle. And I have also considered Theodore Caplow's idea of the importance of the sociological-situational elements of one's environment on career development. However, the major emphasis in my process is on the *inner* development of the individual.

In psychology: The titles in the bibliography all have had some influence on me. In the field of psychology, my prime influence has been Jung, along with his disciple Alberto Assagioli; both give a place in their systems for the mystical aspect of the personality. The theories of Jung, with their emphasis on myth, symbol, and the universal consciousness, have furnished the basic framework for my process. Assagiolo, who further developed Jung's ideas into a formula called Psychosynthesis, provided a counseling system, in which I have been trained by Martha Crampton and Harry Sloan, who studied with Assagioli. Some of my exercises come from this particular discipline.

I have been an experimenter in Gestalt therapy methods, having gone to Esalen Institute first in 1968 and then in the 1970s when I met Fritz Perls. I also explored Transactional Analysis (TA) and I have included both Gestalt and TA in my work.

Freud, the dear old father, was also part of my preparation. His writing focusing on the creativity process (see Bibliography) was particularly relevant.

In addition, I am a graduate of est (Erhard Seminars Training). The graduate seminars "About the Body" and "Self-Expression"

stimulated some of my innovations in connection with the idea that
the ultimate symbol of reality is the body. They also influenced my
concept that a person's career evolves from experiencing the self,
using the body as the instrument through which this reality is
expressed, and for which the world will reward according to how
it meets society's needs.

The est "About Money" seminar strengthened my ability to connect the idea of money more directly in my own fee structure. It
also helped me encourage clients to integrate the symbol of money into the reality of the self to meet their own economic goals. The
"Communication" workshop so closely follows the principles of
creativity that I wrote the following paragraph as a quote for their
use:

> In my work as a psychologist, specializing in career development,
> people come to me when their lives have fallen apart. The Com-
> munication workshop heightened my awareness that I can
> empower them to experience their chaos as the first step in creat-
> ing a new life. Our bodies become metaphors through which the
> recreating energy flows. In these moments of mutual joy the gap
> between client and consultant disappears, and we both
> experience a leap toward solving the problem.

Existential concepts have found their way into my thinking, too.
Albert Camus and Jean-Paul Sartre lured me out of my childish,
romantic ideas of human nature. Their ideas helped me to embrace
the "nothingness" that I was struggling with in the late 1950s and
60s.

My consulting psychiatrist, Dr. Ralph Burk Dawson, whose special field of interest is psychoanalytical and analytical existentialism, guided me for many years as I explored my own psyche while
formulating a workable concept relating to career development.

Rollo May's works have spanned for me the space separating philosophy, theology, and psychology. His writings relating to creativity especially have had an influence on me, including *Man's Search
for Meaning* and *Courage to Create*.

A year spent in graduate study at Columbia University included work in developmental psychology, especially adult development, psychology of social change, and group dynamics (T-group
method). There I also studied Abraham Maslow's theory of the hier-
archy of needs, which influenced me in guiding clients to build
careers around their particular needs.

I took National Training Laboratory (NTL) in 1968, focusing on Community Development. This emphasis helped me to see the individual client always within the context of the environment. From Edgar Schein and Warren Bennis, among others, I learned about group development methods, which I have appropriated in the many seminars and workshops I have conducted.

Theodore Reik's *Listening with the Third Ear*, which I read in the early 1950s, profoundly impressed me. I liked the way Reik the psychoanalyst connected what he was doing in his work to his own inner development. Some of his ideas became a part of the body of knowledge out of which I developed my own way of guiding people. Concurrent with writing this book, I dealt with my own creation myth by recording my dreams and nightmares. This material probably grew unconsciously from the same kind of need Reik described.

My early exposure to Karen Horney's *Feminine Psychology*, followed by my reading Irene Claremont de Castillijo's *Knowing Woman* and Jean Baker Miller's *Toward a New Psychology of Women*, made me aware of the special concerns related to counseling women in a society still greatly influenced by sexism.

I have read most of the relatively large body of "how to" books for women, addressed to the particular problems of "making it" in a man's world. (See Bibliography.) They have a special place in the career development field. Even though I consider myself a vibrant part of the feminist movement and have a great number of women clients, I have chosen to focus here on the human being as an individual who is both male and female; to go a step *beyond* the battle of the sexes and explore the universal dimensions within both sexes that provide a climate for developing mutual affirmation.

In creativity: In summer 1955 I bought my first copy of *The Creative Process*, edited by Brewster Ghiselin. I remember sitting in the Mall at Central Park, waiting for the Goldman Band to play one of their free concerts and reading the book. Ghiselin's ideas then were as electrifying to me as was the *Bolero* the band later played. I read and reread his accounts of how famous artists, scientists, writers, composers, and inventors of all kinds got their ideas, inspiration, and energy to create. The concept took hold of me. At last I had found out that I wasn't necessarily inept just because I had to struggle so much to accomplish any task that called for investment of my self. That book literally opened up a new world to me. I took it with me to India in 1960, and it has become the lodestone around which I have set a number of other jewels of ideas. I am now on my third copy.

In *Creativity, the Magic Synthesis*, Silvano Arietti pulls together the major theories of creativity and offers a psychological analysis. Even though its textbook style is rather ponderous, I found validation in the book for many of the ideas and exercises I had already incorporated in my career development process.

Joseph Zinker's *Creative Process in Gestalt Therapy* shows how therapists experience creativity, as well as how their clients experience it. I agree with Zinker's premise that all of life is creative, and that working with a client is itself an experience in creativity.

I have absorbed much of the literature concerning the use of dreams as indicators of how the subconscious breaks through to tell us the truth about where we are in our development. I include specific assignments for reporting dreams in the process I use with clients. Some of the material I have used is from authors already mentioned. Two specific books that have influenced me recently are *Creative Dreaming* by Patricia Garfield and *The Dream Makers* by Richard Corriere and Joseph Hart.

Toward a world view: Since I have worked in the Eastern cultures, as well as here in the West, I needed to formulate a working model that would span cultural and geographical distances. Even though it is impossible to name all my influences in this broad area, I want to pay a special tribute to those Western writers who pointed the way toward the East for me—Joseph Campbell, Alan Watts, and Paul Tillich.

Joseph Campbell's *Myths to Live By, The Flight of the Wild Gander,* and *Hero with a Thousand Faces*, as well as two of his seminars that I attended in 1978, sharpened my awareness of the universality of myths as a way of knowing. His focus on the Greek myths was especially stimulating to me. Since then, Bill Moyers has done the extraordinary television series with Campbell, *The Power of Myth*, which subsequently spawned the book of the same name.

Alan Watts, especially with his books *Nature, Man and Woman*; *Psychotherapy East and West*, and *The Way of Zen*, excited me and lured me into new, multidimensional experiences.

But it was Paul Tillich, the existential theologian, who gave me a basis of hope as a Westerner, built on his ideas in *Courage to Be*. I have read his entire writings, and he has become the one theologian who makes sense to me. I consider him my spiritual father. Tillich's concept of God as Ground of Being; his inclusion of the Greek strain into Christian theology; his definition of faith as the asking of the ultimate question rather than getting the answer (in *The Dynamics of Faith*); his method of correlation as a way of doing theology (in *Systematic Theology*, Volumes 1–3), his ability to speak directly to the human condition, presented in *Shaking of the Foundations* and *The New Being*; his openness to building a bridge from Western Christianity to the Eastern religions, thus giving me a basis for daring to explore the possibility of a transcultural experience as a foundation for evolving a universal philosophy of career development—all these dimensions make him a giant. He was a giant who dared to speak to artists, psychologists, theologians, and ordinary people like me who could no longer embrace the "way of faith" they were given as children. Hannah Tillich's book, published after her husband's death and revealing their personal life, has only made his ideas more relevant to me, rather than diminishing his image. Paul Tillich's friend Rollo May, who wrote a touching tribute, *Paulus*, also added new understanding for me of why Tillich's kind of existentialism is such a pertinent way to *look* at life philosophically and *experience* it simultaneously.

Even though I am familiar with the basic tenets of classical Hinduism, Buddhism, Islam, Sufism, and some of the African and American Indian spiritual traditions, plus a few gleanings from modern mysticism (such as the teachings of Avatar Meher Baba), as well as the Judeo-Christian tradition, I have been influenced more directly by contemporary writers in the fields of consciousness and science, including Pir Vilayat Inayat Khan, Lyall Watson, Karl Pribram, David Spangler, Reb Zalman Schacter-Shalomi, Itzhak Bentov, Charles Muses, Frijof Capra, and Jean Houston. In the section entitled "Recalling the Creation Myths" at the end of each chapter in Part Two of this book, I indicate how I relate these ideas to the creation myths.

The creation myths: Using the creation myths is an effort to bring all of these streams into one river, to give you a synthesis or framework to tap into the universal energy as you create your own career. The world's creation myths offer a recurring theme, a basic pattern of "being" from which "doing" evolves.

In his book *Creation Myths* David Maclagan brought these myths together from many sources. Some of these myths are more fully developed than others; some are mere fragments. All originated in a preliterate society and deal with supernatural beings as primordial types in a primitive view of the world.

Myths continue to fascinate us because they persist in giving us clues for answering the basic existential questions of life. They all attempt to bring the unknown into relation with the known. Specifically, the creation myths ask, "How do things come to be?"

Because of the symbolic nature of myths, their meanings are to be understood not literally, but metaphorically. As Jung stated, myths contain "archaic psychic components which have entered the individual psyche without any direct line of tradition."[4] This idea helps to explain the continued fascination for exploring mythic reality as clues for understanding one's present existence.

The universal nature of myths allows them to be used in a transcultural approach to human development. It is in reference to the individual's "mythic center" that the term *Universal Being* or *Source* is used. Out of my own need to connect my work as a consultant in career development to my "mythic self," I have gradually evolved this way of guiding others. The connecting link is experienced in the commonality I share with all other human beings. I am aware of the necessity to give myself a framework that allows for the mystical and subjective aspects to be included in career development, rather than being closed into a mechanistic way of matching skills to job descriptions. In the final analysis, it allows me to experience who I am while increasing the client's awareness of who he or she is, and thus I further develop my own career while guiding them in developing theirs.

The Lotus and the Pool

🌸 How to Use This Book

You now have in your possession what I believe is the latest and finest tool for enabling you to take charge of your life and come from power instead of reaction. It has been carefully prepared to touch you through your senses, emotions, spirit, and mind. It is designed to guide you into exploring from a positive position your past experiences, to stimulate you to be totally present in the here and now, and to form goals for creating the future according to your inner visions—to set you free to be yourself.

You will be beckoned into giving new messages to your unconscious, to lay over the fear and failure mind-frame that blocks your energy and confidence, and gain new insights through the dynamic presentation of tested ways of learning. Transformation is a slow and arduous process. Old patterns of procrastination and negation die hard. You need to take yourself through the guided meditation exercise on page 245 at least once a day for seven days at the beginning of this process. This step is a key factor in helping you get in touch with the source of your power. Let the flashes of insight you germinate each day give you clues to the wisdom that is stored in your subconscious. In your relaxed state, you will allow this wisdom to rise into the conscious mind in many forms—memories, desires, symbols, and ideas for action. Pay close attention to *anything* that comes up for you. Purchase a notebook to use as a companion to this book. In it, record what happens during this visualization exercise. Also keep it beside your bed to write down your dream images each morning (or during the night if you awaken). These will furnish important clues for you to know how to move ahead. You should also keep a journal to capture the stray ideas that pop into your consciousness each day. Some of them may seem unrelated to your career goals at first, but later you will find that they provide missing links to your plans.

If you would like to supplement this book with personal counseling services, Hilda Lee Dail and Associates International are avail-

4   able for consulting. We can arrange for individual appointments in person, by correspondence, or by long distance telephone. Contact:

Hilda Lee Dail & Associates International
1807 Legion Street
Myrtle Beach, South Carolina 29577
(803) 448-3270

✿ Creativity

A Universal Process

But if you have nothing at all to create,
then perhaps you create yourself.
—C.G. Jung

This first section of the book is a journey through the ancient creation myths of peoples all over the world. The purpose of our journey is to explore the nature of creativity as a universal experience that we can all recognize and observe in our own lives. I am not concerned with presenting abstract definitions as such. Rather, I focus throughout on an *existential* approach. In other words, I am not only interested in presenting *ideas* about creativity, but I also want you to *experience* the process of creativity in the many ways that it manifests in life.

To know that there is a tree in the orchard is one kind of knowledge; to actually taste the fruit is another. Knowledge of ideas is like knowledge that the tree exists. My hope is that you will be open to the kind of knowing that comes from the apple in the mouth. When I talk about the ancient creation myths, I want you to be consciously quickened by the universal reality out of which these myths sprang and to experience the eternal "now" in this moment—and through this experience to discover the framework for developing your life work.

It is always difficult to know where to take hold of a subject that is both pervasive and elusive. I am aware that as I write these words, I am experiencing the chaos that precedes creation, that I am pulling back from taking the plunge into exposing myself. The doubts of my ability to do what I set out to accomplish grab hold of me and nag me into a state of immobility. I fix a cup of herb tea, open the window, pull back the drapes, reread what I have written, make a meatloaf for lunch, cut my toenails, browse through a stack of books I have gathered around me, become aware of a pain in my left leg, go to the bathroom. I recall a fragment of a dream last night

5

in which someone read a manuscript I had written and pointed out that I had used the word "younguns" instead of "children." Suddenly I chuckle to myself. Here I am sitting in the middle of Manhattan Island, with the muffled traffic sounds from Lexington Avenue rising to my tenth-floor apartment, working on a book on creativity. A word that symbolizes my own beginnings more than a half-century ago becomes the handle for me to take hold of my work today.

"Younguns" came to me from my subconscious as I slept. It is a word full of affection, with a touch of humor and veiled derision. I examine it for clues and discover that it is a vibrant reminder of the combination of truths with which I am trying to deal. To go back to the creation myths, I must first get connected to my own creation story, accept my origin, embrace the quaint remnants of Elizabethan language as a symbol of both my glory and my limitations. Whatever I come up with in connection with creativity—all the research I have done—first must be cradled and nurtured in this "youngun" from Georgia before it can be communicated through this grown woman. I feel amused at this fact, delighted at the creativity of my own psyche in presenting me with this dream fragment that puts me into the state of childlike wonder that I need in order to play with myths.

So come with this "youngun" from Georgia, and let us have a story hour together. For my approach to creativity is through creation myths. I cannot, of course, give a complete account of these myths here; there are in any case many excellent books on the subject available. I wish only to give some of the relevant highlights and to show how the same themes occur in creation stories from all over the globe.

By absorbing the meaning of these original stories in all the world's culture, we get a view of the human condition today. The remnants of mythical symbols line the walls of our psyche like dim paintings in a cave or fragments of pottery in an archeological site.

The images of God as creator are many. Joseph Campbell referred to them as the "masks of eternity" that both cover and reveal "the Face of Glory." The tenets of all world religions point to "Truth as one." All our images and names for the ultimate reality are metaphors of the universe and the creations that are a part of it. In looking at the various mythic stories we are called to a keener awareness of the very essence of being alive. The deeper that we dare to look at ourselves, the more clearly we experience a universal

consciousness that is hidden in the recesses of our own uncon-
scious. Here the language is symbolic, bursting forth in dreamlike images that match the metaphors of the creation myths. We know the ancient stories are true because our own experiences echo their meaning in moments of insight and inspiration.

David Maclagan in *Creation Myths*[1] says that "creation is involved whenever any new thing, from the quickening of an embryo to the dawning of an image," is brought to life. Emerson expressed the same idea when he pointed out that the whole of nature is a metaphor of the human mind.

We human beings err when we become dull and listless, half asleep, not alert to these connections. The purpose of this book is to help quicken you to your mythic heritage and to the exciting possibilities of participating in the creative act by tapping your inner Source. This is the way you discover your own personal myth of who you are becoming. Like any myth, it is something that is always happening—it has no distinct beginning or definitive ending. It is also a medium through which you can taste eternity. Through awareness of myth we can even hope to reach the place where we cease to struggle with ideology or theology. In moments of integration of the substance of our mythic self with the presence of the Universal Self, we can dance to the music of the spheres. We can experience that all processes have an inner and outer reference simultaneously. We can be ourselves because we dare to go beyond ourselves. We participate in the works of the Creator; we are in the process of creation.

In this creative career development process, we don't focus first on what we are going to *do* with our lives, but we experience the rapture of *being* alive. This is our departure point in the process of life planning or career development. Our destiny is bound up in the quality of our being rather than the list of things we know how to do. The doing grows out of the being.

I shall always remember the words of a wise psychiatrist when I consulted him about one of my clients who was (according to my judgment) stuck in meditation rather than moving on to action. He quietly responded, "The meaning for life is not doing but being." In my many years of working with the development of people, I have found that each one has a rhythm that I had better not tamper with. It is similar to what the educators of small children call "reading readiness." The client will move on when the inner work is done. As a counselor I cannot force, but rather keep on observing, affirming, and using all my professional skills to heighten my client's awareness of every spark of energy, flash of insight, or urge for action.

One of the problems many people encounter is the lack of classical knowledge in today's educational system. Greek, Latin, and biblical literature used to be a part of every Western student's education but have now been largely deleted from the curriculum. Thus the tradition of Occidental mythological information has been virtually forgotten.

In order to recover this loss, we need to listen to all the world's myths. That is why I don't just stop with the biblical stories. When we read them we tend to get caught up in fact and historical narrative. But when we come upon the same truths in some other culture's creation story, we are quickened into a renewal of our own spiritual heritage. We also discover a bridge to the other culture's experience. Amid the great diversity in the world today, without the golden cord of myth to hold us together, we are like what De Toqueville described when he came to America over a hundred years ago: "a tumult of anarchy."

To take a journey into the ancient terrain of creation myths is to travel inward to the dark abyss of our own mythic self where the transformation comes only after we embrace the darkness at the center of our being. Growth takes place in the midst of upheaval, confusion, doubt, fear, anxiety, and desperation. It is a positive movement that always takes place "in spite of" the negative. If you would like to know how to get a clue to the secret of your life pattern, you must follow the same steps the gods followed in creating the universe. When you discern the motifs in the myths examined in this book and grasp their truth, you will tap the flow of your own creative energy.

Let us begin with the creation myth I first heard—probably the one most of you know if you are a product of western culture.

○ **The Biblical Myth of Creation**

If you read the first three chapters of Genesis, you will discover two creation stories. The first chapter indicates ten steps of creativity. They are in this order:

1. Heaven and earth
2. Light
3. Firmament

Even though we get the rhythmic picture of God doing all this work in the seven-day modality, in reading the first three chapters of Genesis, we also see the playful mood of Yahweh, who kept thinking of things to keep Adam amused (having him name the fruits, flowers, and animals, and finally creating Eve as a playmate or "helpmeet"). This innocent playfulness was disturbed when Eve decided to have "her eyes opened and be as gods, knowing good from evil" (Gen. 3:5). Her motivation was to obtain wisdom, and she got it—the knowledge of good and evil, the ability to make decisions and use her influence: in other words, to be powerful like God.

In the second version of the creation story, the sequence is different. God does not create Adam first and then, as an afterthought, form Eve from Adam's rib. Instead, "God created man in his own image, in the image of God he created him; male and female he created them. And God said to them, 'Be fruitful and multiply'" (Gen. 1:27–28). This version pictures male and female as equals, and is the account that many people feel more comfortable with.

For our discussion now, however, we are chiefly concerned with the origin of things as described in Genesis—the process that all created things must go through, from nothingness to being. It was as though the ancient poets who wrote this account shut their eyes and looked deep into the dark recesses of their own dim consciousness to discover the pattern of creation. Here is a truth for us to grasp in our search for the "source" of the powers of creativity: the inner world is composed of the same substance as the outer.

Sir Arthur Eddington writes:

> We have torn away the mental fancies to get at the reality beneath, only to find the reality of that which is beneath is bound up with its potentiality of awakening these fancies. It is because the mind, the weaver of illusion, is also the only guarantor of reality, that reality is always to be sought at the base of illusion....[2]

This recognition that the inner world is of the same creative substance that brought into being the universe is our point of departure. At first we may encounter a chaotic period, but if we are to be creative, we must deal with the illusion and not try to avoid the chaotic period, the shaking of the foundations of our present thought structures. We must confront this chaos, disturbing though it may be. All we may experience now may be a void. Yet when we embrace it, plunge into it with our whole, searching heart, we know that in this chaos lies the potential of the order that will emerge.

In creating any new thing, we must face a deep, existential level where being encounters nonbeing. This truth was dramatically portrayed in the last scene of Archibald MacLeish's play *J.B.* (the modern Job):

> J.B. and Sarah [his wife] cling to each other. Then she rises, drawing him up peering at the darkness inside the door.
>
> J.B.: "It's too dark to see."
>
> She turns, pulls his head down between her hands and kisses him.
>
> Sarah: "Then blow on the coal of the heart, my darling."
>
> J.B.: "The coal of the heart...?"
>
> Sarah: "It's *all* the light now."[3]

The flickering flame of our potential smolders, waiting to spark when we exert the effort. It does not look for the vitality outside, but deep underneath the "coal" of our own pulsating hearts, where the individual being encounters the Ground of Being. And lo, a flame appears.

This meeting is sometimes experienced in fear and trembling, often with desperation and exhaustion. For to discover being is to be threatened with nonbeing. To create is to risk destruction. To be creative is to give up our present state. Unless we go through the chaotic darkness, we cannot emerge into the white daylight that blends with our little internal lights, until the moment of high noon when creator and creation become indistinguishable.

In considering this experience of becoming conscious of the whole self, I have referred to the Genesis account of humanity's emerging from what the theologian Paul Tillich calls "a state of dreaming innocence." Tillich asserts that the movement from essential being, which he describes as "dreaming innocence," to actualized existence involves an estrangement: "The state of dreaming innocence drives beyond itself. The possibility of the transition to existence is experienced as temptation...Adam before the Fall must be understood as dreaming innocence of undecided potentiality."[4]

It is difficult for us to perceive the state of "dreaming innocence," since humanity in its present form has participated in actual estrangement. It seems to be necessary if we are to accept the concept of being and nonbeing, doubt and faith, and all the other opposites that are constantly being balanced in a struggle with reality. Yet, if we are to create, we must affirm the cosmic event in human development experienced as a split between the polarities. The development of "dreaming innocence" into this historical ambiguity is brought on by the state that Tillich describes as "aroused freedom." A deep tension occurs in the moment in which finite freedom becomes conscious of itself and struggles to become actual: "We are caught between the desire to actualize our freedom and the demand to preserve our dreaming innocence. In the power of infinite freedom we decide for actualization."[5]

In the Genesis story (as in other creation myths) we find clues to understanding the necessity for an "I-Thou" encounter between the creature and the creator if we are to participate in the creative process. "All real living is meeting."[6]

In the Judeo-Christian creation myth, Adam and Eve were put into the garden to till it, look after it; and it was then that the first conversation began. God spoke: "Of every tree of the garden thou mayest freely eat; but of the tree of knowledge of good and evil, thou shalt not eat of it: For in the day that thou eatest thereof thou shalt surely die" (Gen. 2:16–17).

This is the beginning of the word, or *logos*, the concept of order. God turns from the outer creation to the shaping of the inner world. Our ears have been ringing from the thunder of this command ever since. "We have heard it as the primal curse and the primal blessing: Curse, because it is aimed at the psyche's primordial inertia; blessing, because as we hear it infancy ends and we are stirred to meaningful action."[7]

In knowing good from evil, Adam and Eve threatened the prerogative of God for full awareness of the world's nature. But this is not the reason they were driven from the garden. The reason seems to be that they might eat of the tree of life and live forever, and remain in some kind of mindless immortality. With the eating of the fruit, human reality is established and violence begins.

From this emerges a new symbol, the Tree of Life, replacing the paradise of mindless infancy.

> The immature psyche experiences the primal urge toward growth and thus toward Creativity as a curse, as the life force is felt to be aimed directly against inertia, and creating anxieties becomes a spur to the awakening mind. Hence the Cherubims with the "flaming sword...to keep the way of the tree of life" were significantly stationed by the poets; at the east of the garden, a symbol for sunlike, dawning awareness....
>
> Therefore the Lord God sent him forth from the Garden of Eden to *till* the ground from where he was taken (Gen. 3:23).
>
> In perfect simplicity the human condition in both the inner and outer orders of experience is depicted here.[8]

This scene serves as a sort of backdrop for the stage from which we have to struggle "east of Eden" to be creative and to fill the gap of separation of ourselves from other fragments of humanity. The meaning of the Genesis creation myth for us today is experienced in our anxiety, alienation, and guilt as we participate in the act of creating.

George Bernard Shaw gave us an example of the price that is required for true creativity. Having attended a concert given by the violinist Heifetz, he wrote the following letter:

> My dear Mr. Heifetz,
>
> My wife and I were overwhelmed by your concert. If you continue to play with such beauty, you will certainly die young. No one can play with such perfection without provoking the jealousy of the gods. I earnestly implore you to play something badly every night before going to bed.[9]

The profound truth is that authentic creativity is an active battle with the gods. And this conflict breeds the fear that carries with it a feeling of guilt, the fear that we are guilty of breaking the status quo. We are acting like gods. How dare we be successful?

Commitment to truth is healthiest not when it is *without* doubt, but when it exists *in spite of* doubt. This is why creativity takes so much courage. Hence the existentialists Kierkegaard and

Nietzsche and Camus and Sartre have proclaimed that courage is not the absence of despair; it is rather the capacity to move ahead in spite of despair.

The word "courage" has as its root the French word *coeur*, meaning "heart." Just as the heart, by pumping blood to the body and brain, enables all the physical organs to function, so courage makes all the psychological virtues possible. We human beings need courage for *being* and *becoming*.

○ Greek Myth

The Greek myth of creation is that Prometheus, a Titan who lived on Mount Olympus, stole fire from the gods and gave it to humankind, thus ushering in the beginning of Greek civilization. The important point to the myth is that the god Zeus was outraged. He decreed that Prometheus be punished by being bound to Mount Caucasus, where a vulture would come each morning to eat away at his liver (which would grow again in the night).

What a beautiful symbol of the creative process! Most of us have experienced the end of the day feeling tired, spent, and so certain that we could never finish a task we were working on that we would vow to forget the whole thing. But during the night "our livers grow back again." We rise full of energy and go back with renewed hope.

In the Orphic myth the silver egg of the cosmos gave rise to an ambiguous figure:

> When time and wailing Need
> split the ancient egg
> out stepped Love the first born
> fire in his eyes
> wearing both sexes
> glorious eros
> father of immortal Night
> whom Zeus swallowed and brought back...[10]

Out of the cracked egg come all the opposites of light and dark, male and female, love and strife: the actions and reactions that energize the structure, in space, time, and particularity, of the created world.

In the Greek creation myth we also find a doubling back in the form of a union that is incestuous and fertile (a notion that is, at different times and places, both sacred and forbidden). Zeus fathered Dionysus/Zagreus with Persephone, his own daughter; Dionysus was torn apart by the Titans; Zeus burned them to ashes; from these ashes emerged the human race. The topography of such switches in identity or function is beautifully expressed by Gary Snyder:

NO MATTER, NEVER MIND

The Father is the Void
The Wife Waves
Their child is Matter.

Matter makes it with his mother
and their child is Life, a daughter.

The Daughter is the Great Mother
Who, with her father/brother Matter as her lover

Gives birth to the Mind.[11]

The literature of the Greeks is rich with psychological insight. For example, Rollo May in *Man's Search for Himself* offers an illuminating analysis of the Greek tragedy of Orestes, from which he draws a modern parallel to the person bound to his own household so that he cannot love outwardly. May describes this struggle as essentially one against one's own dependency. Obviously, the moral of the Orestes drama is not that everyone must kill his mother (as he did), but, according to May: "What has to be killed is the infantilities of dependency which binds the person to the parents, and thereby keeps him from loving outwardly and creating independently....It is a matter of long, uphill growth to new levels of integration—growth meaning not automatic process but re-education, finding new insights, making self-conscious decision, and throughout being willing to face occasional or frequent bitter struggles."[12]

May listed the stages in consciousness of self that have a direct relationship to creativity. The first is that of *innocence* (of the infant). The second is *rebellion*, when the person is trying to become free to establish some inner strength. (This may be a two-year old, or an adolescent.) The third stage he called the *ordinary consciousness of self*. (Here the person begins to see his or her

errors, prejudice, and guilt, and learns to take responsibility for
them). The fourth stage is extraordinary, in the sense that most people experience it only rarely. It is the *creative consciousness of self*. The classical psychological term for this awareness is *ecstasy*, literally "to stand outside oneself."

The Greek legend that Aristophanes tells in Plato's *Symposium* deals with the idea of the split. He says that in the beginning there were creatures composed of what are now two human beings. And those were of three sorts: male/female, male/male, and female/female. The gods then split them all in two. But after they had been split apart, all they wanted was to embrace each other again in order to go back to original harmony. This is what we mortals also keep doing, reaching for the "other" in our search for ourselves.

O Myths of India

The poets of pre-Aryan India thought of a god as the beginning of the first man, referred to variously as Purusha, Prajapati, and Brahma. He was "a personification of the all-containing life—master and life force itself, yearning to develop into teeming worlds, and he was impelled to create by a twofold principle. On the one hand, he felt lonely, destitute and fearful, and so brought forth the universe to surround himself with company; but on the other hand, he felt a longing to let his substance overflow, wherefore he said to himself: 'May I give increase; May I bring forth creatures.'"[13]

The Hindu scriptures known as the Upanishads (dating from the eighth century B.C.) describe the human psyche as containing with it heaven and hell and all the gods, which are manifestations in image form of human energies in conflict with one another. The Upanishads say, "In the beginning, there was only the great self in the form of a person. Reflecting, it found nothing but itself. Then its first word was 'This I am.'" And then it realized: "I indeed am this creation, for I have poured it forth from myself. In that way it became this creation. Verily, he who knows this becomes in this creation a creator." In these words we find an important key: the creative principle is both within us and in the outer world.

David Maclagen points out in *Creation Myths* that in the Hindu scripture *Shatapatha Brahmana*, the year that Prajapati spends with the golden cosmic egg explicitly corresponds to the gestation time for horses, cattle, and humans.

The theme of creation as expressed in the opposites of experience is contained in this poem of medieval India.

> I salute the life which is like a sprouting
> seed, with its one arm upraised in the air,
> and the other down in the soil;
> The life which is one in its outer form
> and its inner sap;
> The Life that ever appears,
> yet ever eludes.
> The Life that comes I salute,
> and the Life that goes;
> I salute the life that is revealed
> and that that is hidden;
> I salute the Life in suspense,
> standing still like a mountain;
> And the Life of the surging sea of fire;
> And the Life that is tender like a
> lotus, and hard like a thunderbolt.
> I salute the Life which is of the mind,
> with its one side in the dark
> and the other in the light.
> I salute the Life in the house and
> the Life abroad in the unknown,
> The Life full of joy and the Life
> weary with its pain,
> The Life eternally moving, rocking
> the world into stillness,
> The Life deep and silent, breaking
> out into roaring waves.
> There falls the rhythmic beat of
> life and death:
> Rapture wells forth, and all space
> is radiant with light.
> There is the unstruck music;
> it is the music of three worlds.
> These millions of lamps of sun
> and moon are burning.
> There the drum beats and the

love swings in play.
There love songs resound, and
the light rains in shadows.[14]

The human longing is for a way of experiencing the world that will open to us the transcendent that informs it and at the same time forms ourselves within it. This truth is beautifully expressed in the traditional Indian gesture of greeting in which the palms are placed together as if in prayer and one bows to the other person; it is a way of saying. "The God in me salutes the God in you." Being aware of the divine presence in all things, one greets a guest as a visiting deity.

In the Laws of Manu it is written that Brahma (the creator god), after he was born from the cosmic egg, brought out from himself the mind, made of being and nonbeing, and from the mind, in turn, the ego—the self-center of the world.

The Upanishads provide a delightful story about creation as depicted in the capers of the god Indra, who is simply a god of history but thinks he is the whole show. It happened in the time when a great monster had enclosed all the waters of the earth, so that there was a terrible drought. After meditating a while, Indra realized that he had a box of thunderbolts. He decided to drop them on the monster and blow him up. When he did that, the waters flowed, and the world was refreshed. Indra said, "What a great boy am I."

With this inflated thought of his identity, he climbs the cosmic mountain and decides to build a palace worthy of such a great creature as he. The main carpenter goes to work, but Indra keeps changing the plans, making them more and more grandiose. Finally in exasperation the carpenter says, "We are both immortal, and there is no end to his desires. I am caught for eternity." So he decides to go to Brahma, the creator god, and complain.

Brahma sits on a lotus, the symbol of divine energy and divine grace. The lotus grows from the navel of Vishnu, the sleeping god whose dream is the universe. He promises the carpenter to cure Indra of his exaggerated idea of himself. The next morning he sends a blue-black boy with lots of children to talk to Indra in his palace. From his throne, Indra asks, "What brings you to my palace?"

"Well," says the boy, "I have been told that you are building a palace like no Indra before you ever built." And Indra answers, "Indras before me? Young man, what are you talking about?"

The boy (who is really Vishnu, the Lord Protector) then recounts all the rhythms of life as revealed in the appearances and disappearances of Vishnu, Brahma, lotus, and of the many Indras before him. He points to a parade of ants marching across the floor and explains, "Former Indras all."

An old yogi dressed only in a loincloth and holding a banana leaf umbrella over him enters the palace. He is actually the god Shiva, the creator and destroyer of the world, come to instruct Indra. He points to the scant hairs on his chest that disappear each time an Indra dies. Most of his hairs are gone and soon he will be bare. He says, "Life is short. Why build a house?"

Indra, disillusioned with life, dismisses his carpenter and decides to become a yogi and just meditate on the lotus feet of Vishnu. But Indrani, his beautiful queen, is upset. She goes to a priest, who explains that Indra and Indrani are really one, and that Brahma is also radiantly present.

With this message Indra gives up becoming a yogi and finds that he can personify the eternal out in the world. He can become a symbol of the Brahma.

Each of us can become the Indra of our own life. We can find a form of activity in the world of achievement and in the family setting that will enable us to live out our own myth.

Finally, from the rich source of inspiration that comes from India, I would like to cite Meher Baba, an Indian spiritual master of modern times, who characterized creation as arising out of God's whim to know, "Who am I?" To answer His own question, God became everything in the universe: "I am stone. I am plant. I am worm. I am fish. I am bird, I am animal." When He reached the human form, He answered: "I am man. I am woman. I am rich. I am poor. I am beautiful. I am ugly. I am black. I am white." And so on. Thus God manifests as everyone and everything, until He realizes His true identity: "I am God." In this image we get a sense of the divine playfulness celebrating all the possibilities of life through infinitely creative ways. It is good to experience this sense of play as we allow our career goals to take shape—to feel that we can joyfully express some quality of the Divine as we discover the particular way that it wants to manifest in our life work.

The search for knowledge of the divine origin is never complete. A verse in Sanskrit says, "He who thinks he knows, doesn't know. He who knows he doesn't know, knows. For in this context, to know is not to know, and not to know is to know."

Native American myths. For the Aztecs the cosmos was highly vulnerable and insecure. Men were bound to offer their blood, or even their lives, to sustain it.

In the Navajo myth there are stages of ascent that are full of intricate cross-references: In one version, man does not appear until the Fifth World, when the Gods combine to create him; he is named "Created-from-Everything" because:

> They made his toe-nails and ankles of the soil of the earth, his legs of lightening....They made him of all kinds of water...And they made his arms of the rainbow. His hair was made of darkness, his skull of the sun.[15]

The Pima Indians describe creation with these words: "I make the world and lo, the world is finished."

Other Native American myths have similar themes. A conjugation of opposites appears in all these creation myths. In some the discrimination and spacing of elements are gradual.

Hawaiian myth. The Hawaiian myth begins with a list of beings which are named as generalized creative processes:

> Te Ahanga: the swelling of an embryo in the body...Te Apongo: appetite...Te Kune Iti: inner conception...Te Kune Rahi: preparation...Te Hune Hanga: the impulse to search. Te Ranga Hautanga: ordering, as of cells in the body...and so on. There is a parallel between the creation of the cosmos and the coming-to-life of an individual.[16]

Japanese myth. The Japanese Nekongi states that of old, heaven and earth were not yet separated, and the yin and yang—the opposites—were not yet divided. They formed a chaotic mass like an egg, which was of obscurely defined limits and contained germs. The purer and clearer part was thinly drawn out and formed heaven, while the heavier and grosser part settled down and became earth.

Chinese myth. Likewise, in the earliest Chinese legends the giant P'an Kou is described as mediator between yang (sky) and yin (earth). P'an Kou, who was in the middle, transformed himself nine times each day, sometimes a god in the sky, sometimes a holy man on the earth.

African myths. In many African myths, the first humans are lowered to earth from the sky. In others God leaves earth, where he lived among humans.[17] What is remarkable is that in all the creation myths similar developmental strains point to a universal consciousness.

The Bassari people of West Africa have a legend that is a similar sequence to the Genesis account. "Unumbotte made a human being. Its name was Man. Unumbotte next made an antelope, named Antelope. Unumbotte made a snake, named Snake....and Unumbotte said to them, 'The earth has not yet been pounded. You must pound the ground smooth where you are sitting.' Unumbotte gave them seed of all kinds, and said, 'Go plant them.'"

○ **A Universal Pattern**

Let us take a look at the universal pattern that emerges from these various myths and see what their implications are for general principles of creativity. (We will examine the relationship of creativity to career development specifically in the next section.)

In the Judeo-Christian myth of Adam and Eve, a highly developed pattern shows ten steps. They do not always necessarily appear in this order or as separate aspects, but for our purpose here we arrange them in this developmental manner:

1. Chaos (darkness, nonbeing, inertia, and destructive force)
2. Being (dawning awareness, dreaming innocence, aroused freedom, light, and the preserving or nurturing force)
3. Encounter (communing between creator and creatures and among the species)
4. Developing Self (separateness, male and female,[18] anxiety, fear of dying, alienation, blaming ["This woman tempted me"] and guilt, hiding)
5. Experience (discovering work through "sweat of the brow," pain in reproduction, knowing ambiguity)
6. Imagination (seeing the possibility of gaining knowledge and power and being as God)
7. Symbol (naming of the creatures and objects)
8. Form (redefining existence "outside Eden")

9. Communication (establishing closeness and trust and becoming as one—"bone of my bone and flesh of my flesh")
10. Eternity (the search continues, and the cycle is closed—"Dust to dust, ashes to ashes"—new forms and new beginnings, new offsprings, the two sons)

In the Greek myth we find a similar pattern:

1. Chaos (Prometheus stealing from the gods)
2. Being (giving "fire" to humankind, trying to become like God)
3. Encounter (God outraged)
4. Developing Self (through punishment by being bound to the mountain and eaten by vultures)
5. Experience (existing during the night and absorbing energy)
6. Imagination (turning the experience into growing a new liver)
7. Symbol (silver egg)
8. Form (split to make male/female and first-born)
9. Communication ('fire" in his eyes—doubling back in form of union)
10. Eternity (Zeus burning offspring into ashes from which sprang the human race)

In the Indian myths we can catch a glimmer of the same pattern.

1. Chaos (confusion between the gods and man)
2. Being (containing all of life)
3. Encounter (yearning to develop)
4. Developing Self (the split)
5. Experience (longing to overflow)
6. Imagination (year Prajapati spent with egg)
7. Symbol (golden cosmic egg)
8. Form (Laws of Manu—mind and ego)
9. Communication (gestation for horses, cattle, and humans; need for company)
10. Eternity (circling back to the self-center of the world)

The medieval poet I quoted picks up all these aspects and keeps the myth alive for us to experience the same reality.

In the Hawaiian myth, a similar sequence is rather striking:

1. Chaos (swelling of embryo)
2. Being (a list of beings)
3. Encounter (the appetite)
4. Developing Self (inner conception)
5. Experience (preparation)
6. Imagination (impulse to search)
7. Symbols, and
8. Form (cells in the body)
9. and 10. Communication and Eternity (cosmos and individual)

In the remaining myths I referred to, all of the steps appear. Some are not so clearly delineated; but the yin/female and yang/male, sky and earth, spirit and gross form, the hidden and the known—all point to a universal consciousness and a pattern of creativity. *Doing* always grows out of *being*.

Creativity is the self escaping into the open. It is an awareness and action of that which is a purposeful core in the service of expressing the self.

○ Back to Our Own Personal Myths

We have been interested here primarily with connecting the symbols implicit in the myths to our own existence and experiences, and with making them explicit as we let them lead us into a pattern of creativity that becomes our model for career development. These symbols serve as channels for our own inward journeys. By focusing on our centers, we connect ourselves to the center of the universe and participate in the act of creativity, out of which we create our own "mythic" careers.

Earlier in this chapter I shared my own struggle in getting started—the nonbeing tactics I used to avoid the encounter with being. Even so, I was ushered gently and somewhat whimsically into activity by recalling the dream fragment to which my identity was connected. The "youngun" from Georgia then ventured out into the world of creation myths.

About halfway through writing the manuscript for this book, I took an afternoon nap, during which I had an extremely lucid dream. I was conscious of being asleep, and yet I was awake enough to think, "This is a dream." I thought I had been talking to an old

man in a rather intimate fashion. The conversation was pleasant
enough, but I was ready for him to leave me. I was then aware that
I was in bed and that I was dreaming. He was bending over me,
pushing my body down with his hands. I was saying, "You have
to let me go. I must get up. I have finished our conversation."

Suddenly the phone rang. I was relieved to be awake and rid of
the force that was holding me down. I again began to write, but
some of the exhilaration I had felt when I remembered the first
dream about "younguns" and had begun writing had disappeared.
It was as though all these ancient myths were weighing me down.
I had had my conversations with them—had heard what they had
to say to me. Now it was time to be up and about my work.

I began to have a deepening realization of the meaning of metaphor as an image that points to something else. All the metaphors
of the creation myths are transcendent. That is, they refer to a reality that is beyond the literal image of the metaphor. It is important
that we try to enter that reality itself and not get stuck in the symbol. Getting stuck would be like trying to eat a description of
chocolate mousse on a menu instead of the mousse itself. We need
to understand that "the finger pointing at the moon is not the
moon" (as expressed in a famous Zen saying). The symbols that
you encounter in this process are meant to guide you to reality, not
distract you from it. The mythic approach to career development
aims to empower you to reach within to find the message of who
you are. Then you will be able to actualize this metaphoric material in concrete form.

PART TWO

✿ Ten Steps of Creativity and Career Development

We carry within us the wonder we seek without us.
　　　　　　—Sir Thomas Brown

"Creativeness in the world is, as it were, the eighth day of creation."[1] It is the activity of continuing the creative process put into motion by the gods of the creation stories. If it took seven days, in the Judeo-Christian myth, for God to complete the ten stages of creativity, then all subsequent creative activity assumed by humankind takes place on the eighth day. We are only continuing what was already begun at the dawn of civilization. Like the creatures in the myths, we participate with the creator by our increased awareness of our origin.

Now you are ready to explore the specific ways the creativity process is at work in your own career development. The ten chapters that follow are a guide to help you create your own career. Each chapter takes a step in the creativity process, deals with career crisis situations, discusses ideas relevant to the problems, and gives case studies of how other people have dealt with these issues.[2]

You will begin to understand how the ten steps relate to you as you gather clues from the material. The total pattern will evolve gradually. Each client I discuss here has been through all ten of the steps, but I chose to focus each case on a specific point to help you experience, in as full a measure as possible, the impact of the total process. You will identify with the aspects that relate to your own experience. You will also become prepared to understand your personal problems within a larger context. Whether you are just beginning your career, overcoming being recently fired, enduring a dead-end job unsuited to you, facing a midlife crisis, or considering a new career after retirement, you will find help in these chapters.

In this part of the book I talk directly to you as though I were your special consultant. In Part Three I give you some "how to" worksheets. You may choose to do them as you read through each corresponding section of this part, or to do them all at once, after reading the ten chapters that follow. Choose the order that suits you best. In addressing you directly as I would my clients, I seek to empower you to make your own decisions.

○ The Orchestra Paradigm

In my work as a consultant, my role is to help increase my clients' self-awareness. The "orchestra paradigm"[3] is a tool that I have found especially useful in this work. It is a model of the self presented in Psychosynthesis, an original method developed by Alberto Assagioli, a Florentine therapist who based his work on Jung's concept of personality types. Assagioli pictured the self as a core personality around which a group of subpersonalities function. The core personality—the "I"—is like the conductor of an orchestra, and the subpersonalities are the various musicians playing different instruments—piano, oboe, violin, drums, and so on. Each instrument—each part of the self—is part of the whole, neither good nor bad (although they may function creatively or destructively, depending on the directions given by the conductor). Each is important but is not allowed to take over the conductor's role. If the piano tries to dominate, or if the drums flourish all through the composition instead of waiting for the conductor's signal, then the harmony will be lost.

All around your core-conductor are subpersonalities with important functions within your total personality. But if, for instance, your "Big Mama" subpersonality takes over and compulsively offers "mothering" when the appropriate behavior would be allowing others space to do their own thing, your conductor-core must signal that subpersonality to tone down.

On the other hand, you may have subpersonalities, skills, or roles that you have never allowed to play their tune within your orchestra. They are waiting to be identified and signaled into action. Your conductor-core must be trained to recognize them and to create a place for them to function within the framework of the whole.

Just as the orchestra conductor must always be aware of the musical composition, your core must be in touch with the melody or theme of your life. What are you trying to say to the world with your orchestrated self? What is your message? The conductor-core must know these things at all times or you will get off beat. Your conductor-core must embody your life's theme or composition so that no one role or function is out of harmony, compulsively overactive, or too often silent.

The conductor of an orchestra is concerned also with the composer's intention. He or she is dedicated to interpreting the composer accurately. In the same way, your core self is connected to the Universal Self. Your being is a part of the Ground of Being. You stand in the direct line of the source of universal energy. When your conductor-core has completely learned the composition-message from the composer–Universal Self, your orchestra (all the subpersonalities, roles, and skills) will be in such harmony that the audience-market will pay well for your performance.

As a career consultant, I give you a practice room for getting ready for the performance—a place for you to become more and more aware of *who* you are, *what* your melody is, and *how* to get the world to pay you to play your tune. This analogy will help you understand the process as we get under way. The accompanying illustration will help you visualize it more clearly.

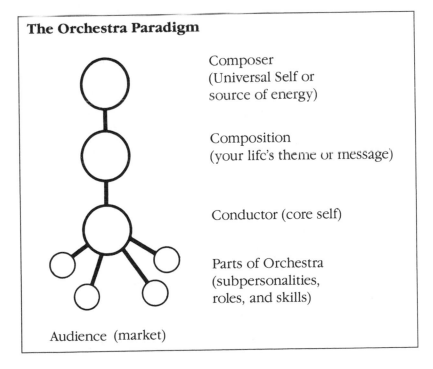

The Orchestra Paradigm

Composer
(Universal Self or
source of energy)

Composition
(your life's theme or message)

Conductor (core self)

Parts of Orchestra
(subpersonalities,
roles, and skills)

Audience (market)

Since the creativity process makes use of images and symbols that often break through the consciousness at unexpected times and in seemingly random fashion, it is important that we explore the ways that our dreams also expand our awareness. During the writing of the original manuscript of *The Lotus and the Pool*, I kept a dream journal that expanded into a volume as large as the book. The richness of these symbolic messages, when decoded, furnished insights into my own creativity as I developed the concepts on paper.

In these intervening years, dream work has been a vibrant aspect of the creative process with my clients. Here I want to focus on a few universal principles in relation to "breakthru dreams" (this is the unique spelling used in *The Dream Makers* by Richard Carrier and Joseph [New York: Bantam Books, 1978]). These dreams furnish us with clues to the activity that is going on below the conscious mind. If we learn to interpret them, we often know what we are ready to do. They can signal us into action that we have been afraid to take before.

As I was preparing in my mind, as I always do days before a word is written, I became aware that I needed a breakthru dream to spur me into action. Then it happened. I had returned home from presiding over a board meeting of a county volunteer agency and was feeling elated and excited at the support I experienced as the members began to assume responsibility for various tasks. I went to bed early, and soon I was asleep. About 2:20 A.M. I gradually gained consciousness with the realization that I had had a significant dream. I lay very still and experienced the intense joy that flooded through my body. In a half-dreaming, half-waking state, I tried to get hold of some action, but all I remembered was that I was viewing an area of landscape that was so vibrant it seemed to be breathing. It had the texture and design of a tapestry. I was standing on the edge of it—just "being there." I stayed alert the remainder of the night, just allowing the various aspects of my life to come before me. Ideas for solving several problems came to mind. The high energy I experienced made me confident that I was entering a fruitful period.

As day broke and I had my tea and toast, I began to sense that the dream referred to the idea that God is the Ground of Being. The term had become more than a concept. It was an experience

of the reality. I knew I was on sacred ground. The earth beneath
me was alive, breathing and exquisitely beautiful. It was an art form, a tapestry, while being also the foundation of reality. And here I stood, connected to it all.

More and more I have found that the breakthru dream offers clues to problem solving. This is true not only in my work with clients, but also in my own dream life. Recently I was facing a financial problem and needed to raise several thousand dollars. At first I tried not to think about the problem, foolishly hoping that somehow I wouldn't have to solve it. Next I half-heartedly went through several false starts, realizing that I was not on the right track. I was about to blunder into another sidetrack when I had a dream. I will tell it in the present tense so that you will get the direct impact. Here it is:

> I am in a play. My part is to be a hen. I am seated, dressed in a fancy feather costume. It is very expensive and extravagant similar to the description I had read of the fish costume in the movie *A Fish Named Wanda*. So I am very special in the play. I am holding a tremendous egg, bigger than an ostrich egg. It fills my whole lap, it seems. I am supposed to have laid it, and had sat on it long enough. Standing at a distance to my right, Roderick, my husband, is smoothing a beautiful layer of meringue on the top of an enormous bowl of vanilla custard.

That was it. Very brief and very clear. I began to free associate, searching for the meaning. I realized that it was a breakthru dream, for I felt energized and curious to see what it meant. I first thought of the principle that you can't rush the hatching of an egg. I am always trying to force things to happen rather than wait for the proper timing. When I told the dream to Jan, my daughter, she immediately said, "There is proof in the pudding," bringing up an old saying that has been passed down through the generations. So my attention was turned to the part Roderick represented in the dream. We know that all aspects of a dream are parts of us. My identification with Roderick is through my sensing, thinking, logical side, which is usually not listened to. So he represented the truth that I need to pay close attention to all the facts so that the egg can not only be cracked but also turned into vanilla pudding with meringue—a dessert.

We all had a good laugh at my creative subconscious, which was working away during the night to produce these symbols that offered the clue to what I must do. I didn't pursue the meaning at that moment, for I had to rush to get dressed and go to the office. My spirit was high, for I knew the dessert was mine. I was certain I would know what to do.

And sure enough, as I was driving down Highway 17, with the sun pouring through my window and my eyes occasionally glimpsing the ocean, the answer popped into my mind. Why had I not thought of it before? I had two government bonds in a bank as security for a loan. The bonds' value was much higher than the amount I owed. So there were resources that were available without my having to do a lot of paperwork. One telephone call took care of the problem. I went over to the bank an hour later to pick up the check.

I am aware that I have a tendency not to look at details. That is the intuitive aspect of my personality, since in the Myers-Briggs Personality Type Indicator, I am intuitive instead of sensing. A sensing person would have kept in mind the details of the financial arrangement. However, my intuition came to my rescue, since dreams originate in the subconscious, where intuition also germinates.

Often a dream will present rich symbols that give us pleasure as we play with them in the process of interpretation. My family had fun with the image of my being an old hen. The laughter and merriment helped us to relax and let the images reveal their message. Of course, the solution seemed very obvious and simple. Answers usually are. When we get the subconscious and the conscious mind flowing together as one, then we have access to the power of the integrated self.

My work with a client I shall call Martha further illustrates this principle. Martha was in trouble with her relationships with her peers. She had been betrayed by friends whom she trusted and had missed a career opportunity that she wanted very much. I had been taking her through the Lotus process. Because of the urgency of the situation, I knew we had to move fast. I suggested she give herself permission to have a breakthru dream that would indicate integration with the power in her subconscious and the ability to cope with the problem. She came a few days later with this dream, and we had the following conversation.

Martha: "It was about five in the morning. I fell back asleep about five-thirty and I dreamed that I was in a building that was on stilts overlooking the ocean, like in Pauleys Island, and I was on the deck on the ocean side. There was beautiful grass and the sea was out there, and I was talking to people about what had happened, the whole story. They were not people who were involved in it. They were people who had heard about it. And we were talking, and when I tried to explain it, it did not make me feel good at all. There was no way for them to enter into my experience, to affirm me through the explanation. It just made it harder. (And a real life experience happened to me yesterday when I was talking to somebody about it; it did not relieve me at all. It made it worse, discussing it makes it worse.)

"So, to continue with the dream, I had been talking to one of the men and I was remembering someone I loved. I thought they were down the beach, so I decided to go down off the deck, walk down the steps onto the sand. As I walked I started to feel a little better in the dream, and somebody who was up on the deck said, 'Hey, you're not walking away without my giving you a hug.' And then all the people came down, maybe seven or ten people. And they all said, 'I want to hug you, I want to hold you. I love you.' And so—each one held my hand or said things to me, embraced me—and then the telephone rang and I woke up. So I never got to the end of the dream.

"The call was from a dear friend of mine who's sort of been on the right side of all this. She said, 'Look, I know you probably had a hard night last night, I'm going to drive over for you. How would it be if I drove the car pool for you today?' And I said, 'That would be really wonderful.' And I staggered out of bed, made coffee, and got my kid ready for school. And then started to get ready to call you."

Hilda: "And that was a very wonderful, perfect manifestation. All right now, let's look at the dream. It is really a wonderful break-through, because what happened was that the subconscious gave you a message that you are not unloved. It's very clear. You said about ten people, not just one person, but lots of people. And they don't want you to leave without getting it, you see. One part of you wants to walk off and remove yourself from love and say, 'I don't deserve it. It's my fault.' That negative part is repeating the same pattern you experienced when your sister died."

Martha: "And the other part is saying, 'No way, we aren't getting out of here!'"

Hilda: "And the other part is saying, 'Wait a minute, we have something to give you. We do love you and here are the hugs.' Now the integration is taking place. That dream shows that it has already taken place, subconsciously. Your subconscious is like the little elves in the fairy story about the shoemaker. They make the shoes during the night and in the morning the message was, 'Here they are, we made them for you while you slept, and aren't they beautiful?'"

Martha: "Now the dark side is that part that doesn't want to . . ."

Hilda: "Doesn't want you to receive it and to enjoy it."

Martha: "Is afraid, is afraid the love isn't there."

Hilda: "Yes, you see, you are so afraid that you're going to lose it again and that it was not real, just temporary. . . . So how do you feel since you told me that dream?"

Martha: "It feels good. But it feels like I could lose it. I mean, I feel in touch with that. But that good part of me isn't as strong as the dark part."

Hilda: "Then let's look some more at the dark. Let's just get all the dark up now so it can disappear."

Martha: "The dark is just like a soft, gray-black color that's in a room, that's like a cloak. But it's square, it doesn't just fit on me; it's in the whole room, so anywhere I walk in the room, it's dark."

Hilda: "So you're completely absorbed in it."

Martha: "Yes, exactly."

Hilda: "It's not inside of you; you're inside of it."

Martha: "Yes, but it's in a room and I could walk out of that room if I knew how, or I could turn the light on or open the curtains or something."

Hilda: "Well, let's look at what was in the dream, the symbols in the dream. You were out on the deck of a house . . ."

Martha: "On stilts over the sea, right."

Hilda: "On the deck, standing on the edge, moving on out into the ocean. The ocean is a wonderful symbol of openness and divinity and love, and all the things that guide us."

Martha: "And that bird! That bird I saw, when I talked to you, that bird's wings . . . it's wounded, it can't fly right now."

Hilda: "Oh, O.K."

Martha: "And yet I know it will be able to fly again, it's not broken, but it's wounded."

Hilda: "That's from several weeks ago, the bird that you saw."

Martha: "Yes."

Hilda: "O.K., so you do have wings, and wings will heal."

Martha: "And only one wing is hurt, the other's fine. And if I think about it, I'm right-handed and it's the left wing."

Hilda: "It's your left wing that's hurt. O.K., what message is your left side sending to you?"

Martha: "It is where the hurt is. When you ask me that, I feel the pain of the fear of not being loved."

Hilda: "Yes, you've said that 'when I am strong, I am not loved.'"

Martha: "That's it. And my loss was that I didn't have my own sister as a woman to be my friend. I was strong and she left me by dying."

Hilda: "O.K., how do you relate to that, to what happened to you? The thing is, you wanted these friends to be your sisters."

Martha: "Yes."

Hilda: "That could give you the bird and could give you all the gifts of their love, and they would not."

Martha: "They were gone."

Hilda: "So you see, you have to be able to embrace the darkness. The hurt is that you wanted these women to be your sisters who could love you. And they failed you, and that brings up all the hurt of your sister leaving you."

Martha: "And being cut off."

Hilda: "Yes, being cut off, and you had no support. The recent experience just opens up the old hurts that are there. So now you dreamed this dream of standing out on the deck looking out at the sea with all the people there in the house saying, 'We love you, here are hugs for you, and don't go until you get them.'"

Martha: "Yes. Don't leave, because they're here. And it's like I'm afraid that there is something about the love that is frightening. Accepting the love frightens . . ."

Hilda: "I was going to say, what happens to you when you love, when people love you?"

Martha: "It feels great."

Hilda: "Yes."

Martha: "But there's something else."

Hilda: "But when they're gone, it hurts."

Martha: "Right. And if you love them, they may hurt you."

Hilda: "If you let them in, you may get hurt. . . . Well, you're still doing great, Martha."

Martha: "Yes, I know. I have some new friends out of this."

Today Martha has an excellent position at a university and has almost finished work on a Ph.D. degree. She has integrated the hurt and has reestablished relationships with her friends. It is exciting to be with her in social settings and observe her energy as she expresses love in her life.

The pattern in working with my own dreams and those of my clients is clear. The breakthru dream furnishes a process of integrating the subconscious with the conscious, releasing the energy that has previously been used in suppressing hurt feelings, and appropriating that energy for creative problem solving.

○ The Ten Steps: A Summary

Here is a brief summary of the ten steps that encompass the process of creativity and career development. (See also the worksheets in Part Three.)

Step 1. Chaos: Exploring Your Confused State. Define your chaos—your career problem. Write out your dissatisfactions with your present situation.

Step 2. Being: Discovering the Reality of Your Situation. Identifying your strengths is the focus of this step, for which I strongly recommend that you take the Myers-Briggs™. See page 218 for further information. Or you can directly contact CAPT (Center for Applications of Psychological Type, Inc.), 2720 N.W. Sixth Street, Gainesville, FL 32609, telephone (904) 375-0180. This test shows you where you are on the continuum between extravert and introvert, sensing and intuitive, thinking and feeling, judging and perceiving. There are sixteen different combinations, and each person is a combination of four elements. For instance, I am an ENFJ type—Extravert, Intuitive, Feeling, and Judging. The testing company furnishes readouts for each type, with suggestions about the strengths of each and some things to watch out for. A summary of the types is given in the chart on pages 220–221.

Step 3. Encounter: Finding Clues for Success in Your Past. List your past successes—things you have done that made you feel alive, and that, when you recall them, put you in touch with a flow of energy. Pay attention to everything that you remember that brought extreme pleasure. The criterion is the level of joy you experienced, not whether the project was of earth-shaking importance or whether somebody else thought it was a great achievement. Perhaps no one even *knew* this was a success story. Free associate. Put down whatever occurs to you, without unduly judging it or analyzing it at this early stage. Your list should include experiences from your childhood. Maybe you will recall the *first* achievement of something you did all by yourself, an event in grammar school or high school, a trip you took, a prize you won, a paper you wrote, a hobby that you enjoyed, a relationship you cherish, a specific project in one of your jobs. Be specific. Don't list categories. Every item you give must be a *particular* achievement.

After you make your list, begin to prioritize each item. Choose the top ten. Then write a detailed story of each of these ten, noting the steps you took, who helped you, the sequence of events, the early planning, the problems solved, the elements that brought the feeling of joy. If you write the stories as though they were for a five-year-old child, you will pay closer attention to details, rather than being too concerned about style and impressive language. The idea is to recapture the event, and reexperience the emotions you experienced.

You can have an added dimension if you share the stories with a consultant or trusted friend, whose task it is to help you identify the skills or success factors in these stories, and to relive the experience with you. The excitement of shared energy will help you begin to get out of your chaos and discover a glimmer of hope from tapping the resources deep within you. In encountering how you behaved when you were at your best, you pick up clues for your next step in your career development. You will feel new energy flowing into your body, and you will shift from despair into a space where creative ideas generate.

Step 4. The Developing Self: Identifying Your Growth Potential. This is the time for continuing to realign with the positive threads of your personality. Here you gradually sense that the chaotic interlude is just the first stage of a new level of awareness. You realize that you are indeed the same person who was so clever as a child, or so innovative in a difficult environment in former years. The quality of affirmation you receive from your consultant or friend is always very important at this particular time since your self-confidence has not yet been stabilized.

Step 5. Experience: Clarifying Your Career Goal. Here you use the master skills list that you formulated from your success stories. Fill out the Success Factors Chart and the Prioritizing Grid. (See

Part Three for exercises related to the process.) Do the skills analysis, values clarification, trait checklists, and executive quotient exercises. These exercises will heighten your awareness and stimulate new ideas. You are beginning to clarify your strengths and to experience a growing synthesis and focus.

Step 6. Imagination: Defining and Projecting Your New Self-Image. In this next step, you replace negative images with positive ones. The Symbol Exercise stimulates this development and helps you make the transition from your past to your future.

Step 7. Symbol: Finding the Appropriate Instrument to Propel You. Discover the true function of symbol in relation to creating your career. The résumé preparation comes in this stage. Your logo, letters of inquiry, clothes, style, manner, telephone personality—everything about you must present a clear, uncluttered symbol of *you*.

Step 8. Form: Planning the Strategy for Getting There. The eighth step guides you to making a quantum leap—to break the patterns, buck the system, get out of the groove, and explore new territory where Form expresses Reality. Researching the career possibilities in areas fitting your new career goal is a part of this stage. Now is the time to decide whether you want to put your energies in a large, medium-sized, or small company, a not-for-profit agency, a government bureau, a multinational corporation, or an educational institution—or perhaps strike out on your own as a consultant, or even form a new company.

Step 9. Communication: What Happens Between You and Others. The ninth step is a time of great excitement. One of my clients enjoyed this period so much that she was reluctant to terminate the activity when it was time to sign a new contract. If you have a consultant or supportive friend, the role has shifted somewhat. The effective communication between you and your helper is valuable preparation for sharpening up your communication skills. If possible, make tapes to listen to your voice and videotapes to see how you come off in relation to other people as you role-play anticipated interviews.

Step 10. Eternity: Assimilating the New Form into Your Life. The next step is the goal for which you have been reaching. When you get there, you will think, "What took me so long?" This step is the natural fruition of all your efforts. The satisfaction you will get from having taken charge of your life in creating your own career more than compensated for your struggles. Here you are participating in the work of the gods. You are now in the "eighth day of creation."

This part, with its ten chapters connecting the creation myths to the creativity process, is the framework and content of a new model for career development, as described in the rest of the book. At the end of each chapter a subsection called "Recalling the Creation Myths" indicates the relationship of the elements in the myths to the specific step in creativity, and points to existential factors in the career development process. The model will begin to come to life for you as you relate your own circumstances to these universal principles.

As you read the ten chapters (the ten steps in the career development process), you may want to follow the directions and do the appropriate matching exercises in Part Three, *Design for a New Creation: Your Personal Career Development Workbook*, as you go, rather than waiting until you finish Part Two.

ONE

🪷 Chaos

Exploring Your Confused State

*Let not young souls be smothered out before they do quaint
deeds and fully flaunt their pride. It is the world's one
crime its babes grow dull. Its poor are ox-like, limp and
leaden-eyed. Not that they sow but that they seldom reap.
Not that they serve but have no gods to serve. Not that they
die but that they die like sheep.*

—Vachel Lindsay

At last, it has happened to you. You have been fired. Always
before, when people you knew lost their jobs, you harbored the
secret hunch that they must lack some skill or have a certain personality flaw. You were sorry, and you expressed some concern,
but you didn't empathize with them very much. You held your chin
a little bit higher, comforting yourself that this couldn't happen to
you, even though a flash of fear may have momentarily shaken your
equilibrium.

Things are different now. Today *you* are standing in line before
the unemployment window, waiting your turn to sign up for unemployment insurance. You look around at your companions and
briefly reflect on your common plight, not having the heart or the
inclination to inquire about them. They may ask how you have
come to this situation, and you don't want to talk about it.

These days you avoid social events where you might run into
former associates or family friends. You may be tempted to ask how
things are, and when they describe what good positions they have,
their answers will only add to your humiliation at being out of
work. Plus what will you say when they ask what you're doing
now?

When you ride the subway or the bus or drive your car, the signs
around you and the faces coming and going seem to jump out in
derision. Television commercials and newspaper advertisements
are more infuriating than ever. They call to you to buy all the com-

modities of the "good life." You won't be a consumer for long, you
fear. Somehow, you have lost your ticket to that blissful place of
unlimited buying power. A ward of the state are you—no longer
a giver, but a taker.

Perhaps such reflection brings up your quarrel with God. A scripture verse from your childhood Sunday school days flashes into
your mind: "It is more blessed to give than to receive." You always
thought the ancient scribe was just writing nice platitudes. Now
that your hand is out to the state, you know what he meant. You
are caught in the dilemma of being both angry and grateful.

You are damned uncomfortable. This shouldn't happen to a good
person like you. Life is *not* fair. All is *not* well with the world. God
is *not* on His throne. You quit going to church or synagogue, or if
you do go, you take exception to the joyous hymns and the plastic smile on the priest, minister, or rabbi's face. When the collec-
tion plate comes around, you are seething inside and feel like
spitting into it. This sensation adds guilt to your emotional over-
load, and you walk out wondering what the hell this religion thing
is all about.

The "job market" is just an illusion, too—an expression used
by politicians to get votes. It doesn't exist. You know first-hand.
Haven't you run down all the ads in the paper that offered jobs that
even faintly resembled your qualifications? Haven't you manipu-
lated your self-image beyond all possible recognition to fit the
description of skills listed?

Your résumé is a mess, and you don't know what to do with it.
You are losing confidence that anybody ever reads it anyway. You
have become convinced that the jobs listed in the employment
agencies, department of labor, or search firms are all imaginary. In
fact, you are beginning to feel unreal yourself. Some days you
would like to fade away. You hide out in your darkened bedroom
for a while, conjuring up various ailments that could incapacitate
you. "Being sick is not disgraceful. Being unemployed is," you tell
yourself.

You have time to overread the paper, and discover that you are
even reading the obituaries—"John Jones, prominent physician dead
at fifty-eight," or "Mary Malcolm, writer of children's books, suc-
cumbs in her Towers apartment." You have nightmares of being
run over by cars or knifed in the the elevator. You are depressed
but you can't afford a psychiatrist (who probably wouldn't know

how it felt to be unemployed anyway). So how could she or he help you? You ponder over the various ways to commit suicide. You are in chaos.

What you need is some reason for hope, a guide through the morass, a road map, and a role model of someone who has been as low as you and survived—someone who emerged from chaos and created a new career.

○ Case Study: Paul
"I'm afraid I won't get any job."

Paul was one such person who created a new career out of his own chaos. When his journey began, he was a fifty-two-year-old top executive in a social service agency, which ran into financial problems and could no longer afford to pay his salary. They promoted a young woman to his position when they cut staff. Paul was out.

I saw him for a luncheon meeting shortly after this happened. He was buoyant and confident that he could land another comparable position without difficulty. He had many connections and had left "like a gentleman." He showed no apparent bitterness. We drank to his new adventure, and I gave my assurances that he could handle things. I vaguely mentioned that he could call me if there was anything I could do for him.

Three months passed; I had no word from him. One morning I awoke with him on my mind. So I went to the phone and called. "Boy, are you psychic," he exclaimed. "I was about to call you. I think it is time we talked."

We made an appointment and our work began. He gave me a brief account of his three months. He had contacted some of his employed friends, tracked down job leads they offered, and carefully checked out the executive search firms and other career development people. Some, he felt, were crooks, others overpriced, most not interested in him. One place was sympathetic but not entirely convincing.

He knew about the effectiveness of my career development process, for we had talked about it on a number of occasions. In fact, I remember I had lunch with him after I had lost my own executive position and was just coming out from the shambles to begin my own business. It was a source of satisfaction to me that he trusted me as a friend—enough to follow the process, now that he was unemployed. His first assignment was to write down the areas of conflict, confusion, dissatisfaction, or problem in his situation. When he returned, he handed me this list:

PAUL'S LIST OF PROBLEMS
1. No job.
2. Unclear about my next career choice.
3. Uncertain that I have a choice.
4. Envious of those who are working.
5. Angry at what seems inadequate caring on the part of friends and family (partly, perhaps, a tribute to my good cheer in the face of adversity).
6. Worried that I won't get a position I care about, one that is worthy of my talents and my capacity for total commitment.
7. Afraid that I won't get any job.
8. Concerned about keeping face—erosion of respect from others and of self-respect, ego damage.
9. Annoyed at my less-than-adequately aggressive approach to solving the employment problem.
10. Concerned about finances; unhappy about using up my savings and borrowing.
11. Bothered by the ease with which I stray into spending time on domestic chores and construction work on my home. My extracurricular activities and the offices I hold in organizations are also too time-consuming in light of my circumstances.
12. Uncertain in making the career choice and in searching out resources, how I can be more certain that the decisions are wise ones, potentially gratifying, rational. How to resolve conflicts between what seems most logical and likely and what is most appealing.

Paul's Personality Type. The Myers-Briggs Personality Indicator revealed that Paul was INTJ (Introvert, Intuitive, Thinking, Judging). Some of the characteristics attributed to this type are "Most individualistic, most independent of all types, logical, critical, decisive, determined, often stubborn, apt to be effective, relentless reorganizers, efficient executives, rich in ideas."

Paul's Past Successes. When I asked Paul to write ten stories from a list of his life's greatest successes, he included a brilliant account of a position as Public Relations Director of a media organization as his number one achievement. Here it is:

Success Story: Director of PR

Simply taking the position of director of public relations represented risk-taking and challenge acceptance. That's good, for I tend to be conservative. Never having done public relations, I nonetheless took the chance offered me. With no preconceptions about PR, I was free to shape the role as I saw it. And I saw my responsibility not as performing puffery, but rather as an obligation to create programs that would give the organization stature, status and viability—and therefore, render it meaningful and respectable to the press and the public, as well as gratifying to its members.

Hence, I proposed and then ran programs for forums and seminars; developed publications, including a regular newsletter, a quarterly journal, and a hard-cover publication—a 20th-anniversary history of an acting school.

In the process, I developed and honed my abilities in organization and administration. As I added staff, I learned how to motivate and direct the work of others, how to recognize and applaud achievement, how to deal forthrightly with ineptitude. As I added programs, I learned how to manage a diversity of activities and roles. And I learned how to achieve and maintain a good balance for myself between creative programmatic work, which gratifies me most, and things like financial reporting, budgeting, doing minutes of meetings, banal correspondence, etc., which are least gratifying to me.

My experience here plus my earlier experience in education, in a rather militaristic environment, shaped a writing and reporting style which is cohesive, has logical progression, and (though somewhat formal) is telling, because it is clear.

Then, upward mobility came as a natural concomitant to these growing skills.

Paul's stories included one about being an actor and another about going to school and working full time simultaneously. Two others involved management of theaters and hotels, and his last position combined his love of the arts, his management skills, and his interest in a social issue. Two of his success stories related to personal development and gave an understanding of the satisfying quality of life he had achieved.

Success Story: "A Neat, Loving, Likable Little Kid"

One of my enduring childhood memories—and they are few—is that of being all scrubbed and in pajamas and going with my mother to pick up my father at the subway a mile or so from home in the Bronx. I guess I was three or four. Because I was physically ill and small and weak until I was six, I was very dependent on care and affection. I recall vaguely a strong nurturing environment from my parents and my older brother and sister.

I took an early interest in helping out at home—cooking, cleaning, caring for plants, and the like, particularly because doing these things was pleasing to me and partly because I knew or sensed that they pleased others. Also, because of my more or less continuous illness, I was in the house a great deal. Cleanliness, interest in and ability to cook well, having a beautiful home, entertaining well are attributes which remain and grow stronger all the time. Sensitivity to others' needs and feelings, care of others (I was my younger brother's official babysitter for years), remembering birthdays and anniversaries—all these character traits developed in childhood stand me in good stead today. My older brother, an introverted engineer type in his youth (much more outgoing now), was a fascinating companion. I would "fetch and carry" for Bill in his basement workshop for hours on end. I still tend more to support the process of physical construction, handiwork, and the like than to lead in the process, but I do like doing that and most often amaze myself with my manual capabilities and physical endurance.

I remember being very genial with adults and liking to be with my many aunts and uncles and parents' friends (my folks were very social), helping to serve them.

Although I was not good at sports as a child (overprotected, I suspect) and to this day do not like to watch or participate in team sports, I was neither timorous nor lacking in adventure. I loved the water (we summered at a beach) and do to this day—swimming and water skiing are favorites, along with boating.

Clothing and appearance were important to me from my earliest recollection. I feel that dressing well and coordinatedly and for the occasion bespeaks personal care, taste, awareness of and respect for others and for place, time and event. I have always liked to "dress up," and decry the informality which prevails now among theater, opera and ballet audiences. I perceive dress as a means of demonstrating position, respect, interest, though I am not slavish in my concern and I am much more modest now in dealing with "fashion," much of which I perceive increasingly as contrived, foolish and wasteful of money and energy.

When Paul focused on priorities related to his skills and characteristics, he came up with these success factors[1], "value system" and "responsibility" tying for top place. In second place were "program development, integrity, adjusting to others," and in third place "in touch with feelings." "Public relations" rated fourth. His next story, one of the most beautiful love stories I've ever read, fits this priority list.

Success Story: A Love Affair of Nineteen Years' Duration

A love relationship which lasts, grows, and becomes richer with each passing year—this is the dream of every human being, I presume. I share such a relationship with Ben.

We met professionally. We were and remain quite different, though as in all relationships of duration, the differences seem to become less and less and the similarities grow as the years pass. Ben is short, blond, handsome. I am tall, dark, not bad-looking. He is detailed, methodical, precise; I am impulsive, quixotic, less precise. It all meshed beautifully, and we have changed and grown and taken from one another our best attributes. We developed mutual trust through shared interests, thinking together but not always alike, doing things and taking chances together that we never would have done alone.

During our first year, when I lived in New Jersey and Ben in New York, he and another friend of mine were visitors every weekend. He was supportive, helpful, generous. I was eager, responsive, the always-prepared host. Then I moved in with him in a cold-water flat in Brooklyn. And I joined him at work at the same company. For the following ten years we were together *24 hours every day*—sharing our growing love, our work, our professional companions, our expanding social and cultural life, our successively better homes.

I adopted so many of his attributes—attention to detail, methodical handling of records, financial management—in our professional and personal lives. He became more outgoing, more impulsive, more mature, easier. Our disagreements, and they have been remarkably few, usually stemmed from different perceptions about our professional roles. What differences we still have usually derive from his tenacity to detail, need for logical progression which is frustrated by my quickness, my shorthandlike assumption of understanding on the part of others, or my presumption of shared perceptions.

When we bought our first property together, we didn't have the $4,000 down payment and had to borrow most of it. But, by practicing economies and by a careful regimen of saving which we sustain still, we parlayed that original purchase into our present two profitable houses. Much of the initiative has been mine, much of the thorough follow-through has been his—but more and more we share both.

I have always tended to be grandiose in my plans, reaching always for the moon. Ben is the pragmatist, prepared to deal with the plodding moves, one step at a time, which carry a project forward. Each of us has learned from the other.

I can recall so many instances of shared discovery and agreement. He saw a painting in a gallery which he liked many years ago, and I went to look at it the next day and loved it. On the third day we bought it together. And so it has been, with furniture, art, so many things. It was I who said that it was ridiculous to go on paying ever higher and higher rent. It was he who contacted real estate agents, started looking, and weeding out good house buys from bad. Together we looked at the good ones, together we chose our present home.

I have succeeded partially in whetting his interest in world affairs, in social issues. Not to the degree of making my kind of commitment to joining organizations, to serving on boards, to subscribing to publications. But I note with great satisfaction his growing interest in the *Times* editorials and Op Eds, his broadening interest in issues. And I have taken the time and effort to introduce him to these, carefully, without pressure, with perspective.

I could go on and on about the moments every day that enrich and reinforce our love; respect for privacy, feeling one another's presence though separated by rooms and floors while reading or writing, working together last weekend to build our garden, planning and then relinquishing our month-long vacation this summer because obviously it wasn't right for me.

One of the beauties of our relationship is the love we have for one another's families. Together we bought and provided a home for Ben's parents. His family is in Oregon, and so visits are special. My family is here, and our entertaining of them is totally shared, and our visits to them the same. What more can I say? We are better by far because we are together.

After we identified Paul's top success factors from the data provided by his ten stories, we created a new, functional résumé based on them. He described related activities in program development, public and press relations, and fund raising, using strong verbs such as *developed, created, conceived, conducted, supervised, wrote, set up, handled.*

Paul's confidence grew as a tangible symbol of his identity, the résumé, came into form. By the time it was polished to perfection, we were ready to start networking to uncover the hidden job or to create one especially tailored to his experience and skills. During this resource-gathering stage, Paul saw people in fund-raising firms. He explored radio and television opportunities, sales possibilities, and administrative positions with corporations and public agencies. He kept a daily log and reported to me. Finally, he settled on the general field of public relations as his first choice.

His research in the library was long and arduous. He ferreted out the names and addresses of companies that interested him enough to explore. Then he wrote letters and made calls to those he selected. In the meantime, he created a basic part-time bread-and-butter job built around one of the social-issues organizations in which he was a national leader. His unemployment was running out, his savings were dwindling, and he had canceled vacation plans. Many leads had fizzled out. His telephone calls went unreturned. Some friends failed to lift a finger in his behalf. No ready-made job appeared on the horizon.

Four months' time had passed since we began working together. Paul acted with clarity, tenacity, and strong purpose. He finally found two public relations firms that were interested in his services. With both he negotiated a careful plan. Gradually, one of them began to appear to promise the most satisfaction. So he accepted it. He moved into the office and began using his creativity and enthusiasm, as well as his many contacts in media and other communicative arts. Soon he was well on his way to achieving his greatest success. He created his own career out of the chaos and disorientation caused by being fired at age 52. In 1982, Paul went out on his own. He formed his own public relations firm, beginning with several substantial clients. He is now flourishing, tapping a level of energy surpassing anything he has previously experienced.

○ **Case Study: Stan**

"Will my rosebush survive?"

Paul's situation is quite different from that of Stan, a young man just out of high school whose chaos arose from a blinding fear of not being able to be his real self. He put his existential question to me like this: "Will my rosebush survive at the Academy?"

Stan's father and older brother had been my clients, and I had been his teacher at a summer camp. His father had wanted him to come to me during the time when he was trying to decide which college to enter and what direction to go in following his graduation from high school, but he had resisted. By chance I saw him at a dinner party. We sat on the floor together and talked about his situation. His mother (who is divorced from his father) had offered to take him to Mexico as a graduation present. Yet he had been accepted in the Air Force Academy to study aeronautical engineering, and had to leave the next Monday—the same day as his planned trip. He had also been accepted at a major university—but without any financial aid—and he did not have the money to pay the $8,000 in fees.

The day after our chat, he called me for an appointment. At this late hour, I was a little apprehensive about what I could do for him, but was willing to try. During our first two-hour meeting, I asked him to tell me whatever he'd like to share. He said he had decided he wanted to fly and to design aeronautical instruments, that the Air Force was the place to get his education. This commitment would take ten years of his life—four years of college, one year of flight training, and five years of service. He would be twenty-seven when he competed his training and service stint.

Our dialogue went like this:

Hilda: How are you feeling about going now that the time is so close?
Stan: I'm feeling negative about the strictness. Pressure throws

me off. That's why I've been to three shrinks. If I go, I'll lose my whole summer. I won't get any trip. No vacation.

Hilda: When is your first leave?

Stan: Thanksgiving.

Hilda: Well, let's see. That's just about four months, isn't it? Not so long to wait, is it?

Stan: No.

Hilda: Are you anxious about leaving home?

Stan: No. I'm ready to leave. I've been away before.

Hilda: Do you have any other options besides the Academy, since you don't have money and don't want to borrow for your education?

Stan: No, not really.

Hilda: O.K. What can I do for you? Help you get rid of your negative feelings?

Stan: Yes. That's just about it.

Hilda: Well, let's first think about an environment where you could function well. Have you had any experiences where this was the case?

Stan: I enjoyed my literature course this year. There was something about the teacher's personality that matched mine. The classes were fun, and I did all my homework, every time. I made a 95 average.

Hilda: All right. Am I hearing that the thing that made a difference in the experience was that the work was connected to human relations?

Stan: Yes. That's it.

Then I asked Stan to tell me his ten biggest success stories. (We didn't have time for him to write them.) The English-class experience was one of them. He also included a story about taking a picture of his sister in the Blue Mountains. She was sitting in the fork of a big tree, and he captured a special look on her face that made him feel proud. He quietly commented, "Sharon is an earth person, and this pose suited her." Later when we talked about his need for the opportunity to be creative in his work, I pointed out that this picture represented creativity—the placing of objects in unusual combinations, since birds, not girls, are usually in trees. He laughed in a delightful, spontaneous way. He had begun to get over his uptightness and to slip out of the depressed mood he had when he met me at the party.

His good mood continued as he told other stories. One was about the time he was host to a youth group from Ohio visiting in New York City and later visited them. "Being Valedictorian of Nursery School" was a story that brought amusement to both of us. He described how he and his classmates wore miniature caps and gowns, and how he gave a speech that was part of the ceremony that was televised over a national TV news program. "I was chosen by the teacher because I was best," he confided. He added another significant bit of information: "My mother was proud of me when she saw me on television."

The account of his visit to the congressman in connection with receiving the nomination for the Air Force Academy revealed his strong need for immediate feedback and the approval of authoritative figures.

His other stories revealed these same characteristics as well as imagination, initiative, independence, friendliness, and sense of values, with top priority to human relations and being in touch with his feelings.

The activity that gave us the greatest insight into his chaos, and also a clue to his resources for facing his fear, was the Symbol Exercise. (See Part Three for full directions for doing your own exercise.) I gave him the directions, which included how to take himself through a mild state of altered consciousness—the awareness exercise. He was told to let a symbol of himself rise to his consciousness. When it was formed, he was to draw the symbol on a paper I furnished him, then to describe the qualities of the symbol and to incorporate them into his vision of himself.

He was to follow the same process in uncovering three other symbols—what he would like to be, what hindered him, and what could help him overcome his obstacle. He came up with two symbols of what he is and two of what hinders him, plus one of what will overcome the obstacle. His symbols and the words that he associated with them are illustrated here.

Stan
First Symbol
What I Am (A)

In motion on turntable
White
Tail that moved and changed
Traveled only in circles
Not in control since there are no wheels
Luxury, not necessary
Freedom if it had wheels
Expensive, can't afford it
Body, but no way to get moving

Stan
First Symbol
What I Am (B)

RAT
Scarred
Former surgery scar
Moving
Eating
Disgusting
In danger of trap
In danger from enemy
Ugly
Not lovable
Came out of wall
Furtive
Not wanted
Might be destroyed
Vulnerable

Stan
Second Symbol
What I'd Like to Be

STAIRS
Lead to doors and new space
Feet use them
Built out front, not hidden
Leading up
Flight—like flying in Air Force
Taking one step at a time
Sturdy
Built by people
Connected to buildings
Lead somewhere
Tool for climbing

FEET AND LEGS
Like the wheels to my car
Means of moving
Part of me
Stand on them
Important
Need caring for
Connected to whole
Go at different speeds
   (tiptoe, run, walk)
Take me where I want to go
In control

Stan
Third Symbol
What Hinders Me

Round window is murky and clouded over: bitterness, anger.

BRICK WALL
Block
Impediment
Strong (won't move easily)
Solid
Keeps out view
Closed in
Can't get going
Can't get around
Not in control
Powerless
Institution

FRONT DOOR OF CHURCH
Not for young people
Religion blocks
Hems you in
Cramps your freedom
Discounting
Not caring
Rules to be obeyed

Stan
Fourth Symbol
What Will Overcome the Obstacle

PICTURE

Rosebush	Colorful part
Woman's navel	Vision
Center—power	Symbol
Part of woman—female part	Artistic
Breast—nurturing	Exhibit
Delicate	Whole
Beautiful	Framework
Sensitive	Balanced

As Stan and I talked about his symbols, the room became electric with energy. He pointed out that he felt like he was a car without
wheels on a exhibit table going around and around without any
control. He said he also felt like a rat, with a big scar on its back
from being hurt as he came out of hiding. Since I knew something
of his background, I could give ready understanding, which was
fortunate since we had only two days for counseling.

The significance of the church door and brick wall was clear. In
describing them he told of his anger at the church for having been
an instrument of blockage rather than of help to him. The rose window was murky with his ire. Nobody listened to him, he said. (I
didn't remind him that he had come to me through a connection
with the church and that for several months I had taught his youth
class on Sunday morning. It was no time to be defensive.) He felt
free to be honest and open. I was grateful to be there with him.

The symbol of what could help overcome his obstacle was brilliant. He saw a picture hanging on the wall, a rosebush on the left
side and the partial outline of a woman's body on the right side.
He laughed; "Look at her belly button." We both studied the picture a while, chatting about how this represented his creative, artistic side. I commented that this was the quality that could enable
him to design aeronautical instruments in the future, as he had
described in his career goal. He could face the rigidity of Air Force
life by "hanging" this picture in his consciousness, to keep this
vision of creativity before him as his goal.

"Someday," I said, "when you've invented a new, important
instrument, you will remember this day." He looked at me, a big
grin on his face, and said, "I guess the question is, 'Will my rosebush survive at the Academy?'"

Stan remained in the Academy for only one year, returned to New
York, worked in a cigar store, and saved his earnings for a year. In
1987 he graduated *cum laude* with a B.S. degree in business and
marketing from a major university. I kept in touch with him infor-
mally and watched him deal with the healing process for his
"scarred rat" feeling and his negative attitude toward authority. He
is certainly no longer a car without wheels. He is on his feet, beginning the climb toward an autonomous, fulfilling life. Today Stan
is manager of a large paint and wallpaper store in a major eastern
city. His apartment is decorated tastefully in Art Deco style. He is
now considering returning to school to study interior design. This

is his way of maintaining structure while keeping his "rose bush" alive. He continues to use the creative process.

○ Recalling the Creation Myths

In the biblical creation myth there was darkness, nonbeing, inertia, and a distinctive force, a "void." This was prior to the creation of "light." In the Greek story, the first step is Prometheus stealing fire from the gods. In the Pre-Aryan Indian myth, the first stage is a picture of confusion between God and man—the creator and the creature. The Hawaiian myth features the ambiguity in the form of the swelling of the embryo. All these symbols point to the first element in anything that is created—chaos, confusion, ambiguity, lack of clarification.

This is the early state of the client seeking career counseling. The old forms no longer hold. No direction or order is discernable.

Where can we look for affirmation in the midst of such uncertainty? There is a clue in turning to the creation myths. I have defined myth as something that never was, but is always happening. The two case studies cited in this chapter illustrate the first stage in the creation myth and in the creativity process. As you ponder your own chaos, get in touch with the myth of your confusion "that never was and is always happening." You can begin to put the pieces together in a new way, as Paul did by first accepting the fact that there is a problem. Allow it to give you a message, and use the occasion to begin the creation of a new career.

Or, if you can identify better with Stan, the academy student whose chaos was experienced as the fear about surviving a rigid situation, find your secret symbol that can hang in the midst of the chaos, and begin to focus on it as the "eye of the storm," and discover Being emerging from it. The aesthetic part of Stan's personality, which he has learned to honor, is finally being integrated into his ordered part.

Go to Part Three, Step 1 (page 216), and write in your notebook. Name your chaos. Describe it, embrace it, and move on.

🌸 Being

Discovering the Reality of Your Situation

To penetrate into the essence of all being and significance and to release the fragrance of that inner attainment for the guidance and benefit of others, by expressing, in the world of forms, truth, love, purity and beauty—this is the sole game which has any intrinsic and absolute worth. All other happenings, incidents and attainments can, in themselves, have no lasting importance.

—Meher Baba

Paul's story—showing how, after he lost his job at fifty-two, he used his rich and varied experiences to give him clues for a new focus—may not give you much hope if you are still in your twenties.

Perhaps you are a magna cum laude graduate from a prestigious women's college. You studied anthropology or English or history. You failed to find the job you hoped for when you entered the labor market three years ago. "Can you type?" was the only thing that seemed to matter to the personnel people who interviewed you. You were faced with choosing between being a secretary or a department store clerk.

You had to do something, but you had no clear idea of a career. You were unsure of your identity. You couldn't decide what to be now that you were grown up.

In the back of your mind, you wondered whether Mother and Aunt Susie were right. Should you find a good (and if possible rich) man to marry? Perhaps he would take care of you for the rest of your life. But what about those friends who found a man, married, and quickly discovered their mistake? Or the others who stayed in the relationship only long enough to have children? They now have to try to build their careers while dealing with babysitters, day-care centers, and schools, and wrangling for enough alimony or child support to supplement the low-level salaries offered to people "without experience."

You know that even women who have stayed married find that a husband's salary is not enough. Some are caught in the two-paycheck syndrome, and often are not offered real "career" jobs, because some employers consider young mothers a poor risk. When the children catch the measles, the mother is usually the one who stays at home. And if the husband is transferred, she probably will have to give up her lower-paying job and move with him.

And, all things considered, you know that being a career misfit is not just a woman's problem. Many of your male classmates aren't doing much better.

○ Case Study: Don
"I need to find the right place for me."

Take Don, at twenty-six, who couldn't find a suitable job after he graduated so he went on to earn a master's degree in accounting. As a child, he had always been "good with numbers," and people advised him that accounting would always come in handy. But now, after four years in the accounting department of a major trust company, he is bored and depressed. He hates to go to work, and once he gets there, he finds he daydreams a lot.

Don came from a broken home. His mother had the sole responsibility for rearing him. When he was sixteen, he lived with his father, an insurance salesman, for one year. After that, he didn't hear from his father for five years. Although his relationship with his father was always a significant problem for Don, he also had difficulties with his mother, whose love seemed to be tied to how well he *did* rather than who he *was* as a person.

When I asked Don to describe his problem, one of the positive clues that surfaced as he recounted his dissatisfactions was his memory of *almost* getting a job as personnel trainee at a major publishing company. This hint helped him to discover the appropriate field for him to pursue now.

Don gradually looked at the pertinent experiences of his previous few years and saw that they could be worthwhile in helping him find a career that would enable him once again "to get up each morning with a smile on my face."

Don's first list of past successes had thirty items, including win-

ning a spelling bee in the sixth grade, having a poem published in
his synagogue's newspaper at age thirteen, designing a wall-sized
sports scoreboard while in grade school, getting his first job as a
stock boy at a supermarket during high school, and deciding to
consult Hilda Lee Dail for counseling.

Since career development includes learning to prioritize, he then
had to limit his list to ten top successes. He would rank them on
the basis of the energy experienced as he remembered each project.

DON'S FINAL LIST OF SUCCESS STORIES
1. Teaching tax seminars
2. Conducting opinion research project
3. Reporting on sports for community radio station
4. Supervising marketing research project for a local bank
   through my college
5. Being promoted in first summer job at the city's leading
   newspaper office
6. Supervising summer personnel at a national insurance
   company
7. Designing various information forms for my present
   company
8. Being promoted to senior assistant
9. Going to therapy and est
10. Clearing up problems with parents

While I listened to Don as he read each story, I not only wrote
down the success factors (characteristics and skills) I heard, but also
noted the expression in his eyes and his body language as he
detailed his successes. The key quotations that formed his "reality discovery" to help him with planning his future included: "I
thoroughly enjoyed the personal contact with my audience...the
challenge of answering their wide assortment of questions and
helping them with their problems." Don made this remark in connection with his first success story, describing the one activity in
his present position that he enjoyed—the opportunity to communicate with people, in meeting their need for tax-related information.

Something Don said in connection with another of his stories
highlights his major skills: "What I enjoyed most was working with
a group of people to reach a common goal...meeting with personnel
to get their understanding of what they felt the problems were,

designing a strategy (writing questions) to discover the problems, interviewing people on the street and over the phone, being selected to oversee the analysis of the results and the preparation of the final report, and making the presentation to the officers of the company." As he shared his stories, a definite pattern became apparent; the same skills were being mentioned again and again. The chart on this page reveals his top skills from the specific data he gave from his top ten achievements.

Success Factors Chart

On a scale of 1 to 5, weigh how much you used each skill in each of the ten stories.

				STORIES							
SUCCESS FACTORS	1	2	3	4	5	6	7	8	9	10	TOTAL
Pride in work	5	5	5	5	5	5	5	4	3	5	47
Courage	4	4	5	3	2	3	4	4	5	5	39
Endurance	4	5	2	3	0	5	3	5	0	5	32
Communication	5	5	5	5	5	4	5	3	5	5	47
Problem solving	4	2	0	5	5	3	2	5	5	5	36
Sense of responsibility	5	5	5	5	5	5	5	5	3	3	46
Public speaking	5	1	5	3	0	2	0	0	0	0	16
In touch with feelings	3	4	4	5	5	5	5	5	5	5	46
Sense of progress	3	3	5	2	5	4	4	5	5	5	41
Preparation	5	5	5	5	2	4	5	5	0	3	39
Trusting	3	4	2	4	3	4	2	2	5	5	34
Human relations	5	5	4	5	4	4	5	4	5	5	46
Need to help others	5	2	0	4	5	4	2	3	0	4	29
Transcultural dimension	5	1	1	1	1	0	0	0	0	0	9
Energy	5	5	5	4	4	5	5	3	0	5	41
Sturdy	4	4	4	5	4	5	5	4	0	3	38
Inspire trust in others	4	5	4	4	4	4	5	4	3	5	42
Reflective	3	4	5	4	3	3	4	2	5	5	38
Research	1	5	4	5	2	0	0	4	0	0	21
Organization	4	5	4	5	5	5	5	5	0	0	38
Enterprising	4	3	4	4	3	3	5	3	0	0	29
Teamwork	1	4	0	5	3	5	2	3	0	0	23
Recordkeeping	2	5	4	5	4	3	5	5	0	0	33
Creative	3	3	4	5	4	3	5	3	0	0	30
Analysis	2	5	4	5	4	5	4	4	5	5	43
Time management	3	5	5	5	3	4	3	5	0	0	33
Strategizing	2	4	3	5	3	4	4	4	0	0	29
Writing	2	5	5	5	4	0	5	3	0	0	29
Memory	4	1	2	2	2	1	0	4	5	5	26

Planning ahead	4	5	5	5	3	4	2	5	0	2	35
Attention to detail	4	5	5	5	3	5	5	5	5	5	47
Imagination	3	3	4	4	3	3	5	4	4	3	36
Broadcasting	4	4	5	1	1	1	0	2	0	0	18
Love of challenge	5	5	5	5	5	5	4	4	3	3	44
Need for recognition	4	4	5	4	5	5	3	4	5	5	44
Identifying with others	4	5	5	5	5	5	3	2	4	5	43
Decision making	4	3	5	5	4	4	5	5	5	4	44
In touch with childhood	1	0	5	1	2	3	5	3	5	5	30
Supervising	0	0	0	4	0	5	0	2	0	0	11
Designing	4	4	4	4	3	3	5	3	0	0	30
Liaison	4	5	3	4	3	2	0	1	0	0	22
Interview	1	5	1	5	2	0	0	2	0	0	16
Initiative	2	4	4	4	4	5	5	3	4	4	39
Troubleshooting	4	0	0	5	4	4	1	3	1	3	25
Enthusiasm	4	5	5	5	5	5	5	4	4	4	46
Management	0	0	0	4	0	5	0	1	0	0	10
Speedy—work fast	3	4	5	4	4	5	0	5	0	0	30
Persistent	3	4	4	4	3	4	5	3	4	3	37
Persuasive	5	5	3	5	3	3	5	4	4	4	41
Self-confident	5	4	4	4	4	4	5	4	4	4	42
Self-understanding	3	2	4	2	3	3	3	3	5	5	33
Observant	5	5	3	5	4	4	4	3	5	5	43
Open	3	4	3	4	3	3	3	3	5	5	36
Control	4	4	2	3	3	5	2	3	4	5	35
Forgiving	1	2	0	0	1	3	2	5	5	5	24
Self-accepting	3	2	3	4	5	4	2	4	5	5	37

When Don took the top twenty factors from his factors chart and prioritized them with the positioning grid (see Part Three for an example), he came up with the top three factors he cherished most and wanted to develop for future use. They were:

1. Communications
2. Being in touch with my feelings
3. Human relations

Don's new career objective became to enter the personnel field. He felt that there he would have the opportunity to *be* who he really is and to find meaning through relating to people rather than balancing books.

Here's how Don filled in his new goal sheet:

IMMEDIATE STEPS TOWARD CAREER GOAL
1. Prepare résumé and cover letters
2. Make contact with people in personnel field to discuss questions I have and suggestions for getting into the field
3. Investigate possible courses to take in personnel

NEXT STEPS (SIX MONTHS)
1. Obtain top-notch position in personnel, a job that will expose me to different areas of personnel
2. Take courses in personnel

FIVE-YEAR GOAL
To get experience in all major areas of corporate personnel, with the idea of possibly specializing in one field. However, this will depend on whether or not this specialization will allow me to reach my ultimate goal—VP of Personnel. Possibly the specialization would prevent that.

ULTIMATE GOAL
VP of Personnel in a large corporate environment.

The following is Don's new résumé, with some details disguised to maintain my client's anonymity.

Don's Résumé

CAREER OBJECTIVE	To pursue a career in Corporate Personnel Training and Management, utilizing my communication, research, and training skills developed during my business career and education.
EDUCATION	M.B.A.,Some University B.S., Other University
EMPLOYMENT	ABC Trust Co. New York, New York First two years as an auditor, working on engagements for a diverse group of corporate clients. Promoted to Senior Tax accountant specializing in individual taxation for U.S. citizens and aliens.

and Management
Supervising ten members of professional staff
Administering performance evaluation process
Creating new training design
Producing related training materials
Conducting instruction sessions

Significant Achievements in Communication
and Research
Presenting tax seminars to groups of up to 100
Developing tax information questionnaires
Negotiating audit settlements with state and
federal taxing authorities
Research and documenting solutions to tax
problems

Long Life Insurance Co.   New York, New York
Assistant Supervisor of 8-member clerical staff in
Group Policy Service Department. Significant
achievements included:
Initiating procedural changes in the department
Handling special research projects for
Departmental Vice President

SUMMER AND   AAA Research Co.   Anytown, Conn.
PART-TIME   Research Analyst on project for gubernatorial
EMPLOYMENT   candidate. Designed data instrument, conducted
interviews, analyzed results, compiled report, and
presented recommendations to candidate.

XYZ Life Insurance Co.   New York, New York
Manager of 20 college students for various
actuarial projects. Reported results directly to the
president.

City Newspaper   New York, New York
Subscription Clerk in Book and Educational
Division, doing customer service work.

It was now time for Don to gather information and resources.
I directed his library research to include the companies that I felt
would interest him. When he had made his initial list, he wrote a

cover letter to them to accompany his résumé. Note how he summarized his past experience, focusing on the things he had most enjoyed doing that would relate to his proposed future position.

Don's Cover Letter

Dear Employer:

Your fine record of economic growth and a proven commitment toward developing your human resources have prompted me to write this letter.

I am currently seeking a new career challenge in corporate management. The leadership, communication, training, and research skills that I have developed throughout my business career make me feel that I can make a significant contribution in this field.

At present, I am a senior tax accountant at ABC Trust Co. Over the past three and a half years, I have assumed a wide variety of responsibilities. My proudest moments have come from the extensive time I spent in the management and training areas. These experiences have included the development and implementation of instructional modules for staff members, the management and evaluation of professional staff, and the presentation of seminars to groups of up to 100 client employees. I have grown to realize that it is the management-related areas of my work that have excited me the most and offered me the greatest challenge.

I am interested in meeting with you to discuss career opportunities with your company. I am enclosing a copy of my résumé for your review. I will call your office shortly to set up an appointment.

Very truly yours,

Donald———————————

Enclosure—as above

When I reviewed Don's data, I noted that his Myers-Briggs Personality Type Indicator showed that he was ISFJ (Introvert, Sensing, Feeling, Judging). The introvert aspect guided me into steering him away from sales and marketing (one of his early trials). His extreme sensing score, plus his needs of feeling and judging, describe one who functions well in a structured situation. His love for report writing, chart making, and questionnaire formulation use his sensing traits, provided that he can connect these activities with a work pattern that offers meaning within his value system.

Don gathered a variety of conflicting advice from his research interviews. However, within a few weeks, I received a message that he had negotiated a position with a large corporate conglomerate. He has now located the appropriate environment for him. He has decided to stay within the general accounting field. A more humane working atmosphere encourage him to be in touch with his feelings and to invest his emotional aspect in his day to day accounting activities.

Don's decision to get out of a negative situation has paid off tremendously. His voice sounds enthusiastic, and his general energy level is high. "What I needed was basically to find the right place for me," he says, "I didn't have to change fields."

○ **What Are the Implications for You?**

No doubt you have observed that in recounting Don's case history, I have not only shared his struggle to discover "being," but have also shown how he went on with other stages in the process. I am not trying to present a picture of my clients as having miraculously solved all of their problems, but rather to show how they learned to allow for the possibility of failure, to give up being controlled by perfectionistic strivings that inhibit the mysterious meshing of their divergent drives. To keep spontaneity alive, we must always be open to the unexpected. Otherwise, we become bound to the past.

In her book *Centering*, potter Mary Caroline Richards writes that at one time she grieved because she could not make a close-fitting lid for a canister, teapot, or casserole. Then a friend sent her an ancient Korean pot, saying she thought Mary might like it because it looked like something she might have made. Mary loved it at once: "Its lid didn't fit at all! Yet it was a museum piece so to speak. Why, I mused, do I require of myself what I do not require of this pot? Its lid does not fit, but it inspires my spirit when I look at it and handle it. So I stopped worrying. Now I have little trouble making lids that fit."[1]

In discovering your "being," you may need to begin to think in terms of a whole new work ethic. The reward may not be in higher wages, another rung on the ladder, or the acclaim of your peers, but rather in sensing the creative forces that flow within you and gradually transform you.

Whether you choose to live your life in the corporate world or to follow an artist's lifestyle, your work must express what is your true "being." You are a creator, and there is no poverty and no poor indifference for you.

The poet Rainer Maria Rilke has some special advice for those who aspire to master an art. His advice has merit for other creative endeavors as well:

> A work of art is good if it has sprung from necessity. In this nature of its true origin lies the judgment of it; there is no other. Therefore, I know no advice for you save this: to go into yourself and test the deeps in which your life takes rise; at its source you will find the answer to the question whether you *must* create....
>
> For the creator must be in a world for himself and find everything in himself and in Nature to whom he has attached himself.[2]

If in working to understand your "being," you discover you are a hopeless egoist, a prima donna who has to have center stage, don't spend your life trying to hide out because of some injunction not to be self-seeking. Instead, subscribe to the creative approach and find an occupation that demands a person with an exalted ego and elevates high esteem. In other words, get a big stage. Show the world how to develop. Be a leader. Don't light a lamp and put it under a bushel.

As Edmund Fuller tells us,

> The new gullibility of our particular time is not that of the man who believes too much, but that of the man who believes too little—the man who has lost his sense of the miracle—the man capable of believing that Creation is in some way an automatic or commonplace thing, or even that man himself, physically and psychically, can be dissected into neat packages susceptible to complete explanation.
>
> When awe and wonder depart from our awareness, depression sets in, and after its blanket is lain smolderingly upon us for a while, despair may ensue, or the quest for kicks begin. The loss of wonder, of awe, of the sense of the sublime, is a condition leading to the death of the soul. There is no more withering state than that which takes all things for granted, whether with respect to

human beings or the rest of the natural order. The blasé attitude
means spiritual, emotional, intellectual, and creative death.[3]

Climb the Truth Ladder.[4] Start at the bottom with step one and move up to step five. Experience the joy of discovering the essence of your being that is "breaking the Truth Barrier."
> 5 State of natural knowing, doing without effort, flowing from being, moment of truth, breakthrough
> 4 Give up, can't do it; turn loose. Relinquish. Surrender
> 3 Belief system, faith, hope
> 2 Trying harder
> 1 Logic, facts, data

○ Case Study: Melanie
"I am a lion, leader of the jungle."

Melanie is a woman who knows with astounding clarity who she is. I am sharing her case with you in this chapter about creativity and being so that you can see from the selected stories how she emerged from high school with a sense of her feminine strength and an ability to compete with other women; and how in experiencing support from her father, she was able to form a strong identity that spells success in the business world, as illustrated in her story about coaching her boss for a speech. Her story about her job with the entrepreneur indicates how her key characteristics—impressiveness, indentification with others, confidence, determination, and response to challenge—point to her own new career as an entrepreneur.

When she completed the Symbol Exercise, Melanie further exhibited her leadership qualities. Her "I Am, I Need, Therefore I Will" paper is decisive. The strategy plan that follows shows she is willing to see her vision come to fruition through careful planning and persistent work.

Melanie began evolving her new business from a strategic base in the position she had when she first came to me. Her peers are very supportive during this transition period, since she knows how to meet their needs at the same time. She is a true lion. Melanie used the business jungle as her natural habitat, where she began merging creativity and being into one.

Melanie
First Symbol
What I Am

Lion—Leader, big, strong, king. Others are subservient. Even the mate goes hunting. He doesn't fight. His presence is what drives other animals away. Beautiful, but inaccessible; wonderful. But there are a couple of things I don't like:

1. Stays in same place, doesn't move
2. *Appears* to be king but is passive
3. Lack of freedom, spirit

Felt very heavy—strength, not fat. Sleek and feminine at same time. Felt regal. I saw a lion, king of forest, most *impressive* of jungle animals. He is leader, not hunter. Hyenas kill caribou; he eats their food. Lion has both male-female qualities. I've had so many thoughts about lion. Day by day, I have so many thoughts since I've been coming to you. When I walked out on the street, everybody was aware of me. I like being noticed. I realized I have this thing about me that appears to be bigger than I am. I feel this density that is lioness, a bigness I feel comfortable with. I've always been attracted to big, dense people—not fat, but warm and human.

Melanie
Second Symbol
What I'd Like to Be

Wild Mustang. Don't want to be caught and made into dog meat. Run with speed. Free, wild, constantly flowing.

Melanie
Third Symbol
What Hinders Me

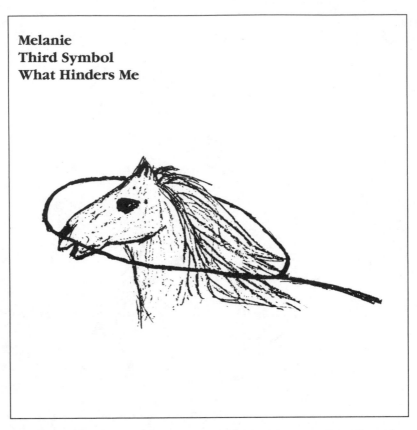

Lasso. My devil; child that supersedes the woman. People and things in my life who have lassoed me, mainly my relationship with my husband.

Melanie
Fourth Symbol
What Will Overcome the Obstacle

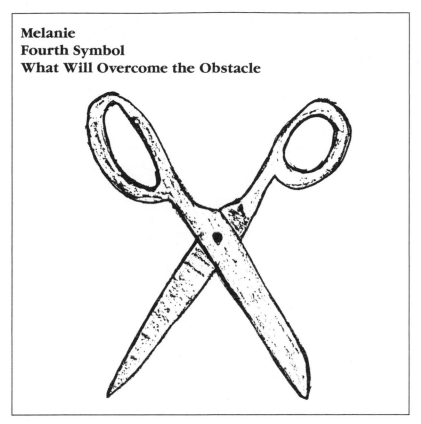

Scissors. To cut off what hinders me (lasso).

Melanie's success stories were a very powerful part of her process of career creation. I have included four of them here because they show so powerfully the essence of her personality.

Success Story: First Day of High School

In my home town in Utah, high school begins in the ninth grade, in a new school—a new beginning. And, in a very real way, everything a young girl or boy has accomplished previous to that first day of orientation is history. So, for a young girl who'd always been the star, and who'd always been comfortable with that identity, that first day at high school was bound to be somewhat traumatic.

Of course, I had no idea my stardom was on the line as I sat in that huge auditorium on that first day right in the middle of my group. In fact, I was feeling delighted at the size of my new class, and I remember the particular excitement I felt when I gazed around that audience and considered the possibilities that existed with so many new people. I was feeling sure and confident surrounded by my friends from my prior school years, and my gaze was broad, encompassing the whole of my new environment.

Suddenly my attention was captured by a girl just a few rows back, also sitting in the middle of what was most definitely her group, and I wondered how it was that such a girl could have existed anywhere in the State of Utah without my having seen her. And there was no question that I'd never seen her before, because I'd never have been able to forget her. We could not have been more physically diametric. She was beautiful in a fragile way. Her hair was long and red-gold. Her nose and chin were fine and elegant and perfection on her delicately sculptured face. She had long, graceful hands and fingers, and when she ran them through that hair, while she easily conversed with her group, I recognized another star, a formidable competitor.

I found myself becoming irritable and distracted by my overwhelming feelings of intimidation and threat. My talk and my laughter rose in volume; my gestures became exaggerated. It had become absolutely essential that she recognize in me what I had recognized in her—that I would have to be dealt with.

I was watching her at the very moment of her recognition. It was a gift from the heavens, allowing me to regain some of my composure, but I knew instinctively that I'd not yet won this battle.

I also felt, instinctively, that my only hope was to know her and to like her, and that to know her and like her would mean discovering her human frailties, and sharing with her mine. I casually and nonchalantly invited her to the ladies room.

When she stood up I saw that she was tall and slender and had wonderful long legs, and I wasn't at all happy that she even had the fashion of the day on her side. Truthfully, I felt there was no hope of ever competing with her physically—she was unequivocally the most beautiful woman I'd ever seen.

We stood in front of the ladies room mirror, brushing and primping and stealing glances at one another. It did wonders for my self-confidence to realize that she was quite as shy and intimidated with me as I was with her. I asked her all kinds of questions about herself, and I really gave myself away when I told her that I couldn't understand why I'd never seen her in town. She liked that, and she smiled at me, and she looked warm and generous. So I told her that I thought she was the prettiest girl I'd ever seen, and that I'd been jealous of her just before, but that I wasn't now that we'd had this time to get to know each other. I said that I wanted us to be good friends. To my great surprise, she expressed the same feelings about me. And so it was settled—we became good friends.

Success Story: Graduation Day

It was the day of my high school graduation. That evening was to be the "wrap-up" of my happy and successful school years, and I wanted it to be appropriately momentous. I spent the morning preparing for the speech I'd been asked to give. I washed and rolled my hair twice until it curled just so, and I put on and took off my graduation dress a half-dozen times to make sure it worked with everything—the shoes, the hair, and the speech. The phone rang incessantly—friends wanting to firm up plans for parties after graduation. It was my favorite kind of day—rushed and hectic and leading up to an event.

But the last time I answered the phone that day, our family doctor told me that my father had been rushed to the hospital. He'd been at the cottage, putting the speed boat into the lake, and his leg had been crushed between the boat trailer and the Jeep. He was going to be O.K., but he would be flat on his back for some time.

Once my fears had been alleviated and I'd recovered from the initial shock, I realized that my father could not be part of my graduation. I felt terribly disappointed and sorry for myself. I might have become unreasonably self-centered about it all, had I not just been sorting out and organizing my medals—the awards for my high school achievements. It suddenly became very clear to me that my graduation night was not my moment alone—it was also my father's moment. I pictured him in his hospital bed, helpless to do anything but lie there, and I thought how frustrated and angry he would be.

I quickly gathered all those medals, jumped in the car, and raced off to the hospital. The first thing he said to me when I walked into his room was how sorry he was that he would have to miss my graduation. He told me that he'd been looking forward to this day more than any he could remember, because he was so proud of me. I told him that I knew he felt that way and that I especially wanted him to be there, because he had championed me through all those happy years. Then I moved his bed tray in front of him and poured my medals on to it. I told him that they were for him, because he had made them all possible.

That night, as I stood in line in my cap and gown waiting for the processional to begin, I felt that what was to follow was now a mere formality. I felt no excitement, not even nervousness. The music began and we marched out into the gymnasium. The bleachers were filled to capacity; the overflow of audience was seated at the opposite end of the gym. The line of graduates was to make a square of the gym before filing into seats placed in the center. Just as I was nearing the end of the gym, preparing to make a sharp left, my eye caught the glint of a wheelchair and then the sparkle in my father's eyes. He was smiling and nodding his head to indicate his absolute pride and joy. I mouthed "Dad, I love you," and then continued my march.

When it was my turn to give my speech, I walked to the podium tall and straight, and very proud. Although I could no longer see my father, I could feel his strength emanating to me. I knew this was the best speech I'd ever given.

They took him away in the ambulance immediately following my speech. The doctor told me later that Dad had been in terrific pain, but that he had raised such hell in the hospital that they put better judgment aside to get him to my graduation. And the doctor also said, "Melanie, greater love hath no father!"

Success Story: The Entrepreneur

My husband and I had ben living in the backwoods of Maine for a
couple of years, so that when the decision was made to return to
New York City, I was more than just ready—I was delirious.

I was 24 then, and although I had worked previously as an
executive secretary, for the two years we'd lived in Maine I
managed a dentist's office, and didn't use my secretarial skills.
Anyway, I'd decided that I wasn't too keen on the idea of
secretarial work per se. I viewed our return to the city as a new
beginning, and therefore I decided I wanted a new start in
something else.

When I got to New York I began my job hunt by reading the
want ads every day. I was searching under that catch-all column
"Administrative Assistant" when finally one day I was struck by an
ad that read "Horse Breeder; Theatrical Producer; Entrepreneur
Seeks Adminstrative Assistant/Personal Secretary. Call X Agency."
And I knew I'd found my job.

I called the agency and told them I wanted to apply for the job.
They thanked me for my interest but asked no questions about
myself, telling me to come in. But I wasn't given a specific
appointment. When I got to the agency I was met with the usual
rigmarole—forms to be filled out, etc. Then I was escorted into a
cubicle office to meet a man. He asked me all sorts of questions
and finally suggested that I might interview with a large law firm to
work in one of their secretarial pools. I explained to him that I was
interested only in the job I'd read about. He said he wasn't handling
that position, but did know that I wasn't what they were looking
for. He liked me, though, that much I could see, so I decided to
trust my instincts and call his bluff. I asked him if he was quite
certain, and when he said yes, I stood up, thanked him for his time
and turned to leave. My instincts were right. He called me back,
explained that the job description called for a mature woman, but
said that he knew he could place me elsewhere. We talked at some
length, and when it finally sunk in that I was determined to get
that job, he said "O.K., give it your best shot."

That was the beginning of a series of interviews with three of
the senior partners of a large, prestigious Wall Street law firm, the

firm that represented the entrepreneur, and, then, the final interview—with her! I had a very difficult time convincing all concerned that I was mature and capable enough to work in her home as her personal secretary. But she was the most difficult to convince. However, I succeeded.

In the long run I became bored with the job, although I stuck with it for close to two years. The victory was my success in identifying what it was that I wanted and then, despite all obstacles, going out and getting it!

Success Story: Ned's Speech

Late in the afternoon of last Tuesday, Ned, one of the partners of the law firm I am now with, mentioned to me that at 8:30 the next morning he would be giving a 15-minute speech regarding bond ratings to members of the investment banking community on behalf of our client, Y Corporation. Since I was interested in the subject matter of his speech but could not attend the seminar, I asked him to practice on me. At 5:00 that evening, just an hour or so before he was to catch a train home, he stood in front of me and began reciting his treatise on bond ratings.

My first surprising discovery was that Ned, under any circumstances, could project himself so inadequately. The fact that he had memorized his speech did not help! He raced through it, slurring words and dropping off ends of sentences. His second mistake, though not surprising, was his overuse of legalese, which would have disenchanted, if not discombobulated, a seminar of investment bankers. But my most horrifying realization was that this speech, for which only 15 minutes had been set aside, was so overambitious, it had to fail.

While he was stumbling through his conclusion, I made some quick decisions as to how to handle this situation. Obviously, some fairly drastic alterations had to occur before he could take that speech before a seminar. On the other hand, we had two, maybe three hours to perfect it—and then only if I could convince him that it needed perfecting. Of course, there was his sensitive ego to deal with.

I suggested to him that he brush up on the new municipal bankruptcy law in case he were asked any questions concerning it. Meanwhile, I read his speech several times until I began to see an outline emerge. I quickly transferred the outline to index cards and

set up a mock podium and microphone. Realizing that time was of
the essence and that a great deal of it would be necessary to
perfect the speech, I decided that our strong point was Ned's
ability to charm the hell out of his audience. I reminded Ned of the
speechmakers we know in common, pointing out their ability to
become intimate with their audience by their facility with humor. I
also pointed out that although 200 people would not hear him if he
did not stand at his podium and speak into his microphone, he
could give in to his need to pace by stepping back from the
podium briefly at transition points in his speech. I proved to him
by demonstration that you can't speak too slowly, nor enunciate
too clearly, particularly when introducing the main points of your
speech. Ned went through his speech three more times, and by the
third time, he had me laughing and applauding.

That night was a victory for me. I was thrilled to discover my
ability to recognize immediately the shortcomings of the speech
and of Ned's delivery and, within the time limit, to coach him
successfully, emphasizing his strong points and deemphasizing his
weak ones.

The reaction to his speech was quite astonishing. He has been
asked to make three more speeches within the next two months,
and he has asked me to write them, coach him, and attend.

○ The "I Am" Treatise

Here is how Melanie did the other exercises in the process.

I am

I am, according to the Myers-Briggs index, an extroverted,
intuitive, thinking type, with a near balance in judgment and
perception. My prioritizing grid indicates that my number one
skill is my impressiveness. In reviewing my work to date, inclusive
of the above, I begin to discern, in the amalgamation of the parts,
an image of the whole of me.

While it is true that I am attentive to detail, thorough, analytical,
and organized, it is good to know that I am also imaginative,
creative, curious, insightful, and instinctive—a balance I'm
delighted with.

And, while on the one hand, I am determined, competitive,
responsive to challenge, comfortable with confrontation, good

at working under pressure, and have loads of energy, stamina and initiative, it is reassuring to know that, on the other hand, I am realistic, flexible, self-understanding, and able to face the truth and accept the facts.

It was no surprise to see human relations emerge so near the top of my list of skills, but it was very good to see it so heavily supported by other skills: critiquing skill, sales ability, persuasive skill, empathetic skill, generous quality, ability to stimulate others, ability to identify with others, social skill, trust-inspiring quality, confidence-inspiring skill, supportive quality, patience, enthusiasm, communication skill, conflict management skill, coordination, ability to compromise, need for center stage, and ability to share center stage.

I am a woman, a professional woman of presence, style, magnetism, confidence, inner calm, and an oceanic quality.

I need

1. Full *self-realization*, i.e., development and use of all my talents and skills
2. *Power*—to initiate plans and to make the decisions
3. Continual *challenge*
4. True sense of *achievement*
5. Contact with *people* to realize the full potential of my human relation skills, but
6. A position of *dominance* to satisfy my needs for *independence, individualism*, and *power*
7. *Recognition* for my work and my position
8. *Wealth*—to be in a position of potentially limitless financial growth and independence

Therefore, I will

Start my own business.

Immediate steps toward career goal

"The idea"—To find a demand that I can supply, by:
1. Defining my qualifications and my personal needs
2. Identifying a variety of needs in the business community

3. Weighing the significance to the business community of each need
4. Determining what product or services will answer each need
5. Analyzing my ability and desire to provide the product or service
6. Researching any business currently supplying products or services to answer the needs
7. Forecasting the short- and long-range marketability and profitability potentials to businesses that would be servicing the needs.
8. Using all possible resources in an effort to arrive at a realistic view of the risks vis-à-vis the likelihood of success
9. Isolating the one need (or related group of needs) for which there is (a) the greatest demand, (b) the strongest growth potential, and (c) a product or service I can, and want to, supply

Next steps (six months)

Once having decided what my business will be, I plan to spend the next six months giving birth to it. I will:
1. Define exactly what my business will do
2. Determine exactly who and where my market is, and what the realistic sales potential is
3. Plan what sales and marketing methods I will employ
4. Identify my competition and why they are, or are not, successful. Will my prices be competitive? What sets my business apart from the others?
5. Decide what I will require for office space. Will it be necessary to rent outside office space, or will I be able to set up in my apartment? What equipment and supplies will be necessary?
6. Consider partners and/or investors
7. Work out detailed budget, and meet with accountants to advise me of my profit potential, my break-even point, tax advantages to the different business structures, etc.
8. Arrange for any necessary financing
9. Form a legal business structure, i.e., sole proprietorship, corporation, etc.

10. Talk to everyone I know who is "going it alone." Get as much feedback as possible

Five-year goal

In five years, my goal is to be running a successful and growing company, and to have achieved personal financial independence, quality and respect in the business community, and true expertise in my field.

I would also hope that, sometime near the fourth or fifth year, my business will be large and strong enough to support a high-quality staff, thereby supplying me sufficient freedom and independence to pursue other ventures.

Ultimate goal

Ultimately I want to be the entrepreneur involved in many enterprises. I see this goal evolving through my business, like branches growing from the trunk of a great oak tree. The possibilities are limitless.

In pursuit of her goal, Melanie later left the legal firm and joined a small financial planning business as the second officer in command. She dealt with offering diverse services that included life insurance for executive incentive programs. She became an insurance agent, a licensed securities dealer and tax shelter expert. She eventually formed a new company, in which she was one of the principals. All of this activity is in direct alignment with the goals she set for herself. She gradually became aware that her family had been in insurance business, and that she actually was following in her father's footsteps. She sees her future as offering fascinating diversification, and she is rather amazed at how well she is doing in pushing toward her ultimate goal.

If your creativity is hidden by a lost sense of identity in the wrong kind of work (work that does not allow your "doing" to emerge out of your "being"), pay attention to the clues provided by Don, who persisted in uncovering his real self by following me in a carefully guided journey into the interior, and out into the clearing.

Or, if you have simply outgrown the concept of your identity that is being lassoed into passivity when, in essence, you are a freedom-loving lion or a wild mustang like Melanie, cut the cords and allow the being to escape.

Go to Part Three, Step 2 (page 218), and experience the exhilaration you deserve.

THREE

🪷 Encounter

Finding Clues for Success in Your Past

Only when my vocation and my avocation
Make two eyes as one in sight
Is the work ever really done
For heaven and the future's sake.
> —Robert Frost,
> "Two Tramps in Mud Time"

Perhaps you have tried everything people have suggested—all the right things. Still nothing happens. You don't know what you want to do. You remember the identification you felt when you saw the front cover of an issue of *Psychology Today* with the headline *I'm 58 years old and I still don't know what I'm going to be when I grow up*. Horrified at the idea of entering middle age or even old age without ever having "found yourself," you rack your brains for a solution.

Unfortunately, sometimes all the thinking and doing in the world gets us nowhere. In Samuel Beckett's play *Waiting for Godot*, the character named Lucky is ordered by his master, "Think!" In response, he blurts out a long speech that has all the pomposity of a philosophical discourse but is actually pure gibberish. This is a perfect illustration of the senselessness of using only our minds to determine our destiny.

In the preceding two chapters we have experienced Chaos and Being. Now we are ready for Encounter, the activity of looking directly at all our subpersonalities in our Orchestra Paradigm and discovering our success factors. Freud wrote that "the creative process taps the primitive and the emotional." For him, artists had unique and special talents that enabled them to delve into the depth of their personalities and give coherent from to ideas and impulses that remain buried and incoherent to others. "The writer," said Freud, "is a person with a certain flexibility of repression and the courage to let his unconscious speak."[1]

My work with hundreds of clients has convinced me that this same power is available as well to *ordinary* human beings who are willing to pay the price of exploration and to risk breaking their familiar patterns of behavior. This belief is in harmony with Jung's idea that everyone is born with universal images in a collective unconscious: the source and the significance of all creativity. The images break through in times of meditation and in our night dreams. They provide clues to the source of our power and indicate that we are ready to move forward in solving our problems. They come from the Ground of Being rather than from our conscious activity.

Charlotte Lackner Doyle, in writing for a Bank Street College symposium on the creative process, asked, "Why has the Mona Lisa smile tantalized people for centuries?" She then offered an answer: "Because it is the tantalizing smile that every infant sees on the tender, seductive, yet unavailable mother whose love each baby yearns for, but ultimately cannot fully consummate." Yet how do we get at this mystery of Being symbolized in the Mona Lisa? Let me suggest that for such an encounter there are three steps—time, medium, and discovery. The creative process begins with a sense of direction, with the hunch that there is something to go after. Spontaneity without a direction may be delightful and wonderful, but without the energy that drives it toward a specific goal, it does not result in creative work. Involvement of time brings us to the medium. That is why words must be used; why I ask people to spell their problem out on paper and then to write stories about their successes. If you tell me you have an idea but can't express it, I will answer that you don't know what the idea is until you say it—until you discover it through some medium.

A friend who taught school years ago in rural Georgia told me about a big overgrown boy in the third grade who kept reading out loud during what was scheduled as a silent reading time. When she reprimanded him, he looked up at her in amazement and exclaimed, "I have to *hear* what it says." The full realization of any idea or desire demands that it be expressed in some concrete form in the world of action. Writing is an important step in this process.

The discipline of writing a detailed description of the things you have done about which you feel proud, and then reading the story to a trained ear (the counselor), brings you to encounter. In fact, the encounter begins when you first see, even in a foggy way, that there is something in a former incident or project that beckons you to come closer.

A Chinese poet beautifully described the encounter of being and nonbeing: "We poets struggle with Non-Being to force it to yield Being. We knock upon silence for an answering music."[2] Perhaps as a result of years of being unconscious about your achievements, of habitually discounting the significance of tasks well done, you now experience only silence when you review your past. Then, at this point, it is time for you to follow what Martin Buber called the "I-Thou" encounter. When you knock upon the silence until you force it to yield its message for you, you participate in the Encounter. For example, let me tell you the story of Mavis, with whom I worked for almost a year as the encounter unfolded a clear sense of direction.

○ Case Study: Mavis

"She kept calling me her 'brick.'"

Twenty-four years old, Mavis was an honors graduate in psychology, having attended a well-known Eastern college. She first came to me because she was intensely bored with her job in a medium-sized public relations firm. We had several sessions, and she was well into the process when her company moved to New Jersey. The added commuting time made her day too long to squeeze in our counseling session. At the new location she forced herself to do her job—detailed list work, research into products, and contact with vendors, as well as handling a variety of clients.

For several months I didn't hear from her. Then one day I got her call, informing me that she had been terminated because her company had lost several accounts. By this time she was living on unemployment benefits and had little money to pay me, so we set up a barter system: I traded her one hour of counseling for one day of her working in my office. During the several months we were together, I watched her grow in awareness and courage, and ultimately break out of her ill-chosen field to compete for and win (over Ph.D. graduates) a significant position as psychological research assistant in one of the country's top research laboratories.

As she read her past success stories and identified her success factors or top skills and characteristics, "determination" was number one. "Response to challenge" and "value system" came in second. "Exploring, foresight, and adaptability" took third place.

However, the important detail that surfaced was not intrinsic in these factors themselves, but rather in the quality of her method of doing things. She took directions with concrete exactness. When I said, "Write as if you were telling the story to a five-year-old child," she produced such clear and elegant prose that I want to give you three of her stories in their entirety. Although they are long, they are worth studying as an example of this exercise. In them, you can see a careful, dependable, alert researcher emerging, one who is capable of complete dedication to projects connected with the development of people along with the progress of science.

As my files grew with the transcripts of our sessions and her diary, dreams, and other data, the element that excited me most was her growing confidence that she *was* what she was encountering in the process. She had begun to embody the winning characteristics, so that by the time she went for interviews, she was "it." And she was hired.

Read the following three stories to experience the qualities in her that gave her the exact skills she needed to be translated into her new career.

Success Story: Handmade Gifts for My Family

Several years ago I decided to made Christmas gifts for my family. I thought about what I could give them. I wanted it to be something special. Something just from me, that nobody else would give them.

My friend Marie showed me a pretty wreath she had made for her mother. I liked it. I thought my mother might like something like that, too. I asked Marie questions about how she made her wreath. It didn't seem very hard. Christmas was coming soon.

When I got home, I made plans. I looked in my closet and found my sewing machine. I got it out and made sure it still worked.

I took two wire coat hangers from the closet. I untwisted their necks. (It was hard! They were stiffly put together.) I unbent them. I knew I would need them for stringing the Styrofoam ball.

I went to the dime store. I couldn't find any Styrofoam balls like the ones I needed, so I asked the clerk. They didn't have any Styrofoam balls for Christmas. I went to another dime store and found the Styrofoam balls myself. They were in a big wire basket.

They looked old. Some were dented in places and some had turned brownish. I picked each one up and turned it over carefully in my hand. I set aside the ones I thought looked best. I counted out twenty. I had decided to use ten on each wreath—one wreath for Mother and one for Martha.

While I was looking at the Styrofoam balls, I saw Styrofoam cones. I remembered how someone in our office had once brought in a white Styrofoam cone with Hershey's kisses attached with toothpicks. I began to think of ways I could do something like that to give to my father and brother. I thought of ways to cover the cone and make it look more like a Christmas tree. I wanted the tree to be pretty and special. I thought about getting green fabric to cover the cones. Then I remembered that we once had bought crepe paper to decorate our house for a party.
I wasn't sure, but I thought that maybe we still had some of that left. I decided to look at home before I bought fabric.

I looked in the candy section for Hershey's kisses to put on the trees. I wanted the kind wrapped in red and green and silver foil for Christmas. I thought they would be prettier than just silver foil kisses. The store had only small bags of silver kisses, so I didn't buy any. But since it was near Christmas, I was careful to remember (in case I couldn't find any colored ones) that I could come back here for silver ones.

I took my purchases home. I was excited. I opened the bags right away and began stringing the balls onto one of the unbent coat hangers. It was fun! I had to be careful to poke through the very center of each ball so they would be balanced. I put ten balls on one hanger. Then I began trying to form the wire into a circle. I had to move the balls back and forth on the coat hanger to make a balanced circle.

I didn't know how much fabric I would need to cover the balls. I found a tape measure and measured the length of the wire with all the balls spaced apart. I measured the circumference of each ball. I decided I could stitch a tube of fabric (with my sewing machine) to go over the balls, and then join the ends of the fabric tube where they met.

After I figured out how much fabric I'd need for the two wreaths (remembering that fabric comes in different widths), I strung the other ten balls onto the second coat hanger. This time it was a little easier and went faster.

I looked in kitchen drawers for the green crepe paper for my trees. I began experimenting, wrapping it all around one of the Styrofoam cones. I wanted it to be smooth and tight, but it was hard to get it to lie flat without wrinkling it. I practiced lots of different ways, until I found a way that looked good. I used straight pins to fasten the paper to the cone.

I looked at the cone and thought it was pretty. I thought of some thin red ribbon my roommate had used to wrap my Christmas present. I thought it might look pretty wrapped around the tree. I went into her room and found the ribbon on her dresser. I brought it out to the living room and began wrapping it around the green cone. It was hard too! I tried lots of different ways and decided it could look pretty. I noticed on the price sticker that the ribbon was from the first dime store I had visited. I decided to go buy some.

I bought the ribbon and looked in a few stores for Hershey's kisses. The grocery store had three bags of the ones I wanted, and I bought two. I didn't know how many I would need.

I went to a department store next. I headed straight for the fabric department. I knew exactly what I wanted to buy for the wreaths. I wanted to cover them in dark green fabric and attach red-and-green plaid bows.

I went to the ribbon counter and looked at everything. There was no plaid ribbon!

Finally I found a checked ribbon that I liked. It was the right width, and it wasn't too expensive. I found some lace ribbon that was very pretty too. I decided I could alternate bows of ribbon and lace.

I picked out some red fabric with which to cover the wreaths. I was planning to make both wreaths the same, until I saw some red embroidered ribbon with hearts. It looked Pennsylvania Dutch, like something my mother would like. I decided to use that ribbon and the lace on the wreath for my mother, and the checked ribbon and lace on the wreath for Martha. I made sure the fabric I had chosen looked pretty with all the ribbon.

When I got home, I practiced tying bows with the different ribbons. The more I practiced, the prettier they got. I cut the red fabric and stitched one piece into a tube. I fitted the tube over one end of the wreaths. I had to experiment a lot, and move the balls around inside. I tried pinning the ends of the fabric closed. I arranged the bows in different ways and decided I could pin them just as well as sew them on.

I kept holding my wreaths up to look at them. I thought they were pretty. I was proud of what I had done. I wrapped them carefully and made the packages look pretty, too.

I experimented arranging the Hershey's kisses on my Styrofoam cones. I cut lots of toothpicks in half. I counted out all three colors so I could arrange the patterns differently on each tree.

I enjoyed making the trees and thought they were so nice that I went out and bought a third cone to make for another friend. And this time, since I had trouble finding colored kisses, I bought chocolate balls wrapped in different kinds of foil. They looked like Christmas ornaments. The tree I made out of these chocolates was so pretty that I decided to give it to my father.

I wrapped the trees very carefully in lots of newspaper to protect them, and then in Christmas paper. They looked wonderful and mysterious from the outside! I wrote something personal and special on each card.

Success Story: Becoming a Lab Instructor

The psych department asked for interested junior psych majors to consider instructing lab sections of D-100, introductory psychology. This was done in the spring for the following fall. I was away in England, but my advisor wrote to me over the summer and suggested I consider it. I was thrilled!
The department approved me, and I became scheduled into the departmental payroll with other bright and promising seniors.

I was able to become a lab instructor because:

I was a committed psych major.
I was a very good student in psych (I had worked hard and applied myself).
I was visible to members of the faculty.
I kept in contact with what was happening in the department during my absence.
I continued to plan for the future and look for every possible opportunity. I knew this would be a good one.

The lab instructors met one evening a week with the director of D-100 labs, and whichever professor from the department whose area of specialization the lab for that week covered. I had to fit all this into my very busy evening schedule. I didn't have any free evenings for studying.

We would discuss the execution of the lab experiment. The prof would give us background information and describe what material we must stress to our classes. Background reference material for us to read was also provided.

I was nervous before each lab. I had never taught before, and some of the material I had to teach my class I had never studied in a course. There were some seniors who had taught labs the year before as juniors. I sat in on one of their classes early in the week to better prepare myself for mine.

I would read all the reference material provided. I would make an outline of what I wanted to tell the class. I would practice explaining the material in my room. I would think of illustrations to draw on the board. I would think of interesting books that dealt with the subject that my students might like.

Since I was always nervous before a lab, I would try to wear something I liked and felt comfortable in. I would make sure my hair was washed.

At the first session I introduced myself to the class and told them what I was studying in the department. I told them I would always be available and willing to help them with any questions they had about psychology. I tried to learn all their names and a little about their interests. I always tried to interject some humor in the class.

As I got to know the class better and felt a little more comfortable in my role as instructor, the classes became easier. When someone asked a question about material I really didn't know about, I hated to say I didn't know, but I would. Then I'd either refer them to the lab director, or find out the answer myself for them. I wanted to know everything, because knowledge meant security to me, and control of the situation.

I tried to be encouraging to all of my students. Some of them were bored with the material and hated the assignments. Some of them would do the assignments but not as explained. I don't think I was always strict enough or demanding enough in what I asked of them. I found it uncomfortable to tell someone that what she had done was wrong, and always bent over backwards to be nice about correcting someone.

During spring semester the lab instructors were responsible for grading our students' weekly lab reports. That was extra work and meant having to be even more familiar with the material. We not only had to know the right answers, but also had to make comments on students' command of the material. A set of lab reports often took me several hours to correct. I would sometimes have to ask the lab director for more information about a topic. Teaching labs was a challenge. It took a lot of time and interfered with other things. (I was paid for it, though.) It was something I guess I believed in. It made me feel important, and I knew it was a valuable experience.

Success Story: Comforting Mother during Father's Illness

Mother called me at 6:00 A.M. the morning of my father's heart attack. Her voice was desperate but controlled. She was beside herself with anxiety, fear, and fatigue. I had been asleep about three hours, having been out with friends at a bar until very late the night before. I could still taste gin. My eyes were red; my mouth and body felt dehydrated. I felt wretched.

I was stunned by Mother's news that Dad had suffered a nearly fatal heart attack and was in intensive care at New Haven Hospital. Mother was all alone and frightened. She asked me to come to her right away.

I was shivering and nauseous, but I became alert immediately. My voice was strong and calm. It didn't crack. I told Mother I would come right away, that everything would be all right, that I loved her. Yes, I had plenty of money. Automatically, I began assembling my clothes and packing them. Part of my mind—my emotions—were numbed. The other part—the emergency, rational, reasoning self—was firing rapidly along. I checked train schedules. I woke my roommate and told her what the situation was. I made a list of people she had to call for me to explain why I wouldn't be at the church coffee hour. I told her where to take the cookies I had baked and who to see. I wrote down my parents' home phone number, my father's full name, and the number of the hospital.

I stepped into the shower. I can't remember if I washed my hair or not. I put on an outfit I knew my parents would like and wore the gold initial pin Dad gave me for my fourteenth Christmas. I drank some orange juice and took two aspirin.

At the train station, I forced myself to drink a cup of coffee and bought a bagel with cream cheese to eat on the train. I bought a newspaper and carried it on the train. I read the first half of the front page. I sat in my own seat by the window. I felt like death warmed over. It took me twenty minutes to finish my bagel. I noticed the people around me and wondered vaguely why they were on such an early train. I stared out the window. The ride was very familiar to me. This train was a local and stopped every few minutes. The doors buzzed every time they opened or closed and were very annoying. But the sun was shining—the day was going to be beautiful.

I sang to myself. I couldn't think of the reality of my father dying. I didn't know what I could expect except that Mother would be in tears and I couldn't be. So I kept looking out the window and singing to myself. I sang "Try to Remember" several times, alternating one of the phrases here and there to make it sound different. I thought about how that song would probably always remind me of this day, and this train ride.

I walked into the hospital confidently. I assumed my on-top-of-everything, professional air. I found out how to go to intensive care, and found my mother alone in the waiting room. She came to me in relieved tears, and we held each other close. I felt like her mother.

The doctor came and explained what had happened to my father. He let me go in to see Dad. Dad was pale and wan and weak and quiet, but very glad to see me. I was cheerful, optimistic, calm. I made him smile. The doctor and Mother came in, and I fed Dad breakfast. I tried to act like I wasn't really standing there feeding him, because I didn't want him to feel helpless. But I did want him to feel loved.

My mother and I waited in the waiting room together. My brother Ray was on his way. Mother had a lot to talk about. She needed to recount exactly what had happened to Dad; how he had collapsed; how she had acted quickly; how the ambulance came immediately; how competent and cooperative and kind the doctors had been. She needed to talk it all out. I listened.

When Ray came, Mother had to tell the story again...and for all of that week she had to relate it to people, probably fifty more times. I thought I'd scream out loud if I had to hear it again. But I never did. I knew it was good for her.

Lots of friends began arriving about noon to see Mother and find out how Dad was. Sitting in the close, warm waiting room (full of anxiety), waves of nausea kept flooding over me. Mother got me some tea and crackers. We had lunch together.

When I felt assured that Mother would not be all alone, I consented to going home to rest. I was exhausted. My brother drove me home. I slept soundly but kept being awakened by the phone, which I didn't want to answer. I had to sleep, to be strong and alert.

Later I found some things to eat and played the piano. The familiar music was good to hear.

All the next three days I stayed with Mother. Sometimes I heard what she said; sometimes I really couldn't listen. But I was there to make the decisions. I called my older brother. I decided when and how to tell my father's sister and parents the news. I suggested when we should eat. When Mother wanted to cry, I held her hand or stroked her hair. When she worried about the future and her job, I suggested lots of alternatives and possibilities for both of them. After the doctors talked to us each time with further diagnoses, Mother and I would discuss together what they had said, and how optimistic things were beginning to look. Mother never saw me cry. She kept calling me her "brick." I stayed at home. I wanted to be there.

A new résumé grew out of Mavis's new synthesis of her personality. Mavis's résumé is one reason why she was hired for a research position. Study it to discern how it revealed her transition process as she participated in creativity and encounter, using clues for success from her past history as a student lab instructor and her early career activities.

Mavis's Résumé

CAREER OBJECTIVE: A responsible position in applied psychological research providing the opportunity for creativity, analytical reasoning, and intellectual challenge.

EDUCATION AND DISTINCTIONS
ABC College, Magna cum laude, 1975, B.S., Psychology. Sigma Xi Honorary Scientific Research Society, May 1975. Honors Thesis read, Linguistic Society of American's Annual Conference, December 1975.

ACADEMIC PREPARATION
Independent Honors Research: A year's primary research investigating the role of redundancy of information and intonational contour of speech in facilitating children's comprehension of language.

Course Work: Concentration in developmental psychology; in-depth personality study of three-year-old over a four-month period; learning disabilities; educational psychology; experimental psychology; statistics; animal behavior; behavior analysis. Designed and implemented behavior modification programs for normal and retarded individuals.

Laboratory Instruction:
Academic year 1974-1975
Lectured introductory lab weekly; taught lab procedures, graded student lab reports. Topics included verbal learning, operant conditioning and techniques, perception, social psychology. My students received high grades on departmental exams and evaluated my teaching as very capable.

PRESENT RESEARCH ACTIVITIES
Assistant to Hilda Lee Dail
Career Development Consultant   New York, New York

Transcription of client tapes and compilation of data for dissertation on creativity and the career development process. Prepared all-day workshop on career transition for the American Society for Training and Development, February 1978. Completed four-month counseling process investigating own career transition.

Vocational Appraisal and Adjustment, two-hour graduate course, Teachers College, XYZ University, Spring 1978.

Mavis's Rationale for Her Career Choice

Implications of Academic Experience
   I graduated magna cum laude from ABC College with a B.S. in psychology. I challenged myself to the rigors of a competitive environment and succeeded well.

   I sought intellectual challenge. I developed creative and analytical skills, and demonstrated competence and thoroughness in research. I was constantly stimulated by the exchange of ideas with peers and professors, and shared my knowledge and enthusiasm for the study of psychology with the students I taught.

   Academic success and honors fulfilled me, and though my professors encouraged me to continue on to graduate school, I wanted to challenge myself in a new environment. The corporate world represented a vast unknown, and I had to learn if I could succeed as well in that domain as I had in the familiar domain of academics.

The business world challenged me in new and surprising ways. The same discipline and determination contributing to my academic success accompanied me through my corporate experience.

I proved my capability in areas unfamiliar to me, and at tasks foreign to my background and nature. I grasped new concepts quickly, was thorough, motivated, and coped efficiently under pressure. My intuitive marketing sense proved keen, and I sharpened it. I learned to assess the marketability of items and to locate potentially profitable products.

I communicated effectively with people on all levels. I learned to circumvent corporate strictures and meet others personably, winning their cooperation and motivating them to work more efficiently than before. I negotiated price among strong competitors in the printing industry and reduced costs. I learned to translate complicated production instructions into a form simple enough for semi-literate machine operators to understand, and increased productivity.

I worked well as a member of a team, sharing responsibilities and rewards, and also thrived when given a difficult problem to solve alone. Meeting the corporate challenge successfully proved a worthwhile and satisfying experience.

Career Planning for Connecting Experiences

Reviewing my corporate and academic experiences, I recognize the time absorbed in psychological research as the most stimulating, most challenging, and most rewarding. The thrill of contributing new information to the body of knowledge of language comprehension is more meaningful than anything I've known in the corporate world. Knowledge, once uncovered, exists forever for others to build upon.

I have concluded from my exposure to the realms of both business and research that I will best realize my potential and find fulfillment by integrating my corporate perspective with my respect and proclivity for applied psychological research.

Mavis's Corporate Experience

<u>Production Manager</u>   Public Relations Firm
May–December 1977
   Scheduled and administered the mailings of 8.5MM direct mail promotional pieces over an eight-month period.

Analyzed response patterns of promotional mailings; recommended expansion or reduction of list universes in 20 product areas.

Executed merge/purge of list universes totalling 3MM; eliminated from 9 to 27 percent duplicate names; reduced mailings costs by $120,000.

Introduced demographic and copy variables for testing in direct mail promotions which identified unprofitable portions of market.

Evaluated and redesigned format of artwork used in promotional mailings to unify types of printing ordered; simplify classes of inventory; reduce printing costs.

Purchased printing and insertion materials for all direct mail campaigns of parent company and clients. Responsible for $400,000 budget.

Negotiated price among competitors in printing and envelope markets; reduced printing costs by 10 percent.

Product Researcher   Public Relations Firm
August 1967–May 1977

Scoured golf market for promotable items. Obtained exclusive promotional rights to golf ball which launched our most successful direct mail campaign, grossing $250,000 from two mailings.

Surveyed and reviewed newly published books in several product areas; recommended acceptance or rejection for testing.

Conceptualized and designed golf newsletter intended to expand universe of names and create multiple buyers.

Assistant Buyer   Home Furnishings Department
July 1975—August 1976   of Large Department Store

Liaison between New York buying department and 12 branch store managers. Informed branches of all sales, promotions, new merchandise.

Supervised sales, clerical and warehouse staff of 10.

Structured and innovated departmental policy which reduced the return of custom ordered merchandise by 50 percent. Such returns cost departments thousands of dollars monthly in unsalable goods.

Tightened operational control over all paperwork contributing to inventory losses; next inventory reflected 0.2 percent overage.

References available on request.

The Encounter stage in the creation myths can point us to a new way of thinking about old problems. The communing between Creator and creatures in the Genesis story, the outraged god (Zeus) in the Promethean myth, the yearning to develop in the pre-Aryan account, and the appetite personified in the Hawaiian myth are all symbols of the principle of Encounter in the creativity process.

The ancient myths were an effort to get at the universal necessity for confrontation of opposites in any substance or situation. Today, old concepts about the separation of matter and consciousness are being exploded. Modern findings in brain physiology indicate a new order in biology paralleling the new order necessitated by discoveries at the quantal and nuclear levels in physics. It is now well known that there has been a major shift in the paradigm of Western science. Karl Pribram, a neurosurgeon and neurophysiologist, has proposed the holographic functioning of the brain and synthesized the implications with recent experiments in physics, suggesting that the entire universe is a hologram.[3]

Pribram defines the hologram as a mathematical plate, a photograph, a detail in pattern, a way of putting on film the frequency of patterns. The brain is a memory bank where no specific memory is lost. His experiments have enabled him to find cells in the brain that are in tune with frequency waves in the environment. A hologram can be divided into small parts and each one will have the complete pattern of the whole.

In a national conference of scientists, psychologists, and other professionals, Pribram demonstrated an image reconstruction by presenting audiovisual slides of a design of squares. Unfocused, they become a blurred picture of Lincoln. He reminded us that images are "ghosts" from the frequency domain. Zooming a lens shows part of an image. The zoom characteristic is the same as a piece of hologram. He concluded that meditation techniques allow us to take more and more of a hologram in a small piece. We begin to make the unconscious conscious, bit by bit.

This is how we think of old problems in a new way. The deductive (cause and effect, purpose and reason) is the old way. The new way is multidimensional and existential. It causes monism, dualism, and structuralism to collapse. There are then no boundaries. We experience a timeless, spaceless domain. This is where mystics have always been—tuning in on the holographic domain. They tuned in thousands of years ago on what we're going to find out tomorrow.

It is now time for you to stand aside and allow the encounter to happen—to "experience knowing" in the new way. Take heart from Mavis's case. She is now a researcher in areas of psychology and technical systems in a major laboratory. She is working on the human factor in engineering. One significant project was concerned with automatic speech recognition, working with a computer that understands human speech, and creating instruction for people to interact with the computer. Recently she presented a paper at an international conference in Europe. After being with the company for years and working alongside others who have Ph.D. degrees, she went to graduate school and got a master's degree. She also married a colleague and is now expecting a first child. She is thriving in this challenging situation and has never regretted taking this direction with her life.

Go to Part Three, Step 3 (page 230). Follow the instructions there.

FOUR

❧ The Developing Self

Identifying Your Growth Potential

*To venture causes anxiety, but not to venture is to lose
one's self . . . and to venture in the highest sense is precisely
to become conscious of one's self.*

—Søren Kierkegaard

As we continue our examination of creativity, you will discover that the encounter cannot be willed or forced. But you *can* will to open yourself to the experience of encounter with intensity of dedication and commitment. Such ability leads you into connecting creativity with the developing self. Here your task is to take responsibility for *becoming* what you already *are* in your essence, to perceive new ways of experiencing the many-faceted self.

Abraham Maslow, the psychologist who developed the theory of self-actualization, viewed creativity not as the making of a work of art, but as a way of living life, to be expressed in the manner in which one eats food, makes friends, decorates a house, or walks in the park. He advised psychologists and educators interested in creativity to focus not on talented neurotics, but on the conditions needed for a life of healthy growth. My work with clients is based on this same principle—that the creative process is experienced in terms of the total life. This book has been written to help you see the many ways in which you can use your past experiences to create a new concept of career as wholeness rather than to persist frozen in the same track, which is only one fragment of your total self. You can become willing to live with the anxiety of change— temporary rootlessness, disorientation, and nothingness—in order to grow. You can gain access to the deep wellsprings of creativity inside you only to the extent that you have developed a healthy, strong sense of self and freed yourself from the psychological umbilical cords that bind you and stifle your creative energy.

Lewis J. Sherrill, in his book *The Struggle of the Soul*, described the beginning development process as "a dread and a fear of

growth, a shrinking back from the hardships, the risks and dangers,
the suffering, which are involved in each stage of growth." He
described the different stages quite graphically:

> It is to be found in some form at every potential stage of growth.
> The infant emerges from the physical womb, but the psyche can
> decide only after prolonged struggle whether to emerge from the
> psychic womb of safety, or to stay enmeshed within it. The youth
> wishes to shake himself free of his parents, yet as the years roll
> on, child and parent may find themselves locked together by
> imprisoning bonds which neither is capable of breaking. In young
> maturity one who has achieved a certain type of free individuality
> may miss the deeper fulfillments of young maturity because he
> is afraid of the mature responsibilities of marriage, parenthood,
> parental love, business, state, and religion. Toward middle life, one
> may find his philosophy of life wholly inadequate to the demands
> placed upon it, and yet from pride or fear he may shrink from the
> frightening task of reorienting life. And as old age approaches, one
> may refuse to face it, clinging desperately to the outward trappings
> of youth, reckoning his golden age as somewhere in the past, and
> thus in his boastful refusal to grow old, he is already dying, but
> does not know it.[1]

When you embrace the full dimensions of the self—the being
along with the nonbeing—you can experience *ecstasy*. This is not
an irrational state, but rather a condition of higher consciousness,
beyond the level of the rational mind. This state integrates the
intellectual, volitional, and emotional functions, moving one toward
wholeness. It is as though, for a moment, you stand on a mountain peak, viewing your life from a wide and unlimited perfection.
From this point, you get a sense of direction that enables you to
sketch a mental map that can guide you for weeks of patient plodding up and down lesser hills, when your effort is dull and inspiration is conspicuously absent.

The great German poet Goethe has been described as a person
who achieved creative consciousness. The philosopher Nietzsche
said of him, "He disciplined himself into a wholeness, he *created*
himself." You don't have to be a genius of the status of Goethe to
create *your* self. In the last section, I emphasized how getting in
touch with past experience provided the channel for encountering the present validity with creativity. This section focuses more
directly on the aspect of growth potential.

The case history I have chosen to illustrate this growth potential concept is that of Dolly, a 45-year-old woman whom I had heard make a presentation at a professional club I belong to. Over a drink afterward, I asked if her company made maximum use of her talents. She answered, "No." So I gave her my card and suggested she call if I could help her in any way.

A few weeks later she came, and we plunged into one of the most fascinating cases I've ever had.

○ Case Study: Dolly
"I was determined to be somebody."

In describing her early life, growing up in a small town in New Mexico, Dolly said, "I rode to school on a Greyhound bus. We lived in such a small place there was no good school. I was determined to be somebody, to get beyond my narrow, restricted environment. Nobody at school knew my family. I lived with my grandmother because my father left my mother when I was nine. As I grew into womanhood, I created my own separate life—a lonely one.

This pattern of strong determination showed up again and again in her success stories. Here is one example that also highlights her need to be on center stage and to get immediate feedback, two other characteristics that came to be dominant as the process continued.

Success Story: The Prince and the Pauper

During my junior and senior high school years I helped to write many plays, variety shows, skits, etc. I also directed and performed in them. I thoroughly enjoyed every aspect of mounting a theatrical production.

The one show that stands out in my mind as having brought me the greatest joy and the greatest sense of achievement was my small role in our seventh-grade production of *The Prince and the Pauper.*

During that year I had my first Speech and Drama course. We studied radio production, dramatic declamation, diction, makeup techniques, the works. We had a fabulous teacher, Miss Jones, a woman I both admired and feared.

She assigned us *The Prince and the Pauper* as a reading

assignment. We analyzed the play, the action, the characters, and the actual era when these fictional events took place. From the beginning of our study of the play, I was drawn to the character who was the maid. She had only one speech, but I saw the opportunity to make that character into an unforgettable person. Even before I knew that this play was to be our big production of the year, I was imagining how she would dress, how she would look, how she would speak. I drove my family crazy practicing my Cockney accent. I had decided that this maid would have to be Cockney. I thought I could steal the show.

When Miss Jones announced that we would use this play as our Spring Drama, I was thrilled beyond words. Then she announced that auditions would be held to select a cast. I had auditioned for a part one other time in my life, and I knew what a terrifying experience it could be. However, I wanted the part I had practiced my Cockney speech to play. Before the audition dates were posted I found out that the richest girl in the school, Nellie, wanted the same part. My heart sank. I knew that her father was a very influential man in town and that she had studied drama. She had been to school in Europe and South America, which made her a very poised, sophisticated person even for a seventh-grader. But *I* wanted that part, so I set my mind to getting it.

My family thought I had driven them crazy before—ah, what they were in store for. I had to have an audience to gain confidence, and so I begged and bribed until I convinced my grandmother, mother, brother, and two uncles to sit and listen to me rehearse my part for hours. I was tireless in my efforts, and I expected them to be. When they would force me to give them a rest, I would stand before a three-way mirror and rehearse alone.

The time came for auditions. No one in my class knew how I viewed this part; I had confided in no one about my Cockney accent. I was the first to audition. I pushed my fear so far away from my consciousness that I stood before the committee and read the part with utmost confidence. I knew that I had done well, but I did not really expect to get the part.

Three days later, the names of the chosen for the cast were posted, and I was to play the part of the maid! It was one of the happiest moments of my life. I had been chosen over Nellie—that meant I was really good. (At that time in my life I had been very confused about what that meant—about money's influence on objectivity, on the *idea* of being educated—or at least being exposed to schools abroad and private lessons—and sophisticated, etc., as opposed to being good because you are willing to work hard.)

Since I already knew my part (so did my family, I might add), I could concentrate on the look I wanted for my character. We had no money for me to buy or rent a costume, and so I scouted around town. I asked older people I knew if they had anything on their attics I could use to make a costume. I found someone with the perfect dress, which she gladly let me borrow. My mother and I tore up an old sheet, and together we made me a long apron and an appropriate hat.

I spent hours trying to decide what to do with my long hair, which to my mind could not be sleek or chic and suit my character. With my mother's help we found a way for my hair to appear slightly untidy without looking downright disheveled. My Cockney maid was a woman who appeared to try to put herself together well, but never quite succeeded. Her hair appeared to be falling, but never fell. Her slip showed—but just slightly. Her shoes were scuffed but without holes. Her personality was one of a high-strung woman who was so terrified of her master that it made her indecisive. She could not decide which of her actions provoked greater degrees of his wrath. Herein lay my unforgettable character.

As I explained earlier, I had only one speech and three lines in one scene of the play. However, my Cockney maid was the only character in a rather lengthy three-act play who got a standing ovation at each performance. And I don't mean at curtain call. As I made my exit, the audience stood up and cheered! Need I tell you that I consider that to be the most thrilling—and shocking— moment I can remember?

Other success stories based on Dolly's being center stage were these:

Danced in recital—age 4
Clothes model—ages 3-6, again as a teenager
Appeared in TV feature—age 16
Appeared in full-length movie—age 5
Created, performed, and directed marionette show
Sang in girls' trio in school choir
Taught in training program in one job

Dolly's intense need to keep learning, which motivated her to take the Greyhound bus to school when she was growing up, has continued to dominate her. The second story I have chosen to share with you describes her strong determination and her organizational skills, in combination with her love of learning.

Success Story: Graduating from College

All my life I had wanted to go to college. For many reasons that was not possible for me at the time most people go. I was married when I was eighteen and had two children by the time I was twenty-four.

But when my older daughter was in kindergarten, that old longing came back: I wanted to go to college so that I could be a teacher. My husband thought my idea was a joke and told me that I could go to college if I could pay for it myself.

To keep myself busy I had worked part time at a local Sears store for a couple of years. When they offered me a full-time job, I decided to take it. For slightly more than a year I worked as a sales clerk in the Home Furnishings Department (selling draperies, curtains, upholstery, etc.) and saved my money.

Many changes were taking place in me; I was learning a great deal about myself. After looking over my old high school report cards, I discovered that all through junior high and high school I had been an A student in English. So I decided to give myself a test. I would enroll in a freshman English composition course at the local college. If I made an A in that course, I would take that as an omen that I should find a way to go to college. I kept all this a secret, except that I told my husband that I was going to go to school two nights a week during the summer and that I would pay all the expenses if he would stay home with our daughters those nights. He agreed.

Everything worked well. I got my high school transcript, new vaccinations, sent for college literature, planned meals in advance so there would be as little conflict at home as possible. After much investigation I registered for the summer session—one course. I knew that because I do not perform well on tests that I would never pass the required entrance exam. I reasoned, however, that since I was only taking one course, no exam would be required. (A call to the registrar proved I was right.) Furthermore, I figured that once I had a student ID number I would not be required to take an entrance exam because I would already "be enrolled" at the college should I decide to go full time. All proved to be accurate.

I went to my first college course at the age of thirty. I was scared to death. I did extremely well, developed a crush on the handsome professor, who was only a few years older than I, and *loved* the academic environment. I made an A in the course. The die was cast. I would go to college full time in the fall.

Only I knew that I had saved enough money to continue for a full semester or more to live as if I were working, plus enough to pay all the expenses for two semesters of college. I announced to my husband that I was leaving Sears and would enroll in college for a full fifteen-hour semester. I told him that I was hiring a girl to come in once a week to clean and do ironing. None of this would be his expense. Therefore, he agreed. Because my husband had chosen to change jobs so that he could work at night, I had use of the car during the day. Everything was perfect.

Things had been growing tense between my husband and me—I should say more tense. For the first time since we'd been married, I was extremely happy. He knew it had nothing to do with him. Therefore, he got himself a paramour, and I enjoyed college!

I finished my first full semester with a B + average. I made the Dean's List and was awarded a tuition scholarship. There was no doubt that I would enroll for the spring semester. But things grew worse and worse at home. By the middle of the spring semester I was determined to get out of the marriage. I confided in my mother, and she agreed that I should do what I want. She offered me a cash gift of $300, which I took. I confronted my husband with the hopelessness of our lives together and we agreed to separate.

In spite of my situation at home, I finished my second full semester with a B average, made the Dean's List and was awarded another tuition scholarship. I enrolled in summer school and started looking for work. I had become a known presence at the college, especially in the English Department, so many of the professors let me grade papers for them to earn a little money.

By June I had managed to get enough money together to move into a furnished apartment with our daughters. My husband had agreed to share the car with me until the divorce settlement was reached.

By the end of July the divorce was final. I had a part-time job as a bookkeeper in a local men's store, and my mother and a friend of mine had agreed to watch after the girls during the hours I was away. By the end of August it seemed far more reasonable for me to move to the same town the college was in and drive to my job. I reasoned that if I found an apartment in walking distance of the college and the girls' school, life would be less hectic for all of us.

We settled into a tiny apartment, and I enrolled the girls in the best elementary school in town. I registered for my third full semester. By now I had negotiated with the loan officers at the school and had been given a $1,000 per year loan. I found a better part-time job in a bookstore and worked on Friday night and all day Saturday at Sears. My husband had custody of the girls on weekends if he wanted them, and during the first couple of years he became my weekend babysitter.

Also, as a part of the divorce settlement, the children got $150 per month from their father. I got a cash settlement of $1,500. This allowed me to buy a used car and put away a small amount for emergencies. (This was a few years ago, when prices were not so high!)

Somehow I managed to keep my grades up and I never had to pay tuition after that first semester. I always received tuition scholarships. And I always worked for the English Department during registration, which always guaranteed my getting into the classes I needed to fit my schedule.

By now my situation was well known to everyone in the English Department. They all knew how I was juggling job, kids, and my course work. So the chairman of the Department called me in for an interview, asking if I could manage to keep up my studies, take care of my children, and work full time there. He explained that he would work my office hours around my courses and let me make up any needed hours by working half days on Saturdays. I agreed.

Now, at least my life centered around a walking-distance radius of the campus. I planned each semester with great care so that my daughters spent a minimal amount of time alone, kept all their doctor and dentist appointments, etc. They were wonderfully cooperative and extremely helpful, especially in terms of doing the household chores and laundry. They proved to have an extraordinary depth of understanding about what I was doing and how important it was.

Our schedule was hectic. I took the girls to school each morning at 7:30 and went to an 8:00 A.M. class. My classes ended at noon; I then went home to prepare lunch for the girls. I went to work at 1:00 p.m. At 5:00 p.m. I picked the girls up from the day school where they went after school, which was only a couple of blocks from their elementary school. I took them home, fed them, got the babysitter and went back to the office at 6:00 p.m. to work until 10:00.

Because I was an English major, I had an enormous amount of reading to do and many papers to write each semester. I learned to go with less and less sleep. My determination to succeed kept me from weakening and/or giving up. It also allowed me to find the time and the energy to be active socially, to take part in the Sigma Tau Delta (Honorary English Fraternity) activities, and to serve as the executive secretary of our chapter for two and a half years. I was also active in the local drama group, serving as house manager and publicity manager for two of their productions. I established many valuable relationships during this time, some of which have lasted to the present time. I learned a great deal about myself and about life as well as the subject matter of my courses. I could never have succeeded in all this without the love and cooperation of my daughters, the help my mother gave me (when she could), and the love and support of my friends. One of the happiest days of life was May 31, 1967, when I graduated *in absentia* from the University, *in absentia* because at long last it was over—I could stay home to relax and sleep!

After Dolly wrote and shared her stories with me, we began to prioritize her skills. Here is one of her lists that proved to be significant:

I ENJOY MOST
Learning
Organizing
Teaching (showmanship)
Influencing others/motivating
Thinking/problem solving, researching

I AM
An achiever
Determined/fighter/survivor
Persistent
Chic and need a job that uses that quality
Extravagant and need a job that pays well
A lover of independence
A freedom-lover, with direction accepted only when needed

I am in conflict because I know I have valuable skills, that I am capable, independent, motivated to work, that I am loyal, strong, dependable. But I cannot identify a composite of skills that, when used, bring me the most joy for the longest period of time. My thoughts are scattered. I can't bring my goals into focus.

Near the end of the counseling period, she wrote this list from all her collected data:

KEY CHARACTERISTICS
Problem solving
Pride in work
Ambition
Management skills
Persuasiveness
Communication skills (written and verbal)
Independence
Training and organization skills

The Symbol Exercise gave Dolly very potent information, as her words and her pictures on the following pages indicate.

Dolly
First Symbol
What I Am

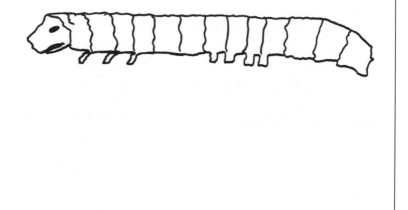

A caterpillar. A caterpillar crawls around and is vulnerable. It is an extremely limited creature. Its only reason for being is for what it is to become. There is nothing special about the worm itself. It is not beautiful, not even attractive to look at. It seems helpless. Because helplessness is associated with weakness, I view the worm as revolting.

This worm is a self-indulging creature. Since its purpose is to be something else, its existence is only one of survival. In this respect, I relate closely to the caterpillar. I have only survived. The self-indulgence of this worm takes form in its eating habits. The worm lives to eat. My self-indulgence is more a self-pity. Because I view myself as "becoming" rather than "being," I feel sorry for myself and allow myself to do as I please—be lazy or to drink or to give in to my weaknesses rather than to deal with them.

A caterpillar can easily be overlooked. It has little opportunity to be in the spotlight. It gets stepped on and smashed, therefore, never evolving into the beautiful butterfly it was intended to be.

Dolly
Second Symbol
What I'd Like to Be

A Butterfly. A beautiful butterfly has a definite ecological purpose to serve. It helps to pollinate plants that are important to keep ecological balance. The butterfly is strong and flies from plant to plant with few, if any breaks. Yet, because of the thin construction of its wings, the butterfly is a fragile being. It can soar to rather remarkable heights for being so small and fragile.

Its beauty is so captivating that most people are fascinated with this creature. Those who don't collect them are still willing to watch and admire the beautiful insect's adventures.

It is important for me to do something worthwhile, and it is also important for me to get attention and admiration for what I'm doing. I've always believed that I could become "famous," but something seems to hold me back.

Dolly
Third Symbol
What Hinders Me

Fear, Self-Doubt, Trapped in a Cocoon. Self-doubt is like a monster with many heads. The heads are nameless. It is very hard to identify what any given feeling of fear or self-doubt comes from. Am I afraid that I'm not intelligent enough? Afraid I'll fail? What?

Self-doubt traps me and prevents me from creating or from achieving. Golden opportunities arise, and that ugly feeling in the pit of my stomach starts to rise. My heart beats faster. It is only when I realize what is happening that the feeling can be controlled—even overcome. So, in fact, all that keeps me trapped inside the cocoon is *me*.

Dolly
Fourth Symbol
What Will Overcome the Obstacle

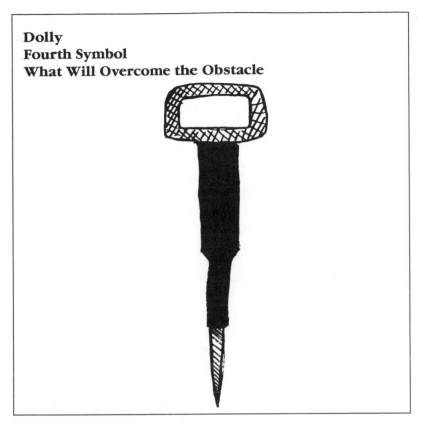

A Pneumatic Hammer. My *self* can be a very powerful force to deal with. As the pneumatic hammer pounds away at concrete and other hard materials, I can use my mind and inner strength to pound away at my self-doubt and free me of this crippling force. This powerful hammer must pound into a surface again and again to weaken that surface. Eventually, the concrete or other substance begins to break away. I see this as being analogous to the forceful drilling I must do to come out of my cocoon.

Now let's see how all these elements fit together to help Dolly find a new career. Dolly's job history had several significant factors. She brought her two daughters and $1,500 of borrowed money to New York after her graduation. Beginning as a receptionist, advancing to office manager, and then to sales and training supervisor, she found she was easily bored once she had conquered the problems each offered. She was impatient with incompetence and lack of recognition for her work. By the time she reached me, she had become head of a training program.

As we continued to unearth her considerable strengths, she became increasingly dissatisfied with her position. She also developed a physical manifestation of this dilemma—a case of hypoglycemia, or low blood sugar, which caused extreme fatigue. Since her present husband (by now she had remarried) had a substantial job, she decided she could afford to resign and take three months off to give full time to the Creativity Process with me and to regain her health.

The work with me was exhilarating. She became increasingly aware of her power. But her dissatisfaction at being unable to come up with a clear picture of what her next step should be in carrying out a new career grew more intense each day. Then one day she called to say, "I've got it." She described how she was riding in the car with her husband when suddenly what flashed into her consciousness, like a "big neon sign in front of my eyes" was *Law*. As she said, "I was filled with energy and excitement. This is really what I want to do—study law. I'll get a job at a university where I can get free tuition, and I'll begin my work toward a law degree. This will allow me to use all my skills to the greatest advantage. Why did it take so long to discover this?"

She immediately set into motion an intense marketing plan—to find the appropriate job to help her to her next goal of becoming a lawyer. Throughout her process she exhibited the same determination that she showed in the *Prince and the Pauper* story. As a result she landed a responsible executive position in a university, over intense competition, and began plans for registering for her first course in law school. Her story, "I Rode to School on a Greyhound Bus," flashed into my mind as I congratulated her on her latest ticket toward her new journey.

The concept of human development is woven into all the creation myths. The actualized freedom exhibited by Adam and Eve as they become aware of their separateness and eventually their alienation from the Creator and each other ("This woman tempted me") is all a part of the picture of the emerging self-consciousness.

Prometheus developed in consciousness by being punished by Zeus (he was tied to the mountain and eaten away by vultures). The split in the images from pre-Aryan Indian myth, and the inner conception that was maintained in the Hawaiian story both focus on the idea of development from conflict and confusion to dawning awareness of separateness and responsible action.

The "mythic self" is undergoing fresh scrutiny in present experiments in developmental psychology and in explorations into how the nervous system functions. Itzhak Bentov, author of *Stalking the Wild Pendulum*, presented an approach to the mechanics of consciousness and the evolutionary process of the human nervous system. He postulated that if we start with the evolution idea that we came from monkeys, we can find a few people who are today's "monkeys," at the bottom of the bell curve. Then we can find some highly developed people. We can go with them to the top of the bell curve and down the other side and be highly evolved.

Monkey People　　　　　　　　　　　　　　　　*Highly Evolved*

Bentov supports the Developing Self aspect of the creation myths. He says people who are evolved can experience sudden evolution—flow of energy through the spine, increased awareness, unsolicited grace.

Dolly's experience of seeing the flash of *Law* before her as she rode in her car, was such a spurt of development after the long pull up the bell curve with me. Even though the position she obtained—as development officer at a prominent university—was so satisfying that she abandoned the idea of studying law, it was the image of herself as someone powerful that gave her the impetus to move ahead. When we examined the skills she used in this work, we found that she had ample opportunity to be at center stage, to be dramatic, influence people, solve problems, have pride in her work, train and manage a large staff, and use communication skills (both written and oral). If you check the lists she made for me, you will see all of these factors there. When I last spoke to her, she was indeed one of the highly evolved people who had progressed to the right side of the bell curve. Looking again at her Symbols Exercises, we discovered that she had become the beautiful butterfly who wanted to "do something worthwhile" and "get attention and admiration for what I'm doing."

Dolly, like Stan, did not follow the exact goal she envisioned. (Stan first thought he wanted to be an inventor, but instead decided to use his creativity to decorate interiors.) The important point here is that skills are transferrable for developing many different career possibilities. This is a viewpoint that I have used over and over in helping people make necessary transitions. Often, because of familiarity of work habits, people get tunnel vision, lose their spark of creativity, and think that life just has to continue with a humdrum sameness. The good news implied by the creation myths is that the saturation point, when energy lags, marks the end of one developmental stage and the beginning of another and higher form of consciousness.

Go to Part Three, Step 4 (page 233), and begin you climb by following the markers placed there for you.

FIVE

❧ Experience

Clarifying Your Career Goal

Nietzsche described the person who has creative self-consciousness when he said about Goethe: "He disciplined himself into wholeness, he created himself....Such a spirit who has become free stands amid the cosmos with a joyous trusting fatalism, in the faith that...in the whole all is redeemed and affirmed—he does not negate any more."
—Rollo May

By now it has become increasingly clear to you that your whole self must be involved in the act of creativity. Everything that has happened to you, whether you consciously remember it or not, becomes a part of the substance out of which your career grows. This is why creativity and experience are so closely interrelated. How you react to your experiences affects the form and substance of your work.

What makes people creative instead of sterile? Years ago a group of psychologists working under a grant by the Carnegie Corporation of New York began a nationwide study of human creativity in the United States.[1] They wanted scientific answers to the mystery of human personality, biology, intelligence, and intuition that makes some persons more creative than others. The researchers wanted to investigate the stereotyped view of creative persons as introverted, neurotic, eccentric eggheads. About six hundred persons participated in the project. The professional groups whose creative members were chosen for study included writers, architects, research workers in physical science and engineering, and mathematics, nominated by experts in their own fields. A brief summary of their findings will help illuminate the creative process.

Although the study found that highly creative persons were, in the main, above average in intelligence, the relationship of IQ to creativity itself was not very clear-cut. Creative writers scored higher than other groups in verbal intelligence—but not so in the spatial arrangement tests, where they had the lowest score.

Creative persons have an unusual capacity to record and retain for easy retrieval the experiences of their life history. They are discerning, observant, alert, capable of concentrating their attention, readily shifting appropriately. Fluent in scanning thoughts and choosing those that serve to solve problems they undertake, they have a wide range of information at their command. They have greater fluency of combination than others have. Therefore, since creativity is defined by the adaptiveness of a response as well as its unusualness, it was apparent that intelligence alone will tend to produce creativity.

Yet intelligence by itself does not guarantee creativity. Regardless of the level of their measured intelligence, what seems to characterize creative persons—and this especially is so for the artistically creative—is the relative absence of repression and suppression as mechanisms for the control of impulse and imagery. Repression operates against creativity, regardless of how intelligent a person may be, because it makes unavailable to the individual large aspects of experience, particularly the life of impulse and experience, which gets assimilated to the symbols of aggression and sexuality.

Openness to experience is one of the most striking characteristics of highly creative persons. It is this openness to experience and the relative lack of self-defensiveness that make it possible for creative people to speak frankly and critically about their childhood and family, and candidly about themselves and their problems as adults.

Creative persons tend to reveal a considerable amount of psychic turbulence. By and large, they freely admit that they have psychological problems, and they speak frankly about their symptoms and complaints. This finding suggests that healthy people are not people who have *no* problems, but people who deal with their problems directly and creatively.

Creative persons are inclined to be more interested and curious, more open and receptive, seeking to experience life to the full. Indeed the more perceptive a person is, the more creative he or she tends to be.

Even though about two-thirds of the persons tested showed a tendency to be introverted, those who were extroverts were just as creative as the introverts. All were impressive personalities who had become in a great measure the person they were capable of becoming.

Since creative persons are not preoccupied with the impression they make on others, nor with others' opinions of them, they are freer. Their behavior is dictated more by their own set of values and by ethical standards that may not be precisely those of others around them. The highly creative are not conformists in their ideas, yet they are not deliberate nonconformists either. Instead, they are genuinely independent.

For the truly creative, it is not enough just to solve a problem; the solution must be an elegant one. The esthetic viewpoint permeates all of creative persons' work; they seek not only truth but also beauty.

If the listing of these characteristics of creative persons makes you feel inferior, let me quickly say that these findings were given to you, not to make you discouraged with your own achievements, but to help you see the goal ahead for all of you who deeply desire to become creative, to be able to use your creativity most effectively. Only *you* can carve your destiny in this respect; you are not responsible for the amount of intelligence with which you were endowed. And you do not have full control of the situation in which you find yourself in life. But you *are* responsible for how you transform these experiences into creative material that can help you function on a high level in your daily tasks—in whatever work you choose. *You* must create your own environment.

O Case Study: Diane
"I don't feel at home in my work environment."

Diane's story seems appropriate here. When she came to me, she was thirty-six and about to be fired from a job in New York's garment industry, much below her ability level. Through a series of events that began a year before with her mother's death, her sister's mental breakdown, and a company's reorganization that resulted in her being fired, she had become unsure of herself.

She had not been able to keep a job for more than a couple of months, and she had lost any sense of career or goal in her life. "I don't feel at home in my present work environment," she said. "I know I'm operating on a lot of different levels. I feel like I'm hiding out, embarrassed about being there. I haven't packaged myself well. I got this job through an agency. I feel like I'm coasting, going backward. I just talked myself into taking it. It's a terrible situation.

My boss is highly disorganized. He runs a one-man show; there's no planning. He treats women like dummies. The owner of the company referred to me as 'this broad.' I have no privacy. Everyone yells."

Diane had a bachelor's degree in textiles and home economics from a state university. She came to New York immediately out of college, got a job with a national fashion magazine. She had several jobs that put her on the professional level; but somewhere down the line she began to discount her achievements, telling herself, "Anyone could do that. I'm not so great."

She came from a prominent Southern family, both parents having been on the national political scene. The home she grew up in was of historical significance, and with both parents dead, she found herself the executor of a valuable estate. Diane keenly felt a split between the concept of herself from her family background and from her work situation. She was cut off from her roots. "I'm pained to the point of embarrassment and shame. Everything about my current job rubs salt into the wound," she says.

As I began to work with her, she grew in awareness of her strengths. Here is how she came to see herself from the data we gathered.

ASPECTS THAT ARE ME
Bright, brighter than most
Independent
Creative/innovative
Analytical
Goal-oriented
Coordinated
Have good instincts
Organized
Team member
Need staff to execute my ideas
Self-starting
Good business head
Good sales type—but of what?
Good with executives and top management

FIELDS THAT MIGHT BENEFIT FROM MY TALENT
1. Clothing
2. Advertising
3. Film

4. TV
5. Real estate
6. Urban planning
7. Politics
8. Management consulting
9. Money and women
10. Writing

(I'm not sure what position in which field I should pursue now to benefit from my past and project me into attaining my long-term goals.)

TOP SKILLS
Lead people with my ideas
Explore unknown
Conceptualize
Act as liaison
Discern
Coordinate
Act as a role model
Develop strategies
Consult

I am

Extremely achievement-oriented.

Currently feeling very individualistic but with a strong need for acceptance and domination of situations or those I'm accepted by.

Also:

I have equal feelings of wanting/needing to belong to a group(s) or just adding people to my life, and of wanting/needing to be by myself (isolation).

Aggression is of equal weight to belonging and isolation and indicates to me that I'm in conflict within myself about these.

Recently I've recognized that I've isolated myself and want/need to involve myself with more people regularly, but am not sure what groups to join. Therefore, I haven't joined any.

I think this aggression is also a result of many recent vocational rejections. I'm trying to find what I want to do and where I want to belong. Not knowing this frustrates me.

Contentment and passivity rank lowest with me and seem to be logical accompaniments to my high sense of achievement.

I am feeling very much in a state of transition and find it difficult to respond to the questionnaire you assigned me as a definite statement regarding my general posture. This transition embraces many questioning emotions and thoughts about myself. For example, if I make a statement about myself today, I immediately question whether it will be true of me tomorrow. This makes me uncomfortable.

I feel that these ambivalent feelings are symptoms of a new growth phase I'm going through right now. I think this is partly why these assignments are difficult for me. Because I'm very conscientious, I want to do them, but I find that I must approach them as games so I can lighten the weight of the answers. (I feel that I'm doing this for "the rest of my life" or that the rest of my life depends on how I answer/respond today.)

I NEED

A work base and a direction
To define what I want to do, where I want to go
To know what results, achievements, or signs of recognition
    will give me a feeling of success and self-satisfaction
To accept on a deeper level the qualities I have
A better sense of my own creativity
More information or substance before I can begin to create
To resolve my pull between my assets and resources in my
    home state and New York to establish a direction for
myself

Diane
First Symbol
What I am

Sunflower. At Grandma's—behind her house edging a freshly plowed and harrowed field. I'm 7 or 8 feet tall. In full bloom. It's warm summertime, but not too hot. In the distance, about 75–100 feet away, I see an old picture of me at two and a half or three years old, with Grandma, Aunt Edith, and a little lamb. I'm petting the lamb with one hand while they're smiling at or looking at the lamb. There are only a few other sunflowers with me—maybe two or three. They're mature, too, but just a day or two into full bloom.

I notice that though we are in a small row as a cluster, I stand apart from them by about 6–12 inches; so I see myself alone. The others, though, are closer together and appear to be in a small group.

My blossom is very golden and bright, almost glowing from its richness and intensity. I'm very proud of my appearance—the evenness of the size of the tufts that comprise my "face" and also the evenness or apparent "smoothness" of my surface. I like my petals too. They're all firm, erect—even purposeful—as they radiate from my smooth yet multifaceted face.

I'm really pleased that no one is missing—from either a vigorous toss in the summer winds or from some bird or person who's plucked one away in admiration or as a test of their firm adherence to myself.

My headlike blossom tilts as do all sunflowers. A part of me resents the daisy part of me, because as everyone knows, daisies face and reflect the sun by their very design. Until now I've thought of myself as a daisy. But a daisy didn't come into my focus this time. Suddenly a daisy reminds me of spring, freshness, and youth with a shining face. It has two colors, a yellow face and white radiant petals. Somehow, the white petals evoke thoughts of fresh, new, untainted youth.

Sunflowers are, or appear to be, two shades of one color. With sunflowers, though, while the face still remains in the yellow family, the tone has deepened as with age or maturity into a rich, golden hue. Both faces are comprised of a multitude of soft little particles, but with the sunflower, these particles are larger, more distinct. In fact, to the viewer, each one is separately distinguishable—as are tiles in a mosaic—though it's clearly integrated into the whole of the design. I like that. Back to the tilt of my head. I guess you could say that's how I view life, a little bit off to one side, as it were. But actually, I don't feel that way about it. I really don't know why my head tilts—or I'm sure many folks think it nods. That's O.K., too, as long as they don't think I'm sleeping. God just planned or designed me so that my head would tilt. I think that's good. I prefer to think of my tilt as enabling me to look at life.

You see, it's fine for daisies to have their heads straight and erect. They're only 12–18 inches tall. But a sunflower is 7 feet tall! Very few people are 7 feet tall—only a few basketball players, not even my tallest basketball-playing brother—and I haven't seen any other 7-foot-tall people at Grandma's! Ever.

So you see, if my head were straight and erect, facing only the sun, clouds, and trees, I'd see very little of human life, save for those that glide above in those big silver birds. But I can't see them. I just know they're there.

With my head at a tilt, I can look at life. I'm always looking down on it, though. I don't really feel that way, though. Until now, I was feeling wonderful about being a sunflower, but doubts have begun to creep into my visions of myself. I will tell you about that, but first I want to describe the rest of me that I'm proud of.

My stalk is very firm and straight and deep green. My leaves are green, too, and wavy. There are a few dry, brown areas on them where beetles have gnawed and where the elements of wind, rain, sun's heat have taken their toll, but that's part of the growth process. I still look prime, though. I like those brown spots. At first I didn't think I would; they'd mar my perfection, or at least perfect image. But after they were there, I grew to accept them, and now I'm glad they're part of me. Each one has its memories that I can choose to share or keep to myself.

All in all, I'm very pleased with my appearance. That surprises me, because I've *never* thought of being a sunflower. I never thought about them, never knew what they did or were for. They were just there—in the summer. I don't know what happens to them in the fall or winter. I guess they just dry up and go to seed...and one day a farmer chops them down like old cornstalks. I've never seen an old sunflower.

At first I was surprised at the thought of being a sunflower, but as I began to visualize and describe myself, I began to love being one and was very proud of that identity.

A page ago I began to see the limitations of a sunflower when I thought about what sunflowers do. Nothing! Horrors.

A sunflower is literally grounded. When it rains, you might even say it gets stuck in the mud. It can't go anywhere. (And yes, Hilda, I realize I've changed my person from first to third. Now I'll go back to first.)

I don't *do* anything. I am passive and have felt active. My doing has been *growing*. Now I'm in full bloom and my activity is *looking* at life. Suddenly I feel negative about myself. I'm so pleased with my appearance, my firmness, my near-perfection, my growth—up from a daisy, but for what I can do, I might as well be a *wallflower*. That's what Van Gogh did with sunflowers. He painted them and hung them on a wall. In a frame, no less. How boxed in can you get?

Well, I do feel good that he noticed me and a few others, and liked us well enough to paint us several times. And did he paint and give one painting to his mentor/artist friend, Gauguin—or was it Cézanne? Well, at least he appreciated us, being an artist too. And you must admit he made us famous with the test of time. But that was *his* interpretation and rendering of me/us. It wasn't because of what *I* did.

Being a sunflower, even though a beautiful one, suddenly feels like a *very* passive existence. Even being a part of the natural-food craze—through my sunflower seeds, not even me—is passive.

Planting seeds that came from me to produce new sunflowers is still not me. Wait until I realize my active role in producing those seeds! But that is mothering, a traditional role literally borne out of nature, part of my design. I don't see any real satisfaction in that except spawning a new generation to carry "me" on.

A sunflower leads a passive existence. Doing all that growing, nurturing self, being beautiful, only to wait to be noticed, admired. But, for the moment, a large part of me just *wants* to be appreciated and enjoyed, *just* for what I am. I want a rest from internal doing and growing. For now, I *just want to be—whatever I am.*

Diane
Second Symbol
What I'd Like to Be

Actress (with flashes of female executive). Pretend world. *Me* still comes through.

Flashes

Eliza Doolittle—From guttersnipe to "lady" at Ascot Heath to lady at the ball. À la Audrey Hepburn—beautiful and impeccable—perfect.

Cassie—In *A Chorus Line.*

Mame—Roz Russell or Angela Lansbury.

Dolly—Carol Channing.

Center of attention, leading ladies, roles are highly individual women. I've always related to Mame or Dolly, but this time Eliza appeared first.

In acting I can use or release all my pent-up feelings, and it's acceptable, even *most* desirable.

Role vs. myself.

Want to be known as *me*, not someone else. As business executive, papers don't want to know if you do/don't make a sale, if you decide *not* to commit a crime. That's not headlines.

I've always said I'd rather make news than read or write about it. Can I handle that *world*?

Can I handle the *rejection*? Would it be any more than I've already felt?

Can I handle the competition?

Many times I've felt that I'm always "on." That I'm not acceptable when I'm just me. When I first noticed that several years ago, I made a conscious effort to try "being me" in situations where I was conscious of this happening—parties and large gatherings of people. I'd do one of two things: (1) Take on a "witty" characteristic, using puns and one-liners whenever possible in a mental challenge with my conversant. Someone once told me that I come across as "tougher" than I really am. I think that was true. (2) I'd be a quiet observer in, but not of, the crowd. I'd move among people so they could see me, looking purposely for no one. I could also look them over and see if anyone caught my eye, enough for me to want to talk to them. I began to realize that these situations subconsciously took me back to being in my large family. I was seeking attention.

Once at a party about ten years ago, I tried a new role. I don't even think I'd made any particular effort to look "different" or distinctive. I was quiet, unfunny, with a sense more of who *I* was than who *they* were. During the party I was very conscious that men came over to me and talked with me, even several at a time. And quietly I was pleased. One or two even asked me for coffee then, or to go somewhere else later. I don't remember if I went for the coffee, but I do remember that I felt very content and pleased with myself, just as I was . . . and I'd go home when I was ready . . . and alone if I wanted, which I think is what I did. I remember it as a good time.

For no particular reason, in the last six months I've been meeting people in the theater or movie business, or who take acting or dance lessons. In advertising, too—that seems related. I've wanted to know more about their fields and business, through conversation.

What occurred to me is that as I met them, I seemed to be saying to myself, "Well, they're just normal people, too." I don't know what I'd been telling myself, but somehow they seemed to belong to a "different," perhaps magic or fictitious world.

Courses I've taken helped me to realize also that people pursuing "glamorous" careers are just people too.

Eliza Doolittle Images

I am in a stage of emergence. I'm in the second of three stages.

The guttersnipe appeared smaller than the "lady" figures, but she was clear (back, left of focus).

The lady at Ascot Heath was also clear and larger (middle, right of focus).

The "princess" at the ball was in the near foreground, but only partially clear and with only the head, or top half, of her showing.

The early Eliza represents who I was when or before I came to New York. I can identify with the unpolished part, but I wasn't entirely without refinement.

The lady at Ascot Heath indicates that I've become more refined, sophisticated, part of a different life with fancier raiment.

While the real Eliza appeared to be part of the scene, she was actually a showpiece with a few limited phrases she had learned well enough to speak. Underneath she was a lively, vibrant, sensitive person who had quite a lot to say.

The third Eliza at the ball is what I'm still becoming. It's a glimpse on my horizon and not yet in full view.

The fact that the first Eliza came into focus first and the second just a little afterward seems to indicate that it's not time for the third stage yet. I must focus on the second stage now. As I do that, the third will begin to come into focus and in view. I'm not able to see the whole image and conclude that I shouldn't try to. (I'm wrestling with that inside and have been trying to put my *whole* life into focus.)

Diane
Third Symbol
What Hinders Me

Family House. I have pleasant memories of that house. At times this year, I've felt that the house was me. These times were when it was in danger of being demolished. (It seemed important that I understand that.) It comes from my past and also present responsibilities on Mom's estate. I spend a lot of time now thinking about that house and what to do with it. I never expected to be thinking about this three years ago. It seems to be intertwined with my identity and career: past, present, and future. Last year I fantasized that the house was one of the locations for a film.

Then, to continue my fantasy, I wrote other stories that became films. The house was my home base and retreat from my busy life in many places I'd travel to in my work, New York, California, places "on location" where I'd need to write or consult on the story to get accuracy and appropriate sensitivity into the story.

I love the idea of saving this house. I would get a sense of achievement from saving it and rejuvenating it. I would have a sense of having "done" something . . . a track record.

Sometimes I think of what my life would feel like without the house in the picture. The pressure and the responsibilities would be gone, but so would my house.

I'm in constant conflict over whether to give up or pursue my idea of recycling the house. Giving it up would be just that, with a feeling of selling out. Pursuing it would give me the satisfaction of knowing I had an idea and gave it a full-fledged try.

Recently I've wondered if I was interested in the house as a matter of principle or to rebel against the family. When I learned that I could pursue the idea without the family's approval, I was immediately excited and eager to make the next step.

Careerwise: Recycling of the house is a new career step and direction. Currently, it doesn't require full-time attention, but later it may. I don't have all the facts for this project. What is needed is time—other resources, finances, human work, studies. This could be my major career direction at the moment.

Diane
Fourth Symbol
What Will Overcome the Obstacle

Typewriter. It doesn't seem to relate to a *quality* I possess. This symbol was the slowest to emerge. It comes from writing a lot in the last two and a half years. I consciously began to write as a matter of record then, when Mom's and my sister's illnesses were detected.

Later I began to write my problems down, to (1) see them in black and white to help clarify my thoughts and feelings, (2) hold them, and (3) see a sense of progress or pattern.

I've been a good letter writer, and people tell me I write good letters. But writing was my biggest problem in school. I hated term papers and compositions. I didn't know how to do them and was too intimidated to ask a teacher for help. I figured all the other kids knew how. (For my college roommate, it was *very* easy.)

Diane's file grew to enormous proportions. After she began coming to me, she was fired from the job she hated. She gave full time to writing my assignments and putting all the facets of her life together in a new synthesis.

At the same time, her personality began to change. A quiet confidence began to replace the hollow laugh she used to put on when she tried to act cheerful.

Here is a copy of the brilliant résumé she formed from dozens of bits and pieces of paper, representing how fragmented her life had become before she decided to take charge of her environment and really *be* Diane, the Discerner.

Diane's Résumé

EXPERIENCE   Fifteen years of multifaceted experience in financial
SUMMARY: management and marketing of products and services

OUTSTANDING ACHIEVEMENTS

Financial Management
- Analyzed marketing operations and product sales of two $25 million firms to determine causes of sharp sales declines over two 2-year periods.
- Approved operational costs and maintained financial records during estate administration of legislator's will.
- Evaluated quality standards and financial estimates of project candidates before awarding $15,000 production project to color card contractor.
- Projected operating budget and established pricing for services of own consulting firm and freelance accounts.
- Produced semi-annual limited-edition trend publications within $2,500 budget.
- Produced testimonial dinner for 10% of projected budget.

Marketing
- Created innovative marketing programs for nine operating companies of $1 billion apparel conglomerate.
- Researched data and consulted with design staff on product development for apparel manufacturers and textile mills.
- Projected idea for and supervised production of first "industry" color card for $20 million fiber marketing firm.

- Advised pattern firm of untapped college market. Implemented resultant program at alma mater.
- Appeared on radio and TV talk shows as sales promoter.
- Updated corporate logo of computer software firm for current projection of image.
- Headed performance list of sales staff for fashion consulting firm.

Communications and Public Relations

- Created and implemented "roundtable" discussion meetings for top management of operating companies to exchange marketing concepts and techniques.
- Introduced the use of videotape and cable TV as marketing tools for apparel firms.
- Projected color and fabric trends to top management and merchandisers of leading U.S. department stores and their merchandising consultant firm.
- Forecast and presented color directives to key personnel of major textile mills and apparel manufacturers for fiber marketing firm.
- Secured free services of international celebrities to be featured editorially in fashion publication.
- Researched and wrote feature editorials on couture sewing and related products for international fashion publication.
- Cut through institutional red tape and enlisted volunteers to provide therapeutic treatment for patient at mental hospital.
- Organized weekend event for 25 people to honor 96-year-old woman.

EMPLOYMENT HISTORY

Owner, Consultant, AAA Associates, New York, 1977-Present
   1973-1976

Marketing Assistant to Group President, BBB, Inc., New York,
   1976-1977

Color Specialist, Trend Forecaster, CCC Co., New York, 1971-1972

Color and Fabric Specialist, XYZ Corporation, New York, 1969-1971

Sales Promotion Representative, Special Features Editor, "ZZZ"
   Magazine, New York, 1964-1969

RELATED EXPERIENCES

Speaker on Career Development, University of State, 1978, 1977,
   1972, 1966, 1965

EDUCATION

Bachelor of Science in Economics, Clothing and Textiles, University
of State

SPECIAL TRAINING AND EDUCATION

Top of the City, 1978

The Present and Future of the Theater, 1978

Night in the City, 1977

Fashion Management and Consumer Lifestyles, Marketing Association, 1977

The Future of the Fashion Industry, 1976

Sales Training Course, 1975

Fashion Merchandising, 1973

Dale Carnegie Course, 1967

PROFESSIONAL AFFILIATIONS AND MEMBERSHIPS

Chairman, Public Relations, Business and Professional Women's Club,
1979-1980

American Marketing Association, 1977-1978

Diane finished her research and referral period, interviewing
people in the theatre and taking an acting course. She also explored
ways of turning her estate into a training center. She developed a
strong support network, getting involved in a professional wom-
en's organization where she could be at home in her environment.
While her first résumé did not have a definite career objective, one
emerged in time as she gathered more information and support.
She landed a very creative job in the fashion industry in a midwestern city.

I focused on her "discernment" as her key characteristic because
she had the capacity to distinguish the fine points of conflict and
ambivalence in her personality structure, as revealed in the material I have shared here. Diane later returned to New York and is using
her expertise in merchandising designer fabrics.

○ **Recalling the Creation Myths**

As the state of human consciousness develops in the Genesis story, we see Adam and Eve learning from their experience, working
and reproducing through sweat and pain. We discover Prometheus

existing through the night, absorbing energy in the Greek creation story; and the same expression is present in the longing to overflow that Purusha exhibited in the pre-Aryan myth.

The ability to learn from experience is an evidence of higher intelligence. Build on your heritage. Rabbi Zalman Schachter-Shalomi says, "Tradition is a treasure that we leave behind in a safe vessel to be used again if we need it." This idea is connected with the fifth aspect of the creation myths, the relationship of experience to creativity. He adds, "A tree grows from the growing edge and not from the center. It takes people who are marginal, who are not in the middle of their generation, to take us to new places. They are the growing edge."

If you are one of these pioneering types—like Diane, the Discerner, you can also reinterpret your traditions, heritage, and former careers, into a new synthesis.

Go to Part Three, Step 5 (page 237), and move ahead with creating a new career. Put some "new rings on your tree."

SIX

🌸 Imagination

Defining and Projecting Your New Self-Image

We are more ready to try the untried when what we do is inconsequential. Hence the remarkable fact that many inventions had their births as toys. In the Occident the first machines were mechanical toys, and such crucial instruments as the telescope and microscope were first conceived as play-things.

—Eric Hoffer

You are ready to consider the place of imagination in the creativity process and in your career development.

Imagination is suspended between experience and symbol. An image or "vision" must be in your mind before a symbol can appear in some concrete form. You build images not out of the gossamer of nothing, but out of the threads of experienced reality which, if you follow them, lead you into the exciting world of symbols. William Wordsworth described something of this event when he wrote:

> Poetry takes its origin from emotion recollected in tranquility: the emotion is contemplated till, by a species of reaction, the tranquility gradually disappears, and an emotion, kindred to that which was before the subject of contemplation, is gradually produced, and does itself actually exist in the mind. In this mood successful composition generally begins, and in a mood similar to this it is carried on.[1]

It is in just such a mood described by the poet that images come before you like birds flying in front of the hunter. The task is to capture them before they get away. The difficulty comes when the mind, like the hunter's eyes viewing the birds, sees images faster than the hand can capture them. The least hesitancy can mean that they are gone. That is why it is so important for you to write down your disconnected thinking, your free association, for often these seemingly unrelated "birds" of the mind are in reality a part of a whole covey of ideas.

Three aspects of imagination produce symbols: emotion, empathy, and identification.

Let's begin with *emotion*. For it is true that imagination, psychologically explained, is not a rational process, but one based on emotional life (which has its roots in the deeper levels of being). Consider for a moment the effect that an emotion like fear has on you. Immediately the image of what can happen to you comes to your mind. If it is a fire you fear, you picture it consuming your home, you and your family fleeing, carrying only a few of your possessions in your hands. If you experience the emotion of love, the fertile mind brings erotic images before you, and you are impressed enough by them to let them guide you to your lover.

When you are trying to decide on a career, never choose one about which you cannot honestly have some emotion. If you don't *care* about it enough to feel something, you had better turn to another idea. Perhaps your lack of feeling is due to ignorance. In that case, make an effort to become informed. If, after careful research, you have not found some *angle* about which you can become emotionally involved, then move on to something else. If you hold a position that constantly demands that you act on things you are not truly interested in, perhaps it is time to seek out a career counselor to guide you to another job.

This brings us to *empathy*, which is more than sympathy. *Empathy* is a word psychologists use to denote the experience a listener has on being informed about another's condition. It demands participation *in* the experience, giving support to another in a common experience. If you as a worker empathize with the people with whom you work, then you will share in your common experience something of the same emotion. You also need to increase your awareness of various aspects of yourself so you can empathize with them to move on to the use of imagination and symbol.

The third aspect of imagination leading to symbol is *identification*, which is empathy taken a step farther. If you expect to work well with the people around you, you have to be "one of them," at least in some respects. Of course, again the emphasis is on the necessity for you to *understand yourself*, as discussed in previous sections.

You have an image that you desperately want to get into focus;

you must let the image speak for itself. You create the vision of the
image, but its inner meaning is revealed without labeling it. What you fail to do is just as important as what you do. You must discover the rhythm of the reality, which helps you avoid action unrelated to your goals. For instance, if you understand that it takes about two years to test whether a new business enterprise is going to survive and make a profit, you will not waste energy in being negative if you don't have instant success.

Inspiration is a word that I've refrained from using before in this book, not because I don't believe in inspiration, but rather because it is embodied in the other words I've used. The poet Stephen Spender says that "inspiration is the beginning . . . and it is also the final goal. . . . In between this start and this winning post there is the hard race, the sweat and toil."[2] The French poet Paul Valéry expressed the idea like this: "One line is given to the poet by God or by nature. The rest he has to discover for himself."[3]

Most of us would be in company with Spender when he described his search for images by a feeling of "something still vague, a dim cloud of an idea which I feel must be condensed into a shower of words." Living our way through the experience of these ideas and images requires a lifetime of patience and watching.

These images often come to us from memory, from our experiencing of the past (as was pointed out in the last section). As Spender has said, "Imagination itself is an exercise of memory. There is nothing we imagine which we do not already know. And our ability to imagine is our ability to remember what we have already once experienced and to apply it to some different situation."

We sometimes use the expression "to capture the imagination." That is an interesting phrase since it brings you to consider just how to use your own images "to capture the imagination" of someone else.

In career development it is necessary to get the image so clearly focused that it blends with the total reality of who you are until the two are indistinguishable. Indeed you will have to *become* your image.

The problem arises when you have to displace an old image with a new one. The original one may be a negative view of yourself based on traumatic childhood experiences. In such a case, you must create some new experiences in which you see yourself functioning in positive ways. Pay attention to the hunch that persists around the edge of your consciousness that you have the resources to project a new image, arising from another aspect of your being.

○ **Case Study: Richard**

"I realized I was not stupid."

Richard, a thirty-eight-year-old artist, struggled with such a problem. He had developed a pattern of frenetic activity, pushing himself into increasingly intensive compulsive achievement as an artist. He was eventually lured into experimenting with drugs and a variety of sexual adventures that helped to precipitate the breakup of his marriage and the loss of his respected faculty position at a midwestern college.

When he came to me, Richard was near despair. He was trying to hold down three insignificant jobs—all much below his intellectual and aesthetic capacity—to support his alienated family while concomitantly trying to reestablish himself in a new career. "Perhaps now the matured artist is trying to become the matured man," he said as he described his reason for seeking my help. Here is the heartbreaking story of the forming of an image Richard had to replace in his work with me.

My Father

My earliest memory is of a beating. I must have been all of three or four years old. More than anything, I remember hiding from him—as I did for the rest of my days until I left for college. Fear of my father was irrational or without reason. When he arrived home—usually around 5:30—everything stopped, including my painting. Dinner was served, and then I went on to homework before bed.

My father was in the construction business. He was in a bad mood when he came home each night. I eventually realized that this was his true nature. And he was rather two-faced, since evidently he was extremely pleasant and jovial when he dealt with people outside of the family. This act was a real act. His manner was then loud and boisterous, something we only experienced when a client or friend was in the house.

As soon as company had left, he was a sour man. Then his so-called humor became cruel. He enjoyed embarrassing my older brother and me as often as possible. We were constantly being put down, told how worthless we were, what we should be doing, and that we should be really grateful he had supplied a nice house, food, etc. Weren't we lucky! Of course, we didn't give him the impression that we enjoyed all those things. I'm sure we did at one time, but after many years of only getting this type of treatment, all talk with him was avoided whenever possible. Dinner was in total silence. He was the only one who talked.

When I was in high school, I had to do a lot of work around the house—polishing floors, cleaning windows. I remember particularly how much pleasure my father received from seeing me on my hands and knees polishing the floor of the kitchen and the laundry. Of course, he always commented on how I could do it better, where I missed a place (which I usually didn't), and what else I could do to be of some use around the house.

By now his favorite term for me was "stupid." I believed him. What did I know? It was never a question of my asking him anything. He just expected me to know what he was doing, how he did it, what he wanted. We never communicated. He never once asked what I wanted to do, if I needed help—nothing. I was too scared of him to ask, and anyway, who wanted his usual answers?

I remember myself during these years as a shy, withdrawn individual, with no confidence in myself at all, save my art. I was desperate for books—there were none. I wanted records to listen to music, which I loved. None were allowed. Even to ask would mean a beating. He didn't need them, or see the need for them, so obviously, I didn't need them. (Maybe this is why I now have a large library of books and records.)

I was extremely thin, had serious dental problems, and was very nervous, except when painting. When I was in tenth grade, my skin erupted with acne. A period of my life I would not like to remember began about that time. Insults and injuries were so painful to me during this time that I felt nothing but hate for my father, who heaped them on me. I was constantly looked at in disgust, told how ugly I was, asked what did I think I could ever do in my life, etc.

I thought so often of running away. Beatings at this point were so frequent. I was smacked, slapped, kicked, thrown against the wall, and hit with the poker stick from the fireplace. Blood would pour off my head. I was cut, bruised, and in pain. Walking sometimes was difficult. What this did to me emotionally, I cannot even begin to describe. After a while, I just didn't think about it, I suppressed it. Perhaps just got to the point where I went on— knowing that it would happen again, which it always did. (At this point my insides hurt. I feel so empty, hollow, and sweating— perhaps the physical expression of this purge in words.)

What was I thinking about during this time, other than art? Nothing. Absolutely nothing, save trying to get through the next day without a beating or series of insults. I dreaded weekends—he would be home. I dreaded dinnertime, except Wednesdays, when they went out to dinner.

Did I have friends? Yes, one boy and two girlfriends during these years. Obviously, a sexual or romantic relationship of any kind with a girlfriend was impossible. I had no money and had so many chores to do; so time for myself was not very plentiful. I had no sexual experiences during these years. except for masturbation, which I discovered really quite late. I had very few clothes, nothing fashionable. I usually felt extremely self-conscious at school in the same old pants, shirts, jacket, etc.

I did receive treatment for my skin problems. Mostly what I needed was calm. I was so nervous all the time, calm only when I painted.

When I went to college, I remember feeling rather happy to get out of the house. I had a full-tuition scholarship, which covered both tuition and art lessons. I needed an allowance for food and money for my room. These were provided, but not terribly willingly. My father resented sending the money and told me so. My mother provided my food allowance (ten dollars a week) by taking a job as a police school crossing guard.

Ten dollars was hardly enough. I would eat very sparingly. Usually I had no money by the fifth or sixth day. I would have a milkshake—that was all. I simply didn't eat until the money arrived. The allowance was never increased; I was too frightened to tell them it wasn't enough. Yet, my father later accused me of saving his money(!) and using it for a trip to Europe.

Now notice the careful and determined way Richard created a new image of himself in this Success Story.

For all the problems of my childhood, I do remember that when the opportunity arose to do something artistic I would take advantage of it.

In high school I remember one teacher in particular—my twelfth-grade English teacher. I really enjoyed her class, because she really got into teaching—she literally performed each class.

In college I had classes with three art professors who made a lasting impression on me. Each had his own unique way. One was highly disorganized, but he made his points in such beautiful language that I easily forgave him his lack of organization. Another constantly referred to literature to make a point or a particular idea. The third was an art history professor who was highly organized and easy to understand. I felt that in my lecturing I was a combination of the three.

How did I accomplish such a feat? First, I prepared. I thought through all aspects of the material I intended to cover. I read extensively, and let all the material gestate within me. I would study the art I wanted to cover, seeking the best correlation between the written data and the wonderful emotional quality it was describing. Gradually, through assimilation, a total picture would emerge. Then I would write.

I typed all my lectures. I would literally sit at the typewriter and type out the lecture as if I were saying it to a class. This process saved a lot of time. I would polish the lecture as I went. These typed papers served as a guide only. I loved the material and found that I hardly needed to look at my notes—more than likely a result of my memory. While the complete picture remained in me, I stayed at least two or three classes ahead when first typing these lectures. As time passed, I would add pages or make marginal notes and also indicate rearrangement of material when I felt it would result in a clearer understanding of development of idea, point of view, and technique. I earned a reputation as both lecturer and painter and twice received the Outstanding Teaching Award given to faculty members by fellow faculty and students. My classes grew.

Attendance in my classes had always been good. I never took roll. The students knew I was prepared, and they came to my classes ready to work and find what they needed as students of art. The greatest compliment I ever received as a lecturer was when a student told the dean of the school that I had changed his life. I can honestly say that there are several students, many, who have told me this same thing. I feel greatly honored to be held in such esteem and yet humbled at the same time. I serve my art—art, in general. My goal is to be a complete artist-intellect, and I tried to the best of my ability to share that with my students and help them on the path to their own concept of that idea.

I freely gave of myself, which has proven also valuable when talking outside the classroom, i.e., on TV, as a guest lecturer, and in meeting people of all walks of life. I shared willingly and enjoyed every minute of it.

In short, I enjoy communicating with people, I usually find some area of mutual interest and expand from that point. This approach is particularly valuable for winning confidence and helping me accomplish something I value. Imparting enthusiasm and understanding is an aspect of my life that I am most proud of. It has helped me grow as an individual.

In Richard's case, the creativity process was particularly appropriate. He continued to probe into the possibilities open to him in a career that would use his intellect and artistic talent. He wanted to make the transition from teaching. At first, he explored positions in corporations with public affairs programs involving the arts, and in foundations devoted to promoting art. However, Richard was not able to do the Symbol Exercise. When he tried, he came up with words only, no pictures.

Imagination should not be confused with *images* or *imagery*. Imagery is only one type of imagination, the process of producing and experiencing images. Imagination is the capacity of the mind to produce and reproduce several symbolic functions while in a state of consciousness, of awakeness, without any deliberate effort to organize these functions. This is why I use "free association" writing as a part of the career development process. Conscious images emerge from the unconscious, usually in bits and pieces, and furnish clues for what may be a total pattern. Since imagination also can assume nonverbal forms, I guide clients to do exercises using both words and pictures to encourage complete awareness.

If you are not able to receive images spontaneously, you can try rest, solitude, darkness, and meditation. Remember, images are fleeting. You can retain them for only a short time. They shift quickly, revealing only a part of the whole. You must follow them. If you find the totality does not exist, then you *create* it. You literally bring it into existence. That is why action must grow out of imagination. To experience a wish becomes equivalent to its actualization.[4]

It is even possible to get in touch with amorphous material pushed into your subconscious when you were very small, perhaps before the verbal period. This concept is called the "endocept." When you can bring these experiences into focus by connecting them to a specific image, and further let them develop into symbols, you may then be able to synthesize them in a new aspect of yourself, sometimes even leading you into a new career.

This was what Diane was doing in connecting her images of the sunflower and daisy to her grandmother's garden (see Chapter 5). These flower-symbols had a direct bearing on her need to include the estate in her career planning for the present and future.

In Richard's case, the need to wipe out the image of himself as the "stupid" one, as claimed by his father, to become the "brilliant" professor, was not sufficiently dealt with, as indicated by his statement to me, "perhaps the matured artist is trying to become the matured man." This is why a surface, mechanistic type of career planning based only on skills analysis is not adequate for him. Only a holistic approach that begins with a dependable relationship with me as his career consultant and focuses primarily on his quality of "being" could provide a strong enough foundation for a new career.

Richard's imagination has been seriously damaged. His case is not too unlike multitudes of others in our society.

> At the age of five, 90 percent of the population measures "high creativity." By the age of seven the figure has dropped to 10 percent. And the percentage of adults with high creativity is only two percent. Our creativity is destroyed not through the use of outside force but through criticism, innuendo, subtle psychological means which the "well-trained" child learns to use upon himself. Most of us are our own "brain police."[5]

Because I agree with Freud that nothing is ever lost to the unconscious, I work on the assumption that the creativity of early childhood must still be present in the person. It may be latent, repressed, or crippled, but it is present nonetheless. My task is to help the client recover the lost images and to encourage their expression in symbol and form.

You are in charge of your imagination. As William Blake, one of the great creative geniuses of all time, said, "You have the same situation as I. Only you do not cultivate it. You can see what I do, if you choose." Admit that you share the common experience of even those whom you tend to elevate to levels above you. Becoming mature is recognizing that you are no worse and no better than others. Here is an excerpt from a novel by Hermann Hesse, illustrating this point:

> The following spring I was to leave the preparatory school and enter a university. I was still undecided, however, as to where and what I was to study. I had grown a thin mustache, I was a full grown man, and yet I was completely helpless and without a goal in life. Only one thing was certain: the voice within me, the dream image. I felt the duty to follow this voice blindly wherever it might lead me. But it was difficult and each day I rebelled against it anew. Perhaps I was mad, as I thought at moments; perhaps I was not like other men? But I was able to do the same things the others did; with a little effort and industry I could read Plato, was able to solve problems in trigonometry or follow a chemistry analysis. There was only one thing I could not do: wrest the dark secret goal from myself and keep it before me as others did who knew exactly what they wanted to be—professors, lawyers, doctors, artists, however long this would take them and whatever difficulties and advantages this decision would bear in its wake. This I could not do.
>
> Perhaps I would become something similar, but how was I to know? Perhaps I would have to continue my search for years on end and would not become anything, and would not reach a goal. Perhaps I would reach this goal but it would turn out to be an evil, dangerous, horrible one.
>
> I wanted only to try to live in accord with the promptings which came from my true self. Why was this so difficult?[6]

○ Recalling the Creation Myths

No scientist accepts anything unless it is experimental, which is the same thing as experiential. You are always more than you can possibly say. That openness is the extra ingredient—imagination.

When we ask about the limits of consciousness and can't find them, we realize we could also go the other way and assume that consciousness is unlimited—dead and alive, body and soul, matter and mind, left brain and right brain. One absolute statement is that there are no absolutes, only relatives. This is why imagination is such an important element in the creation myth and subsequently in the creativity process. You have to see more than yourself when you look in the mirror. There is oneness with the whole of life, despite the appearance and illusion of separation.

The image that Adam and Eve caught when they decided to eat the fruit and "actualize their potentiality"[7] was that they would "become as God." The audacity that enables human beings to see themselves also as a part of the Divine is the ultimate exercise in imagination. Prometheus "growing a new liver during the night" is an expression of the same kind of audacity.

Richard's case is a glowing example of the same kind of audacity, taking the "stupid" image of himself that his father had given him and "growing a new liver"—continuing to persist in developing an increasingly clear image of who he is becoming. Richard made the transition from college teaching to executive sales. When I spoke with him last, his voice sounded enthusiastic. He has continued to probe into his being for a viable way to express himself. He first took a position as a financial development officer. This led to a sales position in the advertising world. He has moved to the state where his children are living, so he can be in closer touch with them. He is gradually discovering that he has power in dealing with people, with the concrete evidence of sales reinforcing his confidence.

You will move no faster to your career goal than is provided by the clarity of the image of yourself in that place.

Now go to Part Three, Step 6 (page 240), and do your image work.

SEVEN

✿ Symbol

Finding the Appropriate Instrument to Propel You

If we are to remain human and go further into our own discovery of what being human may mean, then it is necessary to accept and endure the pain of knowing those things about ourselves which are neither Godlike nor saintly nor good nor nice. They are as full of energy as their opposites, as the manure heap is as full of energy as the flowering tree.

—H. Westman

You have embraced your chaos, discovered and encountered being in its essence, experienced your growth potential in your developing self, clarified your career goal through examining your experience, and defined and projected your new identity through using imagination. Now you are ready to allow a *symbol* to emerge from your imagining. This is the summit to which you have been climbing.

Some of you may have crumbled under a snowslide of being, been knocked down by encounter, frightened by a look into the pool of self, frostbitten by experience, lost your way in the jungle of imagination, and are suddenly in danger of stumbling over the boulders of symbol. To stop at any of the stations before you hoist your victory flag on this high pinnacle of achievement is to have climbed in vain.

But now it is time for those of you who have survived this struggle to this lookout point to check your mountaineering gear, rearrange the load to accommodate your weary bones, and plant flags of symbol on the summit called New Career.

A symbol is a means of communicating a reality beyond itself. It has no meaning apart from reality. As Paul Tillich has said, a symbol *participates* in the nature of the reality it represents. The theologian Lewis Joseph Sherrill put the same truth this way: "A symbol is a sign representing something else to which it points. It represents that to which it points, not because it has been arbitrarily chosen for that purpose, but because it is intrinsically related to it in some way, such as by association with it or participation in it."[1]

Erich Fromm lists three kinds of symbols:

Conventional—No apparent connection or similarity
Accidental—Incidents that bring symbols to mind
Universal—Intrinsic relationship between symbol and
    reality[2]

If your fleeting images are to develop into useful symbols related to your career, you must concentrate. You must keep your symbols alive long enough so that they can convey the reality behind them to you. Stephen Spender described the elusive quality of imagery when he wrote, "Concentration may be disturbed by someone whistling in the street or the ticking of a clock. There is always a slight tendency of the body to sabotage the attention of the mind by providing some distraction."[3] Your task is to maintain the integrity of your purpose in spite of everything.

Language is symbol. That is why your résumé must use the right words to describe *exactly* who you are. I will never work with anyone's résumé unless I first can take that person through the process that precedes résumé writing. I will not participate in contriving a slick résumé full of fluff, with no resemblance to the true person. The résumé, like any other symbol, must be a part of the reality of the person whom it represents.

The words used in a résumé must be carved from the substance that emerges in the person's struggle for identity *before* the time for writing. When the words match the reality, the effect is very powerful. It has been said of the great French writer Gustave Flaubert that "he suffered the agony of the damned in bringing his book into existence. Days were spent in quest of the right word, the only one; a week, and more sometimes, was required for the exact transitions; entire months were spent writing and rewriting paragraphs."[4] In a lighter vein, Mark Twain quipped that "the difference between choosing the right word and the almost right word is as great as the difference between lightning and the lightning bug."

If, after the agony of examining yourself, you have come to an understanding and acceptance of what kind of person you are, then you must let the words you use to describe yourself fit your discovery. If you are a methodical, matter-of-fact person, your résumé will not ring true if you flavor it with frilly, extravagant words. "Languages are more to us than systems of thought-transference. They are invisible garments that drape themselves about our spirit and give a predetermined form to all its symbolic expression."[5]

One of my favorite quotes in reference to language as the embodiment of reality is from James Joyce's *Ulysses*: "Unsheath your dagger definition. Horseness is the whatness of allhorse."[6] To achieve the quality of "allhorse" in your letters of inquiry and introduction, your résumés and your proposals of what you can do for the corporation or organization to which you are trying to sell yourself, you must have the courage to risk exposing your true nature.

You can't try to get by with anything less than what is required. Reality is never on sale. Its price is never marked down in a bargain basement. And you are not presenting "someone." You are laying *yourself* on the line. Martin Buber describes what is required:

> "What are we to do?" "What is to be done?" If you mean by this question, "What is *one* to do?" there is no answer. *One* is not to do anything. *One* cannot help himself. With *one*, there is nothing to begin. With *one*, it is all over. He who contents himself with explaining or asking what he is to do, talks and lives in a vacuum.
>
> But he who poses the question with the earnestness of his soul on his lips and means, "What have *I* to do?" he is taken by the hand by comrades he does not know but whom he will soon become familiar with and they answer, "You shall not withhold yourself."[7]

It is not always easy for persons to come up with symbols. Often a basic resistance occurs in the inner core. Maslow writes:

> This inner core, even though it is biologically based and "instinctual," is weak in certain senses rather than strong. It is easily overcome, suppressed or repressed. It may even be killed off permanently. Humans no longer have instincts in the animal sense, powerful, unmistakable inner voices which tell them unequivocally what to do, when, where, how and with whom. All that we have left are instinct-remnants. And furthermore, these are weak, subtle and delicate, very easily drowned out by learning, by cultural expectations, by fear, by disapproval, etc. They are *hard* to know, rather than easy. Authentic self-hood can be

defined in part as being able to hear these impulse voices within oneself, that is, to know what one really wants or doesn't want, what one is fit for and what one is *not* fit for, etc. It appears that there are wide differences in the strength of these impulse-voices.[8]

Throughout this book we have talked about the Symbol Exercise and have examined examples created by some of my clients. If you have been able to reach the instinctual level and your images are becoming symbols that will find their place on paper, try to use them in your career development process. But not too quickly. The next step is to work through the medium—as the painter does in form and color; the poet in images and words; the playwright and novelist in characters, dialogue and events; the manager in program and product development. Jungian analyst Marie-Louise von Franz, in discussing the creative process, cites Faulkner describing how he evolved his novel *The Sound and the Fury*:

> It began with a mental picture. The picture was the muddy seat of a little girl's drawers in a pear tree, where she could see through a window where her grandmother's funeral was taking place and report what was happening to her brothers on the ground below. By the time I explained who they were and what they were doing and how her pants got muddy, I realized it would be impossible to get all of it into a short story, and that it would have to be a book. And then I realized the symbolism of the soiled pants and the image was replaced by one of the fatherless and motherless girls climbing down the rainpipe to escape from the only home she had, where she had never been offered love or affection or understanding.

From the image, Faulkner developed the characters and events, forming a fictional medium. Von Franz goes on to offer suggestions for how we can respond to our fantasies:

> If you notice an unconscious fantasy coming up within you, you would be wise not to interpret it at once. Do not say that you know what it is and force it into consciousness. Just let it live with you, leaving it in the half-dark, carry it with you and watch where it is going or what it is driving at. Much later you will look back and wonder what you were doing all that time, that you were nursing a strange fantasy which then led to some unexpected goal. For instance, if you do some painting and have the idea that

you could add this and that, then don't think "I know what that means!" If you do, then push the thought away and just give yourself to it more and more so that the whole web of symbols expands in all its ramifications before you jump at its essential meaning.[9]

○ Case Study: Violet
"No answer to 'What do you do?'"

Violet's story is a poignant example of the long, patient climb back to productivity following a breakdown. She was able to wait and ponder, to explore the hidden value of her experience in coming to a complete halt in her life. I share her story here because the way she has been able to achieve a beautiful synthesis of all her dimensions is an effective example of the true relationship between symbol and reality.

Violet grew up on an isolated ranch in the Southwest in an extremely fundamentalist religious atmosphere. Her fantasy world was rich and romantic in contrast to her actual drab environment. Even though she longed for a life of adventure, she followed her mother's determined choice to become a rural schoolteacher.

After two years of teaching in the public schools, Violet mustered up the courage to break away. She came to New York to study acting and singing. During this period her life followed the classic mode of the struggling actress—working in boring office jobs to make the money to survive and pay for classes, hoping for the professional breakthrough. In her case, she was fortunate enough to "make it." Several of the success stories she wrote for me were descriptions of significant roles she played in the theater. The one included here capsulizes both the genius she possessed and the "demon" that finally eroded her personality structure.

Success Story: Playing Lyuba in Solzhenitsyn's Play

I was offered the role of the female lead in a play by Alexander Solzhenitsyn. There was no script available, and I was given only a description of the role. It was to be directed by an internationally known director, someone I didn't know personally. But I'd heard much about him and how creative and demanding he was. I was nervous about rehearsals at first.

The play was set in Russia when the leader of that country was doing terrible things to his people, putting them in prison in Siberia. These people underwent tremendous deprivation. Most were locked up for no valid reason.

My character was twenty-two years old and had been in prison since she was sixteen. She had learned how to survive in the prison camps. She was called the love girl because she knew how to win the affections of the men in position to make her life a little easier. In the play she is offered love by someone who can't help her and whom it would be dangerous for her to love. She has to decide whether to love and die or survive without love. She also sings in the play because one night the camp put on a show for the officers. Her songs were filled with her fragile strength and the pain of her life.

I read many books written by the actual survivors of those camps so I could get an understanding of what their life was like. I became deeply involved in the horror of that time and the pain of the people. Mostly, I was struck by a person's ability to endure the most horrendous conditions of deprivation and survive.

I worked hard to close the gap between my own life and Lyuba's. I knew a lot about being imprisoned by my mind. I also knew something about survival and deprivation and the fear of love, I was able to pour my own pain, fears, and needs into the role. I learned a lot about myself and gained a deep respect and understanding of the spirit and the life force within humankind.

Doing the play made me feel beautiful, as I was the love girl. I had to feel as if everyone could be seduced by me, that is, made to love me. That was challenging and fun because I'd never felt really loved or allowed myself to enjoy being lovable. Now, because I was playing a character who was, I got to act as if I too were lovable.

I worked slowly and felt at times the director's impatience. I was impatient too, but I always had to immerse myself in the situation of the character before I could begin to do anything that resembled her. My realization of Lyuba had to be thorough and slow and based on a truth I knew through research and my personal experience.

I was experiencing myself more fully than I ever had, and my life on the stage was satisfying and fulfilling. I felt I was part of a valuable theater company offering an experience to people that would enable them to experience "man's inhumanity to man," the enduring qualities of human strength, and the need for love, not simply survival.

Following this success, Violet had a prolonged struggle with depression and spent ten years with a Freudian analyst. Then came three years of Rolfing and Gestalt-TA (Transactional Analysis) therapy, where she was supported with a nonjudgmental love throughout an intense, highly dramatic, agonizingly painful period. She was never made to feel she was sick, only that she was experiencing pain that was deeply suppressed. Her therapist never stayed with a single format, but was constantly growing and changing himself. Eventually they dropped the Gestalt-TA work and continued deep focusing, confronting her many parts, and deep inner sensing, always integrating and finding her wholeness through a body-mind-spirit discipline.

She stopped smoking, drinking, and using drugs. She was committed to natural whole foods and an understanding of the importance of nutrition in the developing and evolving consciousness. Their work had now progressed from therapy to grasping consciousness.

In addition to her internal work, Violet also earned a master's degree in art therapy. She also created and taught a university course for actors. Still, she had no abiding sense of career when I met her after the course had been discontinued. She could not answer the question "What do you do?" She said, "It's a terrible thing to have no socially acceptable answer to the question. I couldn't very well answer that I was working full time searching for my soul. I would answer that question with whatever was my latest interest—pottery, classical guitar, fashion design, master's degree."

In her journal, Violet summarized her problem this way:

Finding work has been an obsession with me for several years, ever since I quit my career in acting, in which I had been intensely involved. I have been on a search for something that would involve me fully and use my resources. Even now, I'm not clear what those talents and resources are, what my skills are, where I could go to work without further study and training. I often run up against the feeling that I know a little about a lot of things, but I am not really prepared to do any one thing.

I have had a difficult time making a decision and staying with it for fear of cutting off options. In some way I feel I'm going to be stopped short in my development—whether in my deep commitment to change, personal growth, work on body-mind-spirit; my intense interest in consciousness and healing; and my need to pursue and be involved in the arts in some way.

I confuse myself by being interested in too many areas, and yet I'm afraid of cutting off one of them. My major conflict seems to be the need to be true to myself and yet not be limited by what I feel I should do. Thus I could be keeping hidden from myself what I could do now.

My big need is to be in a responsible position, earning my living, without being financially dependent any longer on my husband, but contributing my share materially in our relationship. This is coming from me; I feel no big pressure from him. I need independence, and yet I also need structure.

Violet worked with me for twenty-three sessions over a period of six months. She wrote other beautiful, detailed stories, and she came up with dynamic symbols. As you study them, note that they reveal her unceasing effort to hold on to her center while expressing herself in outer activities. They show that the harmony is still in the process of emerging.

Violet eventually developed an impressive résumé. During her research and referral period, I put her in contact with a number of professionals who affirmed her rich background of experiences and assured her that she had a significant place in the working world. Together we explored a number of possibilities. There seemed to be a missing link in the integration of her experiences.

One day she called to thank me for putting her in touch with an actress who was working on a master's degree thesis entitled "Towards a Holistic Method of Acting." Like Violet, she was deeply committed to evolving consciousness and was successfully integrating that commitment into her teaching of acting, private coaching, and her own work as a performer. This woman confronted Violet with the fact that she too was an actress and could no longer afford to avoid embracing that part of her being. Violet quickly grasped the truth of this, and even though both shaken and elated, she realized she had found the missing link—she could not ignore what was essential to her true nature; she would now have to integrate "the actress" into her career choice.

Gradually Violet evolved a plan of action that combined all the skills developed in her former careers. She became a true entrepreneur, creating her own career in a "major synthesis"—training students in "Sensing for Actors." She has become focused and energized, moving from the center of her being, using her*chaos* as material for a new *creation*.

Here are examples of the beautiful way she began "packaging" her new "symbol of the organism" that is Violet. One was a workshop for actors. Here's what her flyer said about it:

Acting through Sensing

As an actor, you the artist have to perform on the most difficult instrument to master, that is, your own self—your physical being and your emotional being. Only in theater do we have the emotions, soul, spirit, mind, and muscles of the artist as the material of art.

Since you are your own instrument, your scales or exercises must be done through a full use of the senses in order to establish your presence in a larger and more comprehensive way. This workshop is designed to aid you in strengthening, heightening, and channeling your sensory faculties and your inner technique. We will explore how a solid foundation for acting is built through:
- Becoming aware of the body and breath
- Letting go of excessive tension
- Developing a disciplined inner focus
- Deepening powers of concentration and observation
- Evoking the imagination
- Finding sensory and physical involvement in objects
- Establishing a sense of truth

Our primary tools of learning will include:
- Nonverbal experiences of the body-mind connection
- The use of art materials

Her other workshop was offered to a group of businesswomen:

Learn to Take Your Whole Person to Work
A Workshop in Sensing: A Practice in Being Alive

You are an instrument of your own success, but only if the total instrument is being utilized. Sensing is a practice of getting in touch with what one needs to function harmoniously.

Through simple, nonverbal, direct experiences of the ways we breathe, sit, stand, walk, touch, and perceive ourselves and others, we can gradually begin to:
- Become aware of how we function from moment to moment
- Learn to quiet disruptive thoughts
- Allow messages essential to our well-being to come to consciousness
- Call on the strength of our physical grounding
- Let go of excessive tension
- Experience dimensions of ourselves that are beyond judgment
- Connect with the self activating forces within
- Establish our presence with confidence

But Violet still needed structure. In an effort to provide herself with a daily routine, she became an assistant administrator for a major international art and antiques firm. As a consultant, I knew this was not right for her creative spirit, even though she had excellent skills needed in the work.

Then it happened! I got a letter from her telling me:

> This year has been a good one for me. I discovered children. Truly! I began working at a private girls school, kindergarten through the twelfth grade, offering a top-rated classical education based on Rudolph Steiner's educational theories. I began doing the secretarial work. It's a wonderful place, very nice people, and has a stimulating, cultural, intellectual atmosphere. I was also in a study group at the school and assisted in a first-grade play group.
>
> I then decided to be trained in the Steiner education method, which takes the spiritual life of the child seriously and integrates the intellectual and artistic parts in educating the whole child. Now I work there full time as an assistant to the handwork teacher.
>
> I'm very pleased. I feel I have come home at last. I have found a base from which to work that allows me to bring into focus and to synthesize all the disparate parts, and to release them into a larger space.

By now I hope you have observed that career development using the creative process is never an automatic meteorlike rise to success. It's more like the pattern that my Irish setter, Shannon, follows when we walk on the beach together. He circles back and forth, sometimes making wide sweeps upon the dunes, then playing in the waves, wildly chasing the sea gulls and starlings, running after a bicyclist, or sniffing at a neighbor's golden retriever. His great energy and excitement are catching, and my spirit too is let loose to enjoy the glory of our surroundings in an expansive, creative way. Shannon is just being himself—faithfully acting out of his bird dog nature. As we walk I begin to let go of my fatigue and allow myself to be. It is at such moments that creative ideas for the next step in my career come to me.

Violet
First Symbol
What I Am

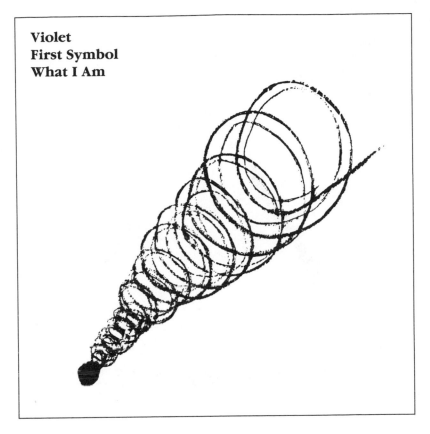

Starting from my center I can move out. I need darkness and light to travel with me. I can start small and grow larger—in fact eventually so large I won't need to spiral but go straight up, or out.

Violet
Second Symbol
What I'd Like to Be

White tube—funneling out, connecting, contacting. A structure freeing white light or container from which light can emanate. Black line insignificant; purple moves in the world—is seen, radiates out.

Violet
Third Symbol
What Hinders Me

Unknown. Held in on left and right sides, free to move out the top. Grayness bubbles and waves rather gently. No base—base is significantly absent. Bars on left and right are thin and not very threatening.

Violet
Fourth Symbol
What Will Overcome the Obstacle

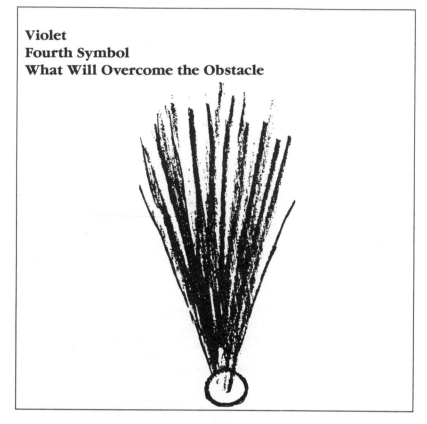

Freed energy from a white or clear, clean center. Holding on to dark exterior. Radiating out of my own center, reaching out to the environment. Free, vital, exultant. Burst through trace of remaining ring of black—black is insignificant.

Symbiosis is an important leap in the process of development. In biology, symbiosis means the relationship between two or more organisms in a close association that may be (but is not necessarily) of benefit to each. This phenomenon appears in the creation myths where we see confusing and conflicting factors or opposing forces coming together to provide a balance of power from which new symbols can spring forth. The myths point to this reality in the natural world and in the human psyche. Ancient myths continue to be meaningful to us today because their language and symbols participate in reality. They arise out of the universal consciousness in which we all share.

Symbols have no meaning apart from reality. They serve as pointers to a reality that cannot be grasped by ordinary intellectual means. That is why we turn to myth in our effort to discover profound truths about reality. Sherrill diagrams the relationship between reality and symbol as a "Cone of Reality":[10]

The Cone of Reality

The Symbol

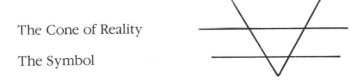

The reality itself stretches away into infinity, like the opening at the top of the V. At the pint of the V lies a small area that we may think of as a symbol of the entire reality.

The symbol-making aspect of the creation myths appears in the Bible in the naming of the creatures. In the Greek and pre-Aryan myths, it appears in the images of silver and cosmic eggs.

Look once more at Violet's symbols. See the connection between what came out of this exercise and the cone of reality. She first experienced herself as a spiral moving upward. Her second symbol is reminiscent of the ancient Egyptian pyramid—the cone in reverse. Her third symbol is a dramatic picture of the amorphous, unfinished parts of her psyche. This was the part that hindered her from moving with force toward a specific goal. Violet's fourth symbol radiates power and vitality, which were always there in potential. This image, being opposite in form to the pyramid, completes the balance of her personality. Her later integration expressed itself in her career as a teacher of small children. Here she lived out her early career goal furnished by her mother. The spontaneity of young children coincided with Violet's "free child" ego state, which she needed to integrate into her adult activity. Happily, a synthesis was finally achieved.

Review the Symbols Exercise illustrations in this book. Now make your own symbols by doing the exercise in Part Three, Step 7 (page 243).

EIGHT

❀ Form

Planning the Strategy for Getting There

*Somewhere deep down in us is stored the secret, and
when we are digging in the wrong place, we know it.
The secret wants to be discovered and will not let us go
in peace a way that is not ours.*

—Elizabeth O'Connor
Eighth Day of Creation

Now you are ready to buck the system—to create a new
form for your existence.

Let us review briefly the creative process up to this point. It starts
with a hunch and a sense of direction, even in the midst of anxiety, guilt, and confusion. It develops and grows through encounter and struggle with reality until the medium comes through in
the form of words, images, and other symbols. From the initial
moment of insight that brings you ecstasy and heightened consciousness, you must persevere through continued commitment
and concentration. You establish a rhythm of work and relaxation,
alternating between material from the unconscious and from the
conscious.

Four stages of creative thought might be identified as preparation, incubation, illumination, and verification. In the fourth stage,
verification, you experience full spontaneity and freedom. This
freedom and spontaneity do not come from nonstructure or lack
of direction in the flow of thought; rather they come from such total
concentration on a task, on its direction and its structure, that all
your resources are directed toward it. You are freed from self-
consciousness, from personal fears and hopes, and can respond fully, freely, and spontaneously to whatever you are centered on.

During your period of total concentration, all the patterns of your
mind are potentially active. All activity flows toward a center. It is
my belief that this center is neither the personal nor the collective
unconscious, but that growing object itself, finding a place in the   *163*

actual world, developing ideas and taking flesh—growing in relation to your initial intuition that started the creative episode and the goal of the consummated statement in the medium.

It would be pleasant to stop here and say that all your creative problems are over; but you know that concentration comes and goes in waves. Discipline achieved one day is lost the next. Aloneness cherished one day because you are surrounded by the reality you are working with is transformed into bitter loneliness and emptiness the next. You try all sorts of tricks to keep yourself at the task—thinking, mental games, yoga, meditation, private rituals, precisely set working hours and conditions, even psychoanalysis, for if you are deeply frightened it is difficult to achieve concentration, which requires that no aspect of the psyche be forbidden territory.

As a creative person you must exercise inner freedom—no matter what the outer environment is. Pasternak, in his novel *Dr. Zhivago*, reveals some of his struggles to create freely in Russia when he has Zhivago speaking to Lara, with whom he was marooned one terrible white winter. In describing the effect of their repressive environment on their ability to maintain their creative energy, he said that the root of all their evil came when they lost confidence in the value of their own opinions, when people thought it was out of date to follow their own moral sense, that they all thought they had to sing in chorus and live by others' notions, notions that were being crammed down everybody's throat. After that, there arose the power of the glittering phrase, first of the tsarist, then of the revolutionary regime. This social evil became an epidemic. It affected everything, even the atmosphere of their homes. Something went wrong everywhere.

Perhaps you are aware that it is possible to lose inner freedom without realizing it. One day you wake up to the fact that it is gone, and you are helpless to act freely. The Indian writer Rabindranath Tagore writes in his short story "Vision":

> Those whom a sudden gust of passion brings down to the dust can rise up again with a new strong impulse of goodness. But those who, day by day, become dried up in the very fiber of their moral being, those who by some outer parasitic growth choke the inner life by slow degrees, such men reach one day a deadness which knows no healing.[1]

Certain tendencies in our society today should warn you about this possibility. When your life is so complex, and the pressures toward conformity and dullness of spirit so great, your struggle to express your true self may take unusual forms at times.

It is at this point that freedom is connected with the development of form. You have the capacity to mold yourself. Freedom is the other side of consciousness of self. If you are not developed enough to be aware of yourself, you are pushed along by instinct or the automatic march of history, like bees riding on mastodons. But by your human power to be conscious of yourself, you can recall how you acted yesterday or last week, and by learning from these actions you can influence, even if only a little, how you act tomorrow.

As you gain more consciousness of self, your range of choice and freedom increase. Freedom is cumulative. One choice made with an element of freedom makes greater freedom possible for the next choice.

Freedom never occurs in a vacuum. It does not come automatically; it is achieved, and must be achieved daily. Goethe expressed the ultimate lesson learned by Faust:

> Yes, to this thought I hold with firm persistence;
> The last result of wisdom stamps it true;
> He only earns his freedom and existence
> Who daily conquers them anew.

When you can achieve the freedom to "choose yourself," then you can move into self-discipline. Then you can stand alone, to trust yourself enough to express what you have discovered about life, and to take the consequences. Creativity, in the final analysis, is a lonely, solitary task. No matter how much energy or inspiration you may draw from another person or the books you read, when you are sitting down alone at your desk, taking your pen in hand, striking the typewriter keys, or speaking into a tape recorder or dictaphone, you know you cannot escape your *self*. It is like entering a door and hearing it clicking shut. You are in and have to put up with what the space offers. Then you can begin to design the form your career will take.

You may be *free* to say what you please, to defy the company policies or the national heritage, the mores of society or anything else; but in doing so, you must also be willing to take responsibility for your words and actions. Freedom and responsibility are the mature person's companions.

When I lived in India, I had an experience that illustrates my point about being open to new forms. I had to manage a meeting of the Literary Society of the college where I worked. I was arranging the first in a series of programs on the theme "Understanding India through the Arts." I had asked the faculty of the Department of Fine and Applied Arts of the government's polytechnical college to present an art exhibit and program. I had worked closely with the five young artists who participated. They included a sculptor, a painter, a commercial artist, a photographer, and the head of the department. The teacher of batik (the art of painting on cloth) was absent, but his work was on exhibit. The program was an aesthetic experience for faculty and students, and it emphasized the universal reality that we were all experiencing. The night I first talked with these artists in the classroom at their college and saw their works, I dreamed that I had returned to my home village in the red hills of Georgia and was looking at a bridge that had been built *over* a "free-stone" spring near home. I exclaimed, "Here are the springs of creativity!"

I felt refreshed the next day. It was a healing experience. Here I was, an American woman struggling in a strange land to describe the creative process, to experience the source of it by fusing the childhood world with the Indian world; and I discovered that the reality is shared by artistic souls the world over. In a sense I was realizing anew that destiny lay somewhere *beyond*, in a universal mingling of minds, that we were experiencing then only the "springs" of creativity. The full flow was to be channeled through the "covered bridge" that connected the two worlds.

I thought of this again as I helped the student who was to write the feature story in the college magazine about the exhibit. I went through the exhibit with him and guided him in choosing one piece of each kind of art to discuss in the story. He then asked each artist to tell him the story *behind* the creation of the chosen object. The light in the student's eyes as he jotted down his notes made me believe that he had grasped the reality we were all experiencing, and that it would be present in his story.

One of the things I had to remember as I taught young Indians about writing is that they have a rich store of expressions that were fresh to my ears since their background is so different from mine.

They had to be helped to express their own forms rather than par-
rot Western style in their writing.

One night as I sat in my living room waiting for dinner to be served, I heard footsteps outside. Four young students from the Engineering College nearby wanted to talk over their plans for organizing an International Youth Organization in the university. The vice chancellor wisely told them they must draw up a statement of purpose for the organization. Someone had sent them to me. I had never seen any of them before, but as I listened to them talk of their desire to learn about people from other countries, I realized that here was an open door for me to enter, to extend myself again beyond my own college walls. I tried to encourage them and guide them in affiliating with the International Student Organization, whose magazine I had on my table. I gave it to them, along with directions for getting information.

The next day while I was sitting at my desk, the leader of the group bounced into the office with a copy of the paper he was presenting that day to the vice chancellor. One of the sentences struck me as being exceedingly fresh and expressive. He had written: "We are through with the idolatry of Geography." Here was an original, positive statement against extreme nationalism. Not only had I met a potential engineer, but a creative person as well.

The important factor in creating form is to be wholly discontented with the present. As J. Krishnamurti has said,

> For such total discontent is the beginning of the initiative which becomes creative as it matures; and that is the only way to find out what is truth, what is God, because the creative state is God.
>
> So one must have this total discontent—but with joy. Do you understand? One must be wholly discontented, not complainingly, but with joy, with gaiety, with love. Most people who are discontented are terrible bores; they are always complaining that something or other is not right, or wishing they were in a better position, or wanting circumstances to be different, because their discontent is very superficial. *And those who are not discontented at all are already dead.*
>
> If you can be in revolt while you are young, and as you grow older keep your discontent alive with the vitality of joy and great affection, then that flame of discontent will have an extraordinary significance because it will build, it will create, it will bring new

things into being. For this you must have the right kind of education, which is not the kind that merely prepares you to get a job or to climb the ladder of success, but the education that helps you to think and gives you space—space, not in the form of a larger bedroom or a higher roof, but space for your mind to grow so that it is not bound by any belief, by any fear.

Can you and I, who are simple, ordinary people, live creatively in this world without the drive of ambition which shows itself in various ways as the desire for power, position? You will find the right answer when you love what you are doing. *If you are an engineer merely because you must earn a livelihood, or because your father or society expects it of you, that is another form of compulsion; and compulsion in any form creates a contradiction, a conflict. Whereas, if you really love to be an engineer, or a scientist, or if you can plant a tree, or paint a picture, or write a poem, not to gain recognition but just because you love to do it, then you will find that you never compete with another. I think this is the real key: to love what you do.*

But when you are young it is often very difficult to know what you love to do, because you want to do so many things. You want to be an engineer, a locomotive driver, an airplane pilot zooming along in the blue skies; or perhaps you want to be a famous orator or politician. You may want to be an artist, a chemist, a poet or a carpenter. You may want to work with your hands. Is any of these things what you really love to do, or is your interest in them merely a reaction to social pressures? How can you find out? And is not the true purpose of education to help you find out, so that as you grow up you can begin to give your whole mind, heart and body to that which you really love to do?

To find out what you love to do demands a great deal of intelligence; because, if you are afraid of not being able to earn a livelihood, or of not fitting into this rotten society, then you will never find out. But, if you are not frightened, if you refuse to be pushed into the groove of tradition by your parents, by your teachers, by the superficial demands of society, then there is a possibility of discovering what it is you really love to do. *So, to discover, there must be no fear of not surviving.*

But most of us are afraid of not surviving, we say, 'What will happen to me if I don't do as my parents say, if I don't fit into this society?' Being frightened, we do as we are told, and in that there is no love, there is only contradiction; and this inner contradiction is one of the factors that brings about destructive ambition."[2]

As a nonconformist, you may not always be in profound disagreement with the current form of society. You may simply wish to add your views, to render your own personal account of the world. The degree to which nonconformity is allowed, both in yourself and in society, is an indication of the measure of health that is present.

○ Case Study: Catherine
"I'm looking through the narrow end of a cone."

In working with hundreds of clients, I have found that one of the persistent forces blocking many people from creating their own new forms is rigid religious training. Catherine's story of emergence from a cloistered religious order into the business world is a classic example. Her long, arduous journey has been characterized by courageous efforts to move forward and by times slipping back into static immobility.

She was forty-nine years old when she came to me. Following a three-year leave of absence from the order, she was stuck in a dead end clerical job with no status or upward mobility. She repeated the same static pattern in working with me. After a period of a year, she maintained an open-ended agreement with me to return for further training when she was ready to make a definitive move.

The oldest daughter of an Irish emigrant family, where the father was a chauffeur and the mother a maid, Catherine took over the running of the home at sixteen, when her mother died at the birth of the seventh child. The Catholic Church loomed large on the landscape of her childhood in a rural section of Connecticut. She and her brothers and sisters walked two miles every Saturday to a monastery where the priests gave them religious instruction. Two of her brothers entered orders. There were few other models for emulation. Thus, after Catherine had the children reared, she entered the cloistered order at age thirty. Her life experiences had been extremely limited—domestic achievements and religious activities. She had only a high school education, and the order allowed no secular reading. For fifteen years she existed in a very sterile environment, negating all the vital forces and dulling her sensitivity to any independent thinking.

The order was organized according to sixteenth-century norms, its rules having been written by the Holy Mother, with no provision for self-governing. Priests came from the outside to say mass. In this way, the nuns were constantly reminded that women were the "lesser vessels," not worthy to administer the sacraments. Their role in the world was to pray. "We were to pray for the Pope, missionaries, and other specific items given on billets," Catherine wrote. "I began to have the gradual awakening that all this holiness was not fostering holiness at all. I remember two sisters had to get up with baskets and brush crumbs from the table bowing to the cross. This whole rigamarole on top of the work! To get the house cleaned was getting ready for Jesus. I began to question all this stuff that was put on us after all these hundreds of years."

I encouraged Catherine to talk about her life in the order and asked her to give me a detailed report of her daily schedule there. I am including it here so that you can understand the all-invasive discipline she experienced.

CATHERINE'S DAILY SCHEDULE IN CLOISTERED ORDER

5:40 A.M.	Get up, get coffee (fought for this)
5:40–6:00	Lauds—communal prayer
6:00–7:00	Mental prayer & solitude (garden, room or choir); trouble staying awake—kneel or lean back or sit on bench
7:00–7:45	Mass—music and liturgy
7:45–8:00	Divine Office—prayer
8:00–8:10	Breakfast (coffee and bread)—after 1972, eggs, cereal, etc.; stand up to eat
8:10–11:00	Work—maintenance, cooking, alter, bread, packages to parishes for support, gardening (vegetables and flowers)
11:00–11:25	Divine Office—prayer
11:25–11:55	Meal—fish and cheese (no meat ever; on Fridays, no cheese, butter, milk, or eggs)—in 1500s only the very rich had meat

11:55 A.M.–12:15 P.M.	Dishes	
12:15–1:00	Recreation—sat around and sewed or went to garden (later, 1968, began to have sports, jigsaw puzzles, Scrabble)	
1:00–2:00	Free time—go to room, rest, sew, quiet time	
2:00–3:00	Work—sew, etc., made clothes	
3:00–3:30	Spiritual reading (lives of saints, books or prayers)	
3:30–4:25	Work	
4:25–5:00	Vespers—evening prayer, recited (Sundays and feast days, chanted or sung)	
5:00–6:00	Prayer and solitude—in choir—people went to sleep	
6:00–6:30	Supper—collation (coming together), a measured meal, including vegetables, soup, cereal, eggs, cheese	
6:30–7:30	Recreation	
7:30–7:38	Examination of conscience	
7:38–8:00	Compline (night prayer) ritual	
8:00–9:00	Free time—went to room to work on "pretties" (dainty work), make bookmarks, write letters, or do spiritual exercise	
9:00–9:45	Matins (prayer) with breviary—official prayerbook, Divine Office	
9:45–11:00	More prayers, work—some went to bed	

In the 1970s I realized something was wrong. I wasn't growing. I would sit there, fall asleep, cry, deal with the awful thing of not being true to my vows. I knew I had to leave for my own personal research.

The spiritual feeding had been forced and I left feeling guilty so often. In growing up, I was never permitted to be a child, was given all those religious injunctions, "What will the neighbors think?" This was even compounded by my being the oldest child, and forced to be an example for the others. All of this made me aware of shortcomings.

Catherine's Success Stories were:

1. Learning to Drive a Car
2. Arranging for Sister's Wedding
3. Going to the Store
4. Conducting Choir Practice in Cloister
5. Going to College and Getting Degree at Age 49
6. Rearing Brother Roy after Mother's Death
7. Entering the Monastery
8. Summer of Fifteenth Birthday
9. Leaving Religious Life

I just discovered that she wrote only nine stories! Is this an indication of her unfinished task with me? Is there one more to come?

I am including three of her stories here because each one is a significant indication of the forces she had been dealing with in her development.

Success Story: Going to the Store

Rightly this should be called "Coming Home from the Store" because I don't recall any problem on my solo trip in arriving at the store in our little, mile-long town. But coming home is another story altogether! Such an anxiety when it seemed as though each block was the one that had our house, with its stone wall, and then the end of the block arrived and no familiar house! I was six years old and we had just moved to this little town. In our former town I frequently went to the store, walking on the overpass of some very busy expressway and then across the street, with its trolley and truck traffic. So it wasn't going to the store that was frightening. It was finding our house. I recall wanting to go back some of the blocks, thinking that I surely had passed it. But I think I didn't because I felt my mother would be looking for me and wouldn't have let me.

As I recall, the temptation to do so was strongest when I came to a grassy slope of lawn that I couldn't place at all. Well, don't you know that was the yard next to ours and it didn't have a stone wall on that part because their yard was twice as wide as ours was! I was so near and I didn't know it. Well, sure enough, I saw the stone wall further on, so I decided to keep going and that's when I heard a familiar call—"Catherine."

I have prioritized as number one the success I accomplished in raising Roy, my youngest brother. It's not my success, really, but somehow we do tend to look on ourselves as a success or failure in raising children depending on how they turn out. Roy is now married, has a new job opportunity with his company, and has two lovely children.

He was born by Caesarian section. Our mother died two days later. He was premature, and so he was kept at the hospital for two months, after which my aunt and cousin took him to their home until I finished high school. I used to go to their house almost every day right after school and just watch him. I don't remember feeding or holding him then, yet now I recall walking him to our house. I'm not sure if this was only after school or sometimes on weekends. So much of that time I haven't tried to recall until now. I do remember taking him home with my dad after I had graduated, and my aunt saying she would never take him back. I was scared, I know now, but didn't dare admit that to myself at the time.

He was a love of a baby, not cranky, just peaceful and loving. However, he hated to be put out in his playpen and cried the whole time if I wasn't out there with him. I got very short-tempered with him and all my brothers and sisters, and I slapped them a lot. For a period of time when he was a toddler, Roy and I had what I look on now as a very strained relationship. I think it's because as soon as he was no longer a baby I wanted him to grow up right away. However, I think he sensed he was loved and we could talk to each other. Some of his expressions of affection are so vivid and precious to me. I'm at a loss to say much more. I know I helped him to understand and respect Dad, and I also know his lack of interest in school is a lot my fault because of my impatience and not helping him with his homework. It was my older brother who helped him understand his sexual development and eased his way into adolescence, and our other brother helped him in his studies and to recognize and work with his reading problems.

I coped with Roy's babyhood by mostly doing what my mother had done with the other children. I shudder when I think of all my mistakes during those years and his growing years. It's remarkable that he is the fine young man he is today.

I don't want to write about leaving religious life, but it is something that I have accomplished that is worth mentioning. When I came to the realization that I was not growing as a person in community and that my prayer life was shallow, especially times of private prayer, I asked for a leave of absence for an indefinite period of time. It was granted for a year, then was extended for me because I was studying and still trying to come to grips with myself. I came to realize that the nuns were essentially trying to be free women of prayer, and that this could be achieved and carried on outside of cloister; but neither my community order nor church law makes provision for this. So I have now asked for secularization and dispensation from my vows. I consulted with authorities in the church and with a nun who was given a permanent exclaustration. These steps and the meetings I had with my community are the positive aspects that I wish to highlight because I have so often done things with impetuosity or not done others because of not consulting or speaking up to state my views—in other words, taking the easy way out. This time I took a stand and even though the results are not what I had hoped for, I have come through a very difficult period emotionally and spiritually strengthened. There are two loose ends to be tied up. One is to write to the sister who so freely shared of her correspondence and church documents to help me, and the other is to have the dowry returned, which will come when the papers of dispensation are received.

Catherine's account of going to the store is a touching picture of a little girl who is completely other-directed. In this case, she was directed by her mother, who told her to go to the store and who "called" her back on her return.

The story of rearing her brother Roy is a description of how she "became" a mother herself. Note how she lists this as her number-one priority.

Her description of leaving the monastery is a sad commentary on the limitations of the contemplative life for her and its failure to offer her an opportunity to experience the fullness of her humanity. Having sought solace in Mother Church, she is finally discovering that she now has to become her own mother, and is still in the agony of giving birth to this new form.

Catherine's symbols are especially pertinent to understanding her existential position at the time she drew them.

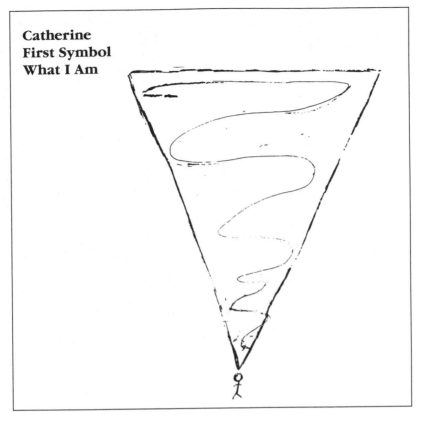

**Catherine
First Symbol
What I Am**

Catherine looking up through a hole in the narrow end of a cone. Sees light at the top (faith, hope and potential for expansion), but view to the top is obscured by wavy, indefinite lines and patterns. (Fuzzy, undisciplined thinking. Cone is big, indicating big, indefinite future.)

**Catherine
Second Symbol
What I'd Like to Be**

An open fan, bringing pleasure and comfort. (The fan is hand-held, not electric, because Catherine wants to be self-motivated. Such a fan also moves the air, indicating a need to get other things moving.)

Catherine
Third Symbol
What Hinders Me

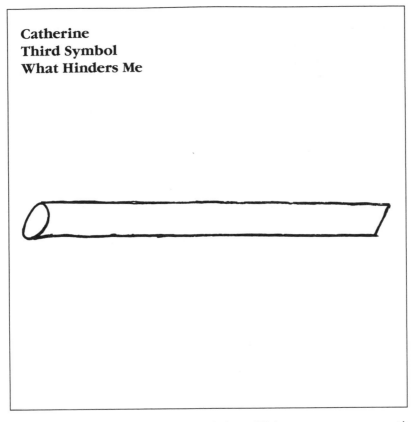

Another image of the fan—folded shut. (This represents procrastination, fear of failure, unsuitability, inability to measure up to own and others' expectations.)

Catherine
Fourth Symbol
What Will Overcome the Obstacle

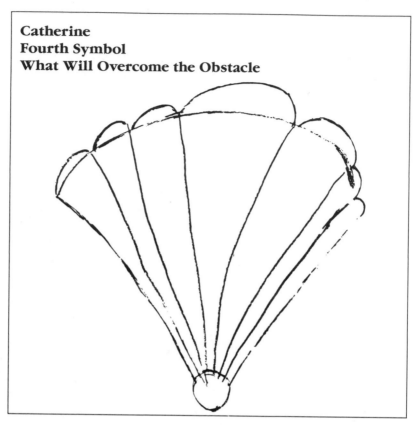

Fan needs to be open, but loose enough to catch wind and billow like a sail.

Early in the process, I sent Catherine for a consultation with the psychiatrist who is my guide and mentor, who is able to evaluate specific clients who I feel I need help in sorting out a solid program of development. He worked with her on her relationships with men and other authority figures.

I began guiding Catherine in a reading program, some of which related to increasing her sexual awareness and her enjoyment of sensuality in other aspects of her life. I also assigned the observance of a regular existential awareness exercise (described elsewhere in this book). Soon she began to trust her own judgment about various issues. One day she came up with the following list:

THINGS I DON'T BELIEVE ANYMORE
1. Pride is always sinful.
2. Extramarital sex is always wrong.
3. Anger is always wrong.

THINGS I DO BELIEVE
1. It is always all right to be held and nurtured.
2. To be "doing" is all right.
3. I still believe "To be bold is to be a bad girl." That is what my procrastination is all about.

Catherine began to show initiative on her job. She asked for and got special training; she insisted on being considered for a promotion. And even though she didn't get it, she learned that she was valuable to the company, and that her superiors were now *aware* of her as having upward mobility.

She soon moved into another apartment and had her name on a wait list for a better building that was being built. Her growing autonomy was spreading into her lifestyle. Perhaps Catherine herself is her tenth success story. She is evolving a new form in the midst of extremely resistant forces. At the end of her story on entering the monastery, Catherine wrote: "I asked the advice of priests and as with so many other areas of life, was told that one can never know for certain if one has a religious vocation or if one is doing the right thing, but it seemed good to try. And that's what I still do. I try."

A few months later I called the financial company where Catherine works. I discovered she had been given a new title: Service Analyst in the national credit office. She had received a master's degree in business administration by taking courses at night and on the weekends. She now lives in a large cooperative apartment complex, sings in the choir every Sunday, and has negotiated with her sister to share the care of their invalid father. She mentioned that she was aware that she did not finish with me, and that she still owes me part of my fee. She expressed appreciation of the patient way I worked with her, for I said, "When you are ready you will make closure." She answered that it was this kind of affirmation without stern authority that has enabled her to grow. I had successfully guided her through the final stages of being completely separated from the order. She borrowed some money and took her first trip to Europe. I considered the case closed!

○ Case Study: Irene
"I was suffocating in the research room."

You can see by the account of Catherine's long, arduous journey that significant change is often painfully slow. Irene, a twenty-eight-year-old black woman, took sixteen months to move from being an administrative assistant in the litigation department of a law firm to a personnel position in a not-for-profit social service agency.

The career development process Irene underwent with me revealed that her key characteristic was her social concern cultivated by family role models. Her father was a retired social worker and her mother a school teacher. The tedious, boring research activities related to her job with the legal firm did not satisfy her need to be directly involved in the development of socially deprived people, with whom she had a strong identification.

Irene's success stories included one related to this issue, involving a woman in a company where she previously worked. I received a clue for her future in this story.

Success Story: Helping Lena

As administrative assistant, my duties included supervising the clerical staff at the corporate headquarters. This was something I really looked forward to because I know how to communicate and work effectively with other people. I have never felt the need to look down on others or be the "boss." In short, I could and did supervise without supervising. I had a good relationship with the secretaries, and they in turn trusted and respected me.

When I assumed my position, there was only one secretary in addition to the receptionist. Because of recent promotions, Lena had been hired by my predecessor. She had been trained by the company and was from a disadvantaged background. She was inexperienced and very timid. On one occasion I was sitting at the reception desk with her, teaching her how to answer the telephone and other procedures. When the phone rang, she jumped and started shaking and asked me, "What do I do now?" I remained calm and explained and demonstrated the proper procedures. Her performance was shaky for the first couple of weeks, so I never left her alone at the main desk. In the beginning she cut off quite a few people, who would then complain to the president or to others.

I thought the personnel director was understanding of Lena's situation, since she hired her. Unfortunately, she became very critical of her, especially her appearance (too much makeup, lots of jewelry, loud scarves). She spoke to her several times and also to her counselor at the company's training center. She was, in my opinion, unnecessarily harsh, and Lena was afraid of her. On one occasion she told me to speak to Lena about her makeup, and I did. She listened quietly and left without saying a word. A few minutes later the receptionist came to me and asked, "Why is Lena crying?" I was very upset because I had been careful to be gentle with her. When I reported the incident to the personnel director, she snapped, "I don't care if she cries." After that I was very careful what I said about Lena, because I knew she was close to being terminated. Lena was terrified of the personnel director, who, I felt, bullied her.

Lena and I worked closely together. Her confidence and office skills improved 100 percent. For several days she replaced the receptionist. I watched closely, but from a distance so as not to make her nervous. She did a good job, and I noticed she was poised and happy with her job. She still made mistakes, but she had come a long way. I was always careful when I criticized her, including the positive as well as the negative. With Lena, too much negative would have been damaging.

Less than three months after she arrived, the personnel director called me in for a conference. She was pleased with Lena's work performance and was going to offer her a promotion in the accounting department. I was happy, but I was also sad about losing her so soon. When I told Lena that the personnel director wanted to see her, she jumped and started shaking like a leaf. I thought she was going to start crying. I told her not to worry, that everything was all right. She was very happy and accepted the position and was given a small raise.

Lena is still with the company. She is more outgoing and confident than when she joined them. I feel her success was my greatest achievement there in spite of my difficulties with the company.

I began to help Irene explore opportunities in social service agencies where she would have an environment and position that would pay her for being who she really is. The form of her career needed to match her inner core of reality. When I asked her to write a philosophic statement concerning her career goals, this is what she said:

> I am currently searching for a creative administrative position where it would be possible for me to use and extend my current skills. Over the years in my various positions, I have had the opportunity to learn aspects of office procedure. I have been employed by (1) a medium-sized corporation and (2) a well-known Wall Street law firm that represents large corporations.
>
> Since I come from a religious family with strong feelings for other people (my father is a retired social worker, my mother has been a teacher for many years, and my brother is studying to be a priest), I would like to concentrate my efforts on an organization which shares my religious beliefs to reach out to others rather than concentrate on financial gains. This type of work is important for my personal growth.

Irene went through a number of interviews and several months' search. Sometimes she was treated like an applicant for a secretarial position, but gently I guided her to recognize her strengths and to keep pursuing her goal in making a transition. Eventually the persistent networking she did paid off. She got exactly what she was looking for: she changed her field to personnel and moved from the corporate world into the social service arena as assistant director of personnel (with four secretaries under her supervision) in a national agency related to the rights of children.

Here in addition she used her own identity as a minority to create a career that fulfilled her rather than stay in a sterile situation in which she felt insignificant. As a result, she experienced the relationship of creativity and form.

Lyall Watson, former director of the Johannesburg Zoo, has told the story of taking a boat trip up the river in an African jungle when one of the boatmen had a high fever from an abscess at the root of a tooth. He waited until he reached a certain village the next day to see a famous healer. Watson had tried to pull the tooth with pliers but could not remove it. He tried again the next day. When they arrived at the healer's hut, they bargained with two packs of cigarettes. The healer, an insignificant-looking man, reached in the person's mouth and removed the tooth with his hand without much effort. Watson looked at the tooth and also at the hole in the mouth. The healer said, "Wait, I have to take away the pain." The man then sat in front of the healer and started to talk. Suddenly the group of people began to laugh. Watson looked and saw blood coming from the corner of the man's mouth. Then a row of ants came from his mouth, marched down his neck, and down into the bush. Later he found that the word the healer had used to describe the removal of pain was the same word for "ants." Thus ants materialized.[3] This defies all ordinary knowledge or reason,

This story, is a dramatic way of illustrating the idea of form in the creation myths. In the Genesis account we connected form to Adam and Eve's action in redefining their existence outside Eden; in the Greek story there is the split to make the male and female and prepare for the first-born, and in the pre-Aryan Indian myth the laws of Manu present the mind and eggs as two different forms.

In Catherine's story, we see a vibrant spirit underneath all the repression of convent life. The glow never went out completely. She experienced love underneath the superstructure and found enough nurturance to develop the maturity to buck the form eventually and get out.

Irene has moved forward also. She has just received a certificate in personnel and is radiant with the knowledge that her work is connected to a meaning beyond her paycheck.

Go to Part Three, Step 8 (page 256) and continue to create your own new form.

NINE

❀ **Communication**

What Happens Between
You and Others

We are born helpless.
As soon as we are
fully conscious
we discover
loneliness.
We need others
physically, emotionally,
intellectually;
we need them if we
are to know anything,
even ourselves.
      —C. S. Lewis
         Four Loves

Have you finally got the message that no one else is going to "get" you a job, not even if you pay an enormous agency fee? You have to do it yourself. You are in charge of creating your own career.

You are now at a place where some people back away and stall, still cherishing the illusion that there is a fairy godmother, and that if they wait long enough or wish hard enough, she will finally rescue them and give them what they want on a silver platter.

Some clients even begin trying to seduce their career counselor into playing this game with them. My "Big Mama" subpersonality often tries to take over my core person at this point, and I have to be very careful to remain in the appropriate role as consultant!

If you have been experiencing me as your consultant as you read this book, perhaps you are ready for another analogy: Here we are, you and I. How can you move ahead to the goal line? I am the ball coach who has trained you well from the sidelines, been with you through all these weeks of strenuous practice, whispered secrets of success in the "back room," following a fumbled ball, called out slogans and cheers when you were on the right track. The game is moving to a climax. So far you are winning. The score is in your favor. So don't flub it now.

You are holding the ball, but you are not alone. You are part of a team. Your ability to throw the ball to the right person, standing in the right place, who can in turn pass it on to someone else until the game is won, is now ready for testing. In short, you must experience the relationship between creativity and communication.

If you are now the embodiment of the images that you have had of yourself, you are ready to expose your new form in the marketplace. You can't wait for someone else to hunt you out and discover you.

One more step is necessary. You have to be able to "close the sale," to get a signature on the dotted line. You have to be hired by somebody, or to get clients or customers, in the case that you have decided to go into business for yourself.

This is the stage when you must begin to connect with other people. You now need to become part of a network, to know who your role models are, who will agree to be your mentors, and who are the connecting links. There has to be a lot of activity during that period, in which your consultant is only an observer and enabler.

Another analogy: The weaning process must begin. It is time for you to be thrown out of the nest, where I have been giving you the fat worms and chirping my directions and saying "Watch, this is how to fly." A little nursery rhyme comes to mind here:

> What does mother bird say,
> in her nest, at break of day?
> Rest a little longer
> Till your wings are stronger.
> Then, you, too, can fly away.

But, my little bird, the resting time is over. I'm pushing you out. I'll even remove the nest eventually so you cannot return to your "baby-bird" stage. You have to build your own nest. You know how. You know where to find the sticks, straw, string, or whatever you need. You have wings. You have a sharp beak for catching your own worms, and I have even heard you begin to chirp your own song. But before you go, here is one more lesson, some more material for you to digest. It's called communication.

What is communication? It is a trip from where you are to where you want to be in relation to another person or group of persons. Your task is to close the gap that separates you. You need all the information you have gathered. You must use energy and drive and patience and the ability to absorb lots of ambiguity and deal with seemingly wasted time and effort. Not every connection will pay off. You may have to send out several hundred résumés, write innumerable letters, go to countless luncheons and cocktail parties, visit watering holes of executives in your chosen profession, join organizations and clubs you have avoided before, connect with college chums you had stopped sending Christmas cards to, call up your favorite old professor who will remember how great you were in that course in which he gave you an A, clean up an unfinished task in a prior commitment, straighten out the fuzzy link with a deserted friend or ex-lover, or even take a fresh look at your parents and other relatives. Most of these people will be flattered that you need them. They will probably go out of their way to open doors for you, now that you know what you want them to do for you.

The reasons I have not suggested networking before is that it is useless and perhaps harmful to circulate before you know what you want to do and how people can be helpful.

There are two stages in this connecting phase of your career develpment. One is what Bernard Haldane (a pioneer in the field of career development) has called Research and Referral. During this time you interview people who are doing the kind of thing you think you want to do. Even though you are just gathering information about the field, you can sometimes show so much prior knowledge and exhibit such exquisite interest in the subject that the person will create a job for you in the organization, or will refer you to someone else who can open the right door.

Like some of my clients, you may really enjoy this phase. Sometimes people have such a great time collecting information and relishing all of the affirmation received during this activity that they are tempted to revel a bit longer here than is necessary. It is important to be open to whatever comes up, or you might miss some clues that could lead you to your goal. Don't become rigid or assume that the world owes you anything. No company will hire you just because you need a job. You have to show how you can meet their needs—usually how you can help them make or save more money.

You must be a clear channel—with all the debris about past bad treatment by employers, teachers, family, etc., out of the way, or at least pushed to the side enough for the message you have to give to the world to get through.

You'll find specific help for doing library research to find companies and organizations and other information you need elsewhere in this book, where books and other resources are also listed. What I want to do here is to talk a little about mentors and models. I also share some of the material from my own client case histories that will inspire you and help you envision how you can do for yourself what they did for themselves.

What is a mentor? A mentor is someone who has achieved enough success in a field of endeavor to have the authority to advise you on your course of action, who has enough leisure time to give you the time you require, and, most important, who cares about what happens to you. Mentoring is a conscious agreement between you and your mentor, who is aware that he or she is taking on this role and accepts it. It is a voluntary act, both from your view and from your mentor's, which can be extended over a period of many years and evolve through many stages and levels.

You are fortunate if you have found at least one other person who serves as your mentor, more than fortunate if you have several. You need as strong a support system as possible. So don't settle for less than you need. Remember, a working mentor/mentee relationship is based on your need to receive and the mentor's need to give. Besides, you can often give new insights to them also. As in every healthy relationship, mutual exchange is necessary.

But don't sit at anyone's feet very long.¹ Eventually you will internalize what you need and will, in essence, become your own mentor.

Now let's talk about role models. A role model is someone whom you would like to emulate. The role model need not be aware that you are choosing him or her. The role model can be someone in your memory, whose image you have carried secretly all these years—someone who chanced into your life briefly and passed by, leaving an unforgettable aura that you still cling to. You may have idealized this person out of all proportion. If this is true, you will have to get the imagery into focus with reality before it can be useful. Maybe seeing this role model again will wipe away the magic and help you realize that you can obtain heights just as great or greater. You are in competition only with yourself. You can drop the tension of competing with anyone else or the compulsion to prove yourself to some phantom audience.

You may have any number of role models, each one furnishing a view of heights in areas where you also want to excell. In fact, spread your role modeling around to help keep you from idealizing anyone. Be aware of their warts as well as their halos. Don't trust anyone who claims to have "arrived" or to have achieved perfection. Such people are liars whom you don't want for your role models. Get close enough to the pedestal where you have placed them to see their clay feet. By doing so you will be able to enjoy your own toes, knowing also someday they may briefly occupy a pedestal. Tickle them enough to see the ridiculous aspect of *any* position. Maintain your sense of humor, at all costs. It's your most valuable asset.

Networking is absolutely necessary for career development. It is still true that no one is an island. We are part of a larger landscape. We have followed Adam and Eve east of Eden, having lost our paradise and having been busy acquisitioning other property ever since. We are hunting, fishing, bartering, and enjoying the spoils back in the caves at the end of the expeditions. As a liberated woman, I see myself in the explorer role interchangeably with the long-haired cave woman. My mate can also mind the cave and make the stew as well as I can. I'm a pretty straight shooter, and can tell fish stories, too. Sometimes, "I bring 'em back alive" to add to the joys of adventuring and returning.

Since the dawn of higher education, men have known about the "old boy's network." At last women too are catching on to the as yet largely untapped network composed of their former classmates, some of whom have done something besides get married and bask in motherhood forever after. Whether you are male or female, you must network. Join a professional group, a men's or women's club, civic organization, a religious community, a hobby club, a college association. Become a member of some board of directors (either an institution in which you have an interest or a foundation board that is giving money to your favorite institution), lead a charity drive, get involved in politics or a social cause. In short, be memorable. Go places and see people. Be visible. Be a useful member of society. Travel and attend events. Make speeches and get excited about something.

Nobody except undertakers or ghouls is interested in dead bod-

ies. No one is hiring cadavers. *Be alive.* Love yourself, and in that
spirit reach out to others. Networking is another way of acting out
the Golden Rule—"Do unto others as you would have them do unto
you."

Which brings up another point. Remember that *you* are also a
useful network to somebody else. It's a chain—so don't break the
link.

○ Case Study: Marshall

*"I would like challenging and remunerative
employment."*

The first case history I want to share in this connection is Marshall's.
I had known him for several years and I sponsored him in several
projects and have been his friend, on many levels. Then he came
to see me as a client. It was exhilarating to participate in his career
development, even though he was forty-four years old and was
floundering for an anchor during that period of his life. As a result,
he was still earning under his potential capacity.

Marshall did his assignments carefully. He wrote his stories,
reworked his résumé, and took a new job to bridge the gap between
where he was then and where he ultimately wanted to go. He was
an actor, singer, teacher, producer, entrepreneur, and champion of
"lost causes." He was constantly reaching out to break down the
barriers between races, classes, and religions.

Because Marshall was a natural networker, I chose to feature him
here. His success stories include:

1. Creating a Docudrama Troupe Growing Out of a
   Fellowship with a Major Theatrical Company
2. Getting Straight A's One Year in College
3. Creating a Performing Arts Festival
4. Organizing Centennial Arts Festival
5. Marketing Quilts to Gift Shops
6. Selling for My Father As a Teenager
7. Creating a Tenant's Association
8. Teaching and Directing a Play in a Prison
9. Finishing a Difficult Project Relating to Racism
10. Establishing a Coffee House

Here is one very pivotal episode in his development.

This is by far the most difficult story I have had to write for this process. There are so many feelings of guilt, anger, and pain that are tied up in this chapter of my life that I am glad I am finally dealing with them.

I started working for my father when I was approximately twelve years old. My father sold a variety of merchandise on the installment plan and I worked for him on Saturdays by collecting payments from many of the customers, especially those who lived on the fifth and sixth floors in walk-up buildings. My father's customers were primarily black and they lived in the Bedford-Stuyvestant area of Brooklyn. My father sold them dry goods, clothing, jewelry, furniture and some electrical appliances. At that time, the major department stores did not give credit accounts to blacks, and those who could not afford to buy their merchandise for cash dealt with either credit stores or "credit peddlers" such as my father.

For the first two or three years that I worked for my father, I sold a few items, but primarily collected payments from the customers. When I got to be about sixteen, I became much more aggressive and found that I was a very good salesman, besides having some very creative business ideas. I have great respect for my father's business ability, his considerable salesmanship skills and especially his honesty and integrity. When I was collecting and selling the merchandise that he had handled for years, we got along fine, but when I started to investigate new items to stimulate the business, we really had some epic fights.

I had seen an advertisement in the newspaper for a set which included dishes, sliverware, glasses, etc., for a fairly reasonable price. I sensed that there was a high profit markup on this combination package and I told my father about the idea. He was very skeptical, but I did some research and found the company who manufactured and wholesaled this combination package. I remember going to their showroom and feeling very important as I flashed my business card. They treated me with great respect, thinking I might buy an order of several thousand dollars. I did talk my father into buying a dozen sets. The reaction on the part of the customers was very favorable, and we sold all of the sets. I really don't remember if we reordered these sets or not. It was at this time that I stopped working for my father.

The other story included here is also about selling, for even though most of Marshall's past successes have been connected to the theater, the direction that he seemed to be choosing came out of his deeply personally satisfying sales experience.

As you read the following story, keep in mind the previous story, as well as the dynamics found in the relationship of Marshall to his father, combined with his ability to deal with the unfinished relationship at the time he wrote the story. This second story involves his wife and children in the creation of a new thing. Note how many skills are involved in making the project work.

Success Story: Marketing Quilts to Gift Shops

In the summer of 1974, Miriam, my wife, created the cottage industry Community Quilters. During the first two years of its existence, I was its chief salesman, sales marketing director, etc. I was spending the summer with my children in a small town on the coast, and I had a considerable amount of leisure time.

Miriam sent some sample quilts and pillows to me, and I was very pleased and excited about both the design and craftsmanship. I was confident that I could sell them at some of the local crafts fairs and flea markets. I asked a musician who had lived in that area for most of her life about the flea market that would be the most promising for the sale of these quilts and pillows. She recommended one market which was held every Sunday.

I borrowed two folding picnic tables from a friend, loaded up the car with quilts and pillows, plus markers and cardboard with which to make signs, and I went off over the trail to the flea market. It was a very hot Sunday and the flea market grounds had no shade whatsoever. As I stood and sweated the whole Sunday, I realized that the quilts and pillows were too expensive for the trade that came to the flea market. I was so tired, sunbaked, and discouraged from standing at the flea market for a whole day without selling one item that I got lost going home. But I vowed to try again because I knew that somewhere there would be a market for the quilts and pillows.

My next marketing venture was a crafts fair. I thought the town had some very wealthy inhabitants and since this was an arts show to benefit their museum, the fair would attract the kind of clientele who would want to buy the beautiful products Miriam and her friends had created. Once again, I loaded the car with voluminous plastic bags full of quilts, pillows, potholders, and dish towels, along with the folding tables, and a large plastic cover to protect the merchandise in case of rain. The fair ran for two days. It showered for a good part of Saturday and some of Sunday. The fair did not produce anything significant, other than some suggestions from someone who really admired the quilts about a couple of chic stores in the area that catered to the ski trade.

I tried to market the quilts and pillows at a crafts fair on a university campus, a town fair, and a county fair with relatively little success. The children were having a great time going to fairs and playing shopkeeper, but it was costing me more in gas, ice cream, and other assorted treats than the traveling market was netting.

The suggestion I had gotten kept revolving in my mind and I decided to take a radically different approach to marketing the merchandise. I was going to sell these quilts and pillows to the chic gift stores that catered to the affluent New York City ski trade and vacationers. I then reseached the numerous shopping guides, tourist newspapers, etc., for those gift stores which I thought might be interested in my merchandise. I analyzed their advertisements and spoke to some friends of mine who lived in the area year round. I made up a list of prospects and consulted a local road map to see which places were near each other.

I started to call each store in order to make appointments for the owners to see the merchandise. I gave a history of the nonprofit organization that had created the items and also ascertained whether or not there was any real interest. The majority of these store owners were interested enough to say that they would look at the samples.

The first gift store that I went to was one of the most fashionable ski shops in the area. The store had very elegant products and the owner was very warm and sophisticated. She bought some pillows and ordered a quilt design called the Bicentennial. This success buoyed my spirits and I knew that I was on the right track. On the same day that I sold some merchandise there, I had an appointment with a woman who was opening a new gift store. She ordered a few hundred dollars' worth of merchandise and later reordered other quilts and pillows.

After the summer was over, I returned to New York City with the kids. I made two other weekend selling trips to the same area. I sold three or four quilts and several pillows and got a very large order from a man who later reordered some quilts and pillows.

I decided to end my quilt-pillow selling career because it was taking a good deal of time from my other creative interests and the $155 commission was hardly enough to compensate for all the hours and effort. But I greatly enjoyed meeting this challenge and helping the quilting cooperative get started.

While Marshall was seeing me, he left the job he had when we started working together and took one with a traveling theater as another "bridge" while we continued the process. Today he is earning a good income as a member of the faculty of a business college, while continuing to work on the entrepreneurial projects and to keep up his interest in the arts. All of his activities used his excellent communication skills.

○ Case Study: Rosita

"I did it myself."

Rosita was angry. She worked for an international public relations firm that promoted South American politicians, having grown up in Santo Domingo as a "little princess" in one of the country's leading families. She knew her job was being terminated partly because of chauvinism. She also was aware that if she stayed, she never would have as good a chance to move up as her male peers, even though she is a strikingly beautiful woman.

We spent quite a few sessions dealing with her hurt and anger. She didn't need assertiveness training. Rather, she needed to be affirmed by me as her consultant and mentor until she no longer would need to indulge in hostile encounters with prospective employers.

Rosita identified her skills quickly, and together we prepared an impressive functional résumé. Here is an adapted copy for you to note how her whole life experience was carefully orchestrated to communicate her level of achievement and her special international involvement.

Rosita's Résumé

CAREER
OBJECTIVE:
An executive position in the field of corporate public affairs where there is a need for bilingual

(Spanish and English), perceptive, analytical, creative individual with public relations and communications expertise.

EXPERIENCE
SUMMARY:
Fifteen years experience in political, community and media related programs involving account management, communications (media liasion, editing select audience publications), financial development, sales, project design and direct client contact.

SIGNIFICANT ACHIEVEMENTS
Public Affairs

- Secured services of famous TV personality, free of charge, to assist in fund raising and community awareness effort.
- Arranged for a corporate tax-free donation to a minority-oriented organization providing social services for the community.
- Initiated briefings for traveling executives about the national public affairs of the country being visited.
- Traveled to two countries in South America, to meet with client representatives.
- Organized public relations activities on behalf of the country's Mission to the United Nations and its government.
- Utilized pro-rated plans for tax exempt personal donations and trust endowments.
- Researched public issues and designed governmental and public relations program for U.S. company operating in Spain.
- Secured legal aid services for free consultation by members of the Hispanic community of New York.

Communications

- Designed and produced an LP record commissioned by the Republic of ABC.
- Edited final manuscript in Spanish for several books to be published by the Republic of XYZ.
- Served as media liaison and drafted press releases.
- Researched and prepared articles for a weekly newsletter which was sent to the business community.
- Planned meetings between executives of major U.S. newspapers and magazines and representatives of the government of AAA.
- Reviewed all confidential translations from English into Spanish.
- Represented the company at professional and social events.

- Wrote TV spots on population problems for use in Latin America.
- Acted as interpreter/translator for visiting Spanish-speaking clients.
- Coordinated promotion campaign for a banking organization.

Management
- Structured and implemented mechanisms for an in-house professional library, expanding considerably the availability and utilization of materials.
- Developed logistics for easier follow-up process of research projects.
- Organized an international political conference in France.
- Submitted monthly reports with recommendations on project development.
- Stimulated Board of Directors to become personally involved in fund raising and public relations on behalf of minority agency.
- Assumed administrative responsibility for client accounts in absence of executive director.

Sales and Marketing
- Obtained significant new client accounts on behalf of company.
- Increased considerably the sale of travellers checks for major banking organization.
- Identified principal sources of funding and made oral presentations to executives of Fortune 500 corporations in charge of corporate responsibility.
- Sold contracts for lease channels and telecommunications facilities.
- Made cost analysis to determine better utilization of the financial resources earmarked for international communications.

PROFESSIONAL AFFILIATIONS:
- Member of the Latin American Studies Association (LASA).
- Member of the Foreign Policy Association.
- Member of the Guild of Professional Translators.
- Elected Assistant Secretary of the International Association of Political Consultants.
- Nominated for the Board of Directors of a Latin American Institute.
- Nominated for the Board of Directors of the Urban League of Manhattan.

EMPLOYMENT HISTORY:
Assistant Account Manager/Project Director, BBB Inc., New York, 1975–78

Public Relations Director/Fund Raiser, CCC Family Institute, New York, 1975
Assistant to the Vice President, Population Reference Bureau, Washington, D.C., 1972–75
Sales Representative, DDD World Communications, Puerto Rico, 1970–72
Administrative Manager, A Direct Mail Company, Spain, 1969–70
Account Representative, EEE Bank, Santo Domingo, 1963–69

EDUCATION AND DISTINCTIONS:
B.A. (Magna Cum Laude) 1963, University of XYZ
Major: Psychology
Minor: Sociology & International Relations
Problem-Solving Alternatives Workshop (1970), Government Institution, Washington, D.C.
Course in Altered States of Consciousness (1973), Government Institution, Washington, D.C.
Course in Discovering Our World (Civilized Cultures & Natural State Societies) (1974), National Association, Washington, D.C.
Management Seminar (1977), The Conference Board, New York
Winner of 1st prize in national public speaking contest, Santo Domingo

LANGUAGE SKILLS:
Bilingual Spanish/English; conversant in Portuguese, Italian and French.

PERSONAL DATA:
Have traveled extensively throughout Europe, South America and the United States. Work experience includes New York, Washington, D.C. Spain, Puerto Rico and Santo Domingo.

I am including Rosita's material in this chapter on communication because she provides an example of effective networking and marketing skills. She decided on the criteria for her new career. It must:

1. Be with an international corporation
2. Use her multilingual skills
3. Provide upward mobility
4. Pay adequately
5. Recognize her social position

6. Allow freedom of movement and travel opportunities
7. Be close to her home

She researched the companies that fit these criteria. Next she listed the resources she could use from past connections. She arranged new contacts, set up exploratory interviews, weeded out the inappropriate or non-productive ones, and kept at the process incessantly.

When she had two international corporations competing for her, Rosita negotiated a contract with the one that was her first choice. When she landed her new position as Corporate Affairs Consultant for an international banking firm, she was exultant. "I did it myself," she exclaimed. And I congratulated her on discovering the secrets of communication. She had indeed closed the gaps between herself and the people with whom she wanted to communicate. Her anger had been transformed into creative energy for her new career.

○ Recalling the Creation Myths

In the Genesis myth, Adam in speaking of Eve describes the relationship as "bone of my bone and flesh of my flesh." He is affirming the possibility of closeness and trust. In his *The Diary of Adam and Eve*, Mark Twain has Eve writing, "The Garden is lost, but I have found *him*, and am content." And in his notation "at Eve's Grave," Adam writes, "wheresoever she was, *there* was Eden."[2]

Today there are a number of experimental communities that are seeking to explore ways of rediscovering or re-creating an environment in which the boundaries that separate human beings from one another and from the universal force can be dissolved. I am calling this to your attention because I profoundly believe that there is within you and me the potential for experiencing "here and there, now and then"[3] the quality of being that comes from "being grasped by the Ground of Being" and thus knowing only oneness. I hope you will increase these moments until they become a way of being. Communication is the basic factor here—whether it happens when a solitary person experiences wholeness through communing with nature or when a group of people dissolve the barriers that separate them from one another and from nature.

As you search for the others with whom you can communicate in relation to creating a career, let us take a fresh look at a holistic concept of communication that can offer clues that will give us hope. David Spangler, former co-director of the Findhorn community in Scotland, once said: "Communication is participation in the art of death and rebirth. You are different from me, and what you have to offer might change me. If I'm not at ease with that, my consciousness may need to change and communication may become difficult."[4] The Findhorn community is based on the idea that people, plants, and animals are all parts of a larger Gestalt of environment. When people come into the Findhorn garden, they leave their negative emotions behind. The success of the garden depends on the ability of the human beings to live well together. There is no break between the earth, soil, and the people in the continuum of communication. An ecological balance has been kept.

Findhorn is an experiment based on the willingness of people to open themselves to experience holistic living, to the possibility of transformation. Spangler went on:

> If the New Age has anything, it means the emergence of our ability to communicate beyond where we are now. Some say the human race is an epileptic. Something within us says, "There's a cure for this."
>
> I cannot be a human being, except in form, until I can recognize my humaness in relation to an ongoing life. . . . I used to be a scientist in a practical way. I don't know what a mystic is these days. . . . Scientific community is the only planetary community that exists. The land of mathematics is universal. But we don't know what the language of the spirit is that is as exact as the language of science, except the language of community that says, "I don't know how to communicate with you, but I'm going to find out."[5]

This is the holistic paradigm that is available to us.

In the Greek creation myth, communication is connected to the "fire in the eyes and a doubling back in form of union" of the creation and creature. The pre-Aryan Indian myth allows for "gestation for horses, cattle and humankind and for the need for company" in the process of communication. The concept of gestation as a symbol for communication is apt, whether it refers to the

period carrying the offspring after the coming-together of male and
female or the development of a plan or idea in the mind.

Get in touch with universal consciousness and your own individual yearning as you begin to reach out to others. Be willing to be transparent, to take risks, and to be vulnerable. Communication is not manipulation. It is not "wheeling and dealing" to get something for yourself that you are not willing to see others get also. It is based on mutual affirmation between yourself and others, beginning with the admission that you are not *there* yet. And can never get there without the others with whom you can connect.

Remember that myth is something that never happened and is always happening. One of the most profound experiences in communication I ever had was in India. My husband and I were on a hunting trip with two Muslim friends and one Anglo-Indian Christian. We had ridden in a jeep deep into the jungle but weren't having any luck finding the animals. Finally we saw smoke rising in the woods ahead of us, and our driver headed in that direction. When we got nearer, we discovered a Hindu family sleeping on flimsy cots around an open fire in the courtyard of their primitive house. They were too poor to own enough blankets to protect themselves from the winter's cold dampness that penetrated their bodies after the sun went down. They were uneducated people who could neither read nor write and of course spoke no English. Our Muslim friends spoke Urdu; we knew neither Hindi nor Urdu well enough to carry on a conversation. Only the Anglo-Indian provided a language bridge. He asked the family where the animals were hiding. They gave him the information with many wide sweeps of their arms as they pointed out the direction for us to follow. Since it was too complicated to facilitate any meaningful conversation among all of us, we finally resorted to smiles and gestures of friendship. Before long our hosts appeared with a steaming pot of tea (a ritual that was repeated in every home we visited in India). We produced the lunches we had packed and sat on their cots while they squatted in familiar fashion around the fire. No words were spoken. There was silence except for the night sounds of the jungle and our eating and drinking noises as we enjoyed our feast together. There was a full moon overhead. Gradually a feeling of peace penetrated our beings. Our tired bodies relaxed. Our differences of geography, history, culture, language, race, and religion disappeared. As we stripped away all these barriers, we discovered the common thread of humanity. In this single act of sharing food and drink, in silence, around a fire in the midst of the jungle many miles away from the structures of so-called civilization, we experienced both our oneness as human beings and our unity with the natural world. We also were "grasped by the Ground of Being." We experienced our own mythic selves that transcend both the ancient creation stories of Genesis and the pre-Aryan Indian stories. We dwelt in the eternal now. And our lives were changed. We can never go back to knowing our selves only as products of our own separate environments. We participated in communication on the highest level. We created our own myth.

Now go to Part Three, Step 9 (page 272), and start to "close the gap."

TEN

🌸 Eternity

Assimilating the New Form into Your Life

We shall not cease from exploration
And the end of all our exploring
Will be to arrive where we started
And know the place for the first time.
Through the unknown, remembered gate
When the last of earth left to discover
Is that which was the beginning;
At the source of the longest river
The voice of the hidden waterfall
And the children in the apple-tree
Not known, because not looked for
But heard, half-hearted, in the stillness
Between two waves of the sea
Quick now, here, now, always—
A condition of complete simplicity
(Costing not less than everything)
And all shall be well and
All manner of things shall be well
When the tongues of flames are in-folded
Into the crowned knot of fire
And the fire and the rose are one.
—T. S. Eliot

You know the anxiety of nonbeing. It is a fundamental fear. As part of what is called the nuclear age, you live in the aftermath of the disintegration of matter, the atom. And you may experience the crumbling of yourself as the psychological "fallout" becomes part of your inner terrain. Perhaps your fear as a modern member of the human race is more intense than that of people who lived before you; yet the query, "If a man die, shall he live again?" has been a universal and perennial question.

Maybe you can remember as a child lying in the grass and looking up into the sky. Did you lie there, one tiny child lost in the wide
bowl of the earth, overwhelmed with the minuteness of your
being? Did you think, "What if I, my parents or my grandparents
never had been born?" Did you stretch your mind back as far as
you could go, and then suppose "What if nobody had ever been
born?" Did you ever ask, "What is this thing called life? If the world
had been here, but no people in it, then what would it be? Is it people who give meaning to the universe?" Perhaps you suspected that
human beings are the only creatures who can ask "Why?" Then
no doubt when you asked "Why?" you were never quite satisfied
with the answer you got.

The search for a response goes on forever. Now in this chapter
on Eternity, I confront you with the same issue. For to discover the
purpose of your own individual existence is the eternal human
quest. The possibility that your existence on this earth will make
no real, lasting difference is the ghost that haunts your waking
moments and the demon of your dream images. It may be what
brought you to reexamine your present career.

The desire to perpetuate yourself is the drive that pushes you
into all sorts of frantic activity, like a firefly that flits about sparkling
its little light in the dark summer night. And in all your sparks, you
fear that the moments of light you create are about as powerful as
the lightning bug's sparks. You are haunted by the fear that when
your lightning apparatus has been pinched from your body, it will
be just as dark as were the lights from the lightning bugs that you
used to pinch out and put into a jar. You fear the possibility that
when you have given your last spark, you will be separated from
the source of light and will lie dull and dead in some jar buried deep
in the ground. Or that the light that has been "you" has appeared
for the last time as a funeral fire, and nothing is left of you but a
few brown ashes.

You are told that you are immortal, but the unknown frightens
you and you do not know how many opportunities you will have
to develop in the next life or lives. So sometimes you would like
to dare to think that your work will be one means of achieving
immortality on this earth—that generations after you will rise up
and call you blessed. In this case, you are overwhelmed with the
anxiety that what you do cannot survive even as long as you live,
much less remain vital after you are gone. What are you to do then?

You must get hold of some assurance that there is a principle of eternity built in you.

Even though you affirm that life is not merely a "tale told by an idiot," you want to know how to experience meaning in the midst of meaninglessness, to discover being in the presence of nonbeing, to achieve immortality while accepting mortality. Somehow then you discover that the hope of the life to come is based on the experience of the reality of eternity in the *now*; and the extent to which you as a human being are grasped by the Eternal Truth, to that degree you participate in immortality here. In your moments of inspiration you experience the timeless power of the whole. And in such moments your being becomes transparent to the eternal source of life from which you come and to which you go.

As a writer, I have found a few role models who seem to have achieved this timelessness. I think of the immortal writers like Shakespeare. Why, after four hundred years, do his dramas still entrance audiences all over the world? Even high school students in India like Shakespeare (as revealed in a survey of favorite materials with the Indian secondary school child). While his insight into human nature is so profound that some authorities cannot conceive of any *one* person possessing enough insight into the intricacies of human nature to have produced the volume of works handed down to us, it is the universal quality of his work that keeps it alive even though some of the language has become archaic. The Truth that shines through even the outmoded forms of language and patterns of speech is what makes Shakespeare eternally contemporary. He has transcended time and entered the realm of eternity.

Now this brings me to a further observation. I know Shakespeare only through the characters he created—Othello, Hamlet, Lady Macbeth and Macbeth, Romeo and Juliet, and others. They are the secret of his immortality. Shakespeare achieved an eternal place in literature because he submerged himself in the truth of the people he depicted. Nicholas Berdyaev was right when he wrote: "In the case of man, that which he creates is more expressive of him than that which he begets. The image of the artist and the poet is imprinted more clearly on his works than on his children."[1]

The "brain children" often become more real to the creative writer than the live people moving around him. Somerset Maugham in his preface to *Cakes and Ale* described something of this: "A character in a writer's head, unwritten, remains a possession, his thoughts recur to it constantly, and while his imagination gradually enriches it he enjoys the singular pleasure of feeling that there in his mind, someone is living a varied and tremulous life, obedient to his fancy and yet in a queer, willful way independent of him."[2]

In a sense, then, when I write I lose myself so that my words might live. And this losing myself to find myself is the basic principle of the universe. In the midst of destruction there is also re-creation, and I can experience the reality of this truth here and there, now and then, even though there is not much chance that I will take a luminous place in the galaxy of eternal stars of literature. But one thing I know: I cannot write about what I have not had the courage to embrace in my psychic experience.

Paradoxically, the assurance of eternity comes when I *survive* the threat of destruction. To be able to "be" in spite of the worst that can happen to me is to experience the eternal truth of the universe. You, too, must come face to face with this bewildering, shattering experience if you are to know life at its fullest. You recognize the moments when they arrive, for you come head-on with the reality of possible destruction and know that you lose your fear of it. You discover that it is not in the power of another human being to have the last word about you. You experience something of what Macbeth knew when he said:

> They have tied me to a stake; I cannot fly,
> But bear-like I must fight the course.
> What's he that was not born of woman?
> Such a one am I to fear, or none!
>
> [Act 5, Scene 8]

In considering creativity, you come back to the beginning—to make the full circle. You began with chaos, the confusion of the universe. You end with eternity, still in the realm of the unknown. Your part is to answer the call of creativity within you in the now, to respond with all that you discover as your self, and to communicate this knowing to other human beings through the work you do. You cannot now know the full impact of your present decisions. This is part of the risk you take. Hugh Prather writes:

Everyone but *me* looks back on my behavior in judgment. They can only see my acts coupled with their results. But I act *now*. And I cannot know the results. I give my actions their only possible meaning for me, and this meaning always issues from: "I am responding to this part of me and not to that part."

I don't live in a laboratory: I have no way of knowing what results my actions will have. To live my life for results would be to sentence myself to continuous frustration and to hang over my head the threat that death may at any moment make my having lived a waste. My only sure reward is *in* my actions and not from them. The quality of my reward is in the depth of my response, the centralness of the part of me I act from.

Because the results are unpredictable, no effort of mine is doomed to failure. And even a failure will not take the form I imagine. The most realistic attitude for me to have toward future consequences is "it will be interesting to see what happens." Excitement, dejection and boredom assume a knowledge of results that I cannot have.[3]

You have experienced the pain as well as the pleasure that comes from emerging from chaos into the new creation. Maslow describes the experience like this:

> Growth has not only rewards and pleasures but also many intrinsic pains and always will have. Each step forward is a step into the unfamiliar and is possibly dangerous. It also means giving up something familiar and good and satisfying. It frequently means a parting and a separation, even a kind of death prior to rebirth, with consequent nostalgia, fear, loneliness and mourning. It also often means giving up a simpler and easier and less effortful life, in exchange for a more demanding, more responsible, more difficult life. Growth forward *is in spite* of these losses and therefore requires courage, will, choice, and strength in the individual, as well as protection, permission and encouragement from the environment, especially for the child.[4]

It is important that the career decision you make now fits into the larger pattern of your total life design, your ultimate life meaning. Sometimes I realize the necessity for a client to continue to work in a certain way because he or she is not ready to give up specific behavior motifs. For me to push too much as an outside force to steer toward what will be the ultimate goal would not be appropriate or effective. There has to be a readiness. And I, as a consultant, must be willing to work within the client's timeframe. The case of Max is an example of such a situation.

○ **Case Study: Max**
"I have been in limbo for four years."

I first met Max when I conducted a one-day workshop for a professional organization. Later he came for one free interview (which I grant to anyone who wants to explore the possibility of becoming my client). At that time he decided he couldn't afford to consult me. Then after four months, he returned for the process.

First, he told me he was unemployed, having failed to get tenure as a college philosophy professor. Later, he admitted that he was a taxi driver. He was forty-five years old, with a master's degree and all his course work finished toward his Ph.D. He had been writing his Ph.D. thesis for four years, while earning money driving a cab. Max's master's theses was on Sartre, whose existential despair, reflected in *Being and Nothingness*, was, as he said, "not exactly the most frolicsome reading." He compared Sartre's theories with those of Kant and Spinoza for his theses—a truly intellectual exercise. Can you image how Max fits all of this existential theory into his daily life as a New York cab driver?

As I worked with him, his stories revealed a whimsical sense of humor, a pugnacity mixed with a lot of procrastination, and considerable writing skills. At one point he clarified his decision not to pursue further teaching possibilities but to explore marketing himself as a research writer. The following two stories reveal some of the characteristics necessary for one who is to do research writing. The first, "Cooking," is shared to reveal his thoroughness in going into any subject. The next story is a delightful account of one bit of research that indicates his joy on discovering some desired knowledge.

Success Story: Cooking

Unfortunately, my mother is a poor cook. I grew up on a kosher diet, which restricts what can be eaten. Furthermore, Eastern European Jewish food, although it can be wholesome, tends to be somewhat like American food—bland and monotonous. I still like sour cream, though, and I dote on herring. Nonetheless, after being in the army two years and college four years and having to endure cafeteria food this length of time, I began pondering (in the manner of most philosophy students) whether or not these grim repasts were part of the natural course of things. After getting an apartment in town, I began experimenting with cooking my evening meal—that is, I tried to follow a recipe, and I decided that one need not lead a bland existence at the dinner table. Since that time, I have acquired a great deal of expertise, as well as a library of approximately fifty cookbooks. I feel I am at my best with either French or Indian food.

I made an Indian meal one New Year's Eve. It probably was my best. It required two weeks of long preparation! The number of dishes and their recipes are too elaborate and numerous to mention. They all are found in Singh's *Indian Cookery*—by far the best Indian cookbook. One dish, an elaborate pilaf, required one half-day alone!

Success Story: Research

In many respects, research is similar to detective work. At the investment company where I was a writer, my supervisor read an article in the Sunday *New York Times* where one of the authors made a statement about another author without documenting the source—which was to be expected, since the *Times* doesn't usually have footnotes. My supervisor wanted to get the reference for the statement made by the author, and after looking through all the customary reference volumes, I concluded that the only way to get the reference was to contact the author. I could have written, but my supervisor wanted it right away. I phoned the *Times*. Naturally they wouldn't give me the address. The problem then was to track down the author. My first step was to phone some of her past publishers, who would not reveal any information, although they offered to forward to her my mail. At this point, the genuine research started. I uncovered a volume concerning women authors, and I noted that the author I needed to contact was married to a New York doctor. I looked in the phone book but had no luck. My next step was to find a volume listing authors' agents. I then was able to call her agent, who said that the author was now living in Washington. I simply phoned Washington information and got her number. The author asked how I was able to get her number. I replied, "It was easy."

Max had done a considerable amount of writing on his Ph.D. thesis, but time was running out and he either had to abandon the goal or get it done. I discovered he was not pushing ahead with his marketing process—uncovering companies that needed research writers—or other networking activities. Therefore, I suggested he show me he was serious about research writing by finishing his thesis before we moved ahead. So he took a two-month leave from me and from his cab driving (his wife held a well-paying position) and promised to return when he had finished his thesis.

I didn't hear from him for several months. I had a hunch that his somber, fatalistic philosophy was supporting him in this defeatist career pattern. Before he left he wrote this evaluation of himself, "I believe that self-destruction is an element in my makeup. But I believe I can keep it in rein. A struggle is always present, but I feel that I can emerge victorious."

A few months later, he brought me a copy of his finished thesis, and we celebrated the achievement of his goal. He is now teaching at two colleges and has shaped his skill as a satirist, using it in the classroom and in social settings (where he also tries out some of his many recipes). He has conquered his procrastination by doing things that tap his flow of creative energy.

○ Case Study: Naomi

"I just kept poised."

Naomi's case has a positive outcome, and is also a reflection of her philosophy. I met her through a professional women's organization. She gave me her age as "over fifty." She is one of those delicious-looking "bunny-haired" ladies. With her soft voice and radiant and pervasive smile, she exudes warmth and love. Naomi is an elegant example of one who has tapped into the universal source of energy. She casts an ethereal glow.

Naomi belongs to an esoteric, metaphysical religious group, having been its organist for many years. She expressed her faith by looking after the affairs of two older women, in their late seventies and eighties, and in spending her vacations in religious retreats and conferences. "We are trying to preserve America as a religious haven," she explained.

Naomi was working for a nonprofit agency as a bookkeeper. Even though she had over twenty years of experience, she had not been able to reach her salary level or a staff position worthy of her skills. By attending school at night, she had recently received her

B.A. in management and accounting, and was ready to move into a more responsible position. However, hers was a chauvinistic organization with few opportunities for someone like her. She was beginning to sense that the promise of promotion was an empty one. After a number of sessions scattered over several months, we gradually uncovered her assertive powers. She began to think of her own needs first, and to recognize that it was up to her to create a new situation for herself.

Naomi began to take the initiative. She organized a professional women's group. She was able to express her feelings more freely in threatening situations. From her success stories, her top skills and characteristics emerged—decision making, planning ahead, problem solving, writing, goal setting, and faith.

Here are two of her stories, representing her quiet persistence.

Success Story: Using Public Relations Knowledge

Several years ago, I was working for a large department store two nights a week and Saturdays, prior to Christmas. In our training period they said it was necessary to make friends of the people who came into the store so that if they did not buy on the first visit, they would come again and buy then.

This philosophy worked to my advantage once when I attended a religious lecture on a Saturday evening, after finishing my day's work. Because I was one of the last to arrive at a closed, private meeting, the hostess asked me to stand guard at the door and to admit a young navy man who would arrive later. During a musical contemplation period, there was a loud knocking on the ballroom door. Thinking it was the young navy man, I jumped up to open the door. To my surprise, there stood a union representative, pushing his card of identification under my nose and saying he was "going in there to break up the meeting to see if the musician had a union card."

To prevent his gaining entrance to the meeting room, I put my hands behind my back, and grabbed the two adjoining doorknobs to keep the doors closed. Trying to quiet the man, I was prompted to say that the musician was playing without remuneration for a religious group. The union man still threatened to follow through with his desire to see that only union men played in the ballroom of the hotel.

Thanks to my department store training, I just kept poised and repeated as calmly as I could that the man was a volunteer musician playing for nothing. About this time the music ceased, and the union representative, seeing that he was getting nowhere with me, smiled and left.

After the meeting was over, I repeated the episode to the musician, who said he did have a union card. Fortunately, the concert was not interrupted and he did not have to produce it.

Success Story: Degree from College

In the 1960s the newspapers and magazines were full of articles about the necessity of a college education. I needed some information on taxes for business, and decided to enroll at a community college in Brooklyn for that course.

I was not allowed to take the tax course without preliminary accounting courses, and so I took them, plus other subjects offered for a two-year accounting certificate. At another college my schedule was four classes a week (four different subjects); at the end of two years of night study, I had earned 64 points. I was fortunate to have excellent teachers—many were businessmen giving their time at night for the cause. My name was on the Dean's List several times.

Then I decided it would be foolish to stop there, that I should have a Bachelor's Certificate to show for my efforts. So I transferred to a private college with quite a different atmosphere for a student. If he or she didn't understand, the student could ask questions, but the attitude of the professors was quite aloof. When I was dropped from a calculus class for not being able to keep up with the homework, I decided to try a major university. I had attended there in 1954, and they seemed friendlier and more familiar.

The university accepted my application and I enrolled. It was not easy. I had to stay up all night many times to get my reports in on time and worked at a very busy full-time job the following day. I tried staying up to 4 A.M. to study for my night classes. Then I would sleep a few hours, go to work for a full day, and go to class at night. Sometimes there were classes two nights in a row or sometimes two classes one night apart. After a couple of years I had to limit my courses to two a semester and then to one per semester. Again, students had a lot of work, but at least there was the chance to take a makeup test if one was missed. In some classes I did well, because I set a goal and the professor cooperated with good grades. Unfortunately, at that time, I was very busy with my church work, which took a lot of time that could have been used in my studies.

I changed my sleeping hours when a lot of homework had to be done. I would go to bed as early as possible so I was asleep by 11:00 P.M. and get up early, anywhere from 2:00 to 4:00 A.M. to study until time to go to work. My bosses let me take extra time—two hours or so—before an exam so I could study. This was vacation time, or time to be made up.

Finally, in January, after taking the exam for my final course, the feeling came over me that it was "all over." I wouldn't have to stay up nights anymore! But it wasn't until several months later that the feeling really took hold. I became more relaxed.

Then, in March or April, my diploma came in the mail. Then announcements regarding commencement came in, then congratulation cards started coming. In May I attended a reception given by the Dean of our school, and my family entertained me for having completed the course.

It adds up to my feeling very nice, but also wondering, "Where do I go from here?"

Naomi planned her marketing campaign as carefully as she had her education. Through networking she landed an excellent position as financial manager of the private funds of an internationally known woman philanthropist. She works in an environment that is as elegant as she is, and she now feels appreciated and adequately compensated for her experience and skills. Her retirement program is generous, and she is confident that she will continue to find ways to express her ultimate life's meaning in her career and in her total lifestyle.

O Recalling the Creation Myths

You have probably discerned that even though I offer a practical, pragmatic formula for career development, I present all these activities as operating within a larger context. Some would say my approach is transpersonal, but I am not particularly interested in labels. What I am concerned about is that you join me in affirming that there is a universal consciousness that is a backdrop to our own consciousness. It is that reality which exists unseen behind all appearances.

This chapter deals with our discovering the cause behind the actual fact, to discern (even if briefly) what is happening in the universe. As an organism, we can adapt the environment to our own purpose. As our consciousness moves upward, we experience everything as *always* rather than something *now*. Like an eagle we get a panoramic view, realizing our limitations and sense of time.

In our dreams we retain consciousness even while we sleep. That is why our dreams are part of our working data. Our bodies are formations in time. Our selves are defined as pure intelligence. Space is convoluted in gravitation. A kind of orderliness is set up. It is possible even to go through a chemical process. At times we experience disintegration and then move toward consciousness beyond existence.

The tenth step in the creative process challenges you to accept the disillusion of your body as the condition of your body where there is no death. As the river survives the drops of water, the death of the body makes way for a larger reality. It is like walking in the street with a telescope in one hand and a microscope in the other. We can experience this holistic dimension even now when we embrace the possibility of our destruction.

I was once locked in a sixteenth-floor apartment-office with a psychotherapist who was experiencing a psychotic episode. He slapped me and threatened to kill me. I knew I was trapped. Suddenly a flood of energy filled me. I looked him in the eye and said, "You can do anything you want to me, but you cannot destroy me. *I* am indestructible." I then took him by the hand, led him to a chair, and began to talk quietly to him. Of course, I later realized what danger I was in. I do not claim to have remained unafraid forever. The point I am making is that I *knew* my immortality in that moment when I embraced the possibility of my destruction.

Your ability to experience this wholeness in the midst of your present existence, will determine the measure of power you have to overcome the fear of trying out new paths.

The decisions you make now must fit into the vision you have of your ultimate goal—even beyond your present form. You are completely free if you don't fear what will happen to you when you take the next step. This courage may not be constant, but when you act out of "being in spite of," you move forward.

Here in the Western hemisphere we say "time marches on." We
think in linear lines. The Hindu concept of life as a circle, with no
beginning or end, just cycles and cycles, is a much more creative
way to symbolize the nature of time and eternity. I agree with
Charles Muses, who said, "Reincarnation makes sense—nature
doesn't waste information. It's like renting a car. You turn it in. You
don't junk the driver."[5]

In all the creation myths, there are new forms, new offsprings.
In the Greek myth Zeus burns the offspring into ashes from which
springs the human race. They all circle back and forth from cosmos to the individual. In the Genesis account, Adam and Eve leave
their state of dreaming innocence inside the Garden of Eden, where
they would have lived forever in a mindless eternity. Though they
enter a world where death is their destiny, their seed lives on in the
continuing human race. The life-death-rebirth mystery is still ours
to experience today. So now you come full circle with me. This is
no time to stop. You might just rest briefly every seventh day, and
on the eighth, see what else in new. The tenth step of creativity
is eternity; embrace it with joy and expectation.

Go to Part Three, Step 10 (page 280), and continue the journey.

✿ Design for a New Creation

Your Personal Career Development Workbook

*Creation begins typically with a vague, even a confused
excitement, some sort of yearning, hunch, or other
preverbal intimation of approaching a potential resolution*
— Brewster Ghiselin, *The Creative Process*

The world's creation myths have given you clues for how
to experience the creativity process. In addition, you have learned from the case studies how to connect creativity to career
development. Now it's your turn to write your own creation myth
and design your new career.

Remember that creativity is a zigzag process, never happening
predictably or in a straight line. It often appears to be random to
the casual observer. It is full of surprises and continues forever.

The following pages will guide you to record what you create
now. This is your opportunity to try out this new career development model. Be open. See where it will take you.

In addition to the space provided here, you will need a journal
or notebook in which to write your ideas, goals, and plans, and
recount your progress. A regular spiral notebook will be fine.

Also, at this stage you may want to find a counselor or consultant who will be able to affirm and support you as you take charge
of your own life and learn to do it yourself.

The following instruments are a product of experience in learning. Some are my own invention. I have also used those developed
by others (credited where appropriate); they have been used extensively in the career development field. I have tested them all in my
extensive work with clients.

❃ Chaos

Exploring Your Confused State

○ Your Present Chaos

Here's where you define your chaos. In your notebook, state your areas of conflict, confusion, and dissatisfaction, or list problems in your present situation. Be as open as you can; make your list as inclusive as possible. This information will help you get started. By knowing what you face, you will be more prepared for what lies ahead. If you are working with a counselor or consultant, this can become your agreement statement to guide you in your work together.

✿ Being

Discovering the Reality in Your Situation

○ Myers-Briggs Personality Type Indicator

Find a career consultant or counselor who will administer this test for you. Hilda Lee Dail and Associates administers the test (see page 4 for address); or you may contact the Center for Applications of Psychological Type, Inc., 2720 N.W. Sixth Street, Gainesville, FL 32601 (phone: 904-375-0180), for the test.

By taking this test you will discover whether you are extraverted or introverted; sensing or intuitive; thinking or feeling; judging or perceptive. Everyone is a combination of these four traits. After you take the test, the company or your counselor will give you an appropriate personality type read-out and will interpret how your personality responds to environment. Record your results in your notebook after you have received them (or attach the report). This will be your personality type worksheet, to refer back to later in the process of developing your career.

Summary of Report Form for Myers-Briggs Type Indicator*

Indicator questions deal with the way you like to use your perception and judgement, that is, the way you like to look at things and the way you like to go about deciding things. The answers given reflect four separate preferences called EI, SN, TF and JP. The profile shows your score on each preference. The four letters of your "type" tell how you came out on all four preferences. What each preference means is shown on the opposite page.

*Pages 218–221 © 1976 by Isabel Briggs Myers. Published by Consulting Psychologists Press, Inc. P.O. Box 60070, Palo Alto, CA 94306. Reprinted by permission.

E An E for extraversion probably means you relate more easily to the outer world of people and things than to the inner world of ideas.

S An S for sensing probably means you would rather work with known facts than look for possibilities and relationships.

T A T for thinking probably means you base your judgments more on impersonal analysis and logic than on personal values.

J A J for the judging attitude probably means you like a planned, decided, orderly way of life better than a flexible, spontaneous way.

I An I for introversion probably means you relate more easily to the inner world of ideas than to the outer world of people and things.

N An N for intuition probably means you would rather look for possibilities and relationships than work with known facts.

F An F for feeling probably means you base your judgments more on personal values than on impersonal analysis and logic.

P A P for the perceptive attitude probably means you like a flexible, spontaneous way of life better than a planned, decided, orderly way.

Each combination of preferences tends to be characterized by its own set of interests, values and skills. Following are very brief descriptions of students of each type. Find the one matching your four letters and see if it fits you. If it doesn't, try to find one that does. Whatever your preferences, of course, you may still use some behaviors characteristic of contrasting preferences, but not with equal liking or skill. This tendency may be greater if preference strength on a scale is low (under 15). For a more complete discussion of the types and their vocational and personal implications, consult your counselor.

<table>
<tr><td colspan="2">

ISTJ
Serious, quiet, earn success by concentration and thoroughness. Practical, orderly, matter-of-fact, logical, realistic and dependable. See to it that everything is well organized. Take responsibility. Make up their own minds as to what should be accomplished and work toward it steadily, regardless of protests or distractions.

</td><td>

ISFJ
Quiet, friendly, responsible and conscientious. Work devotedly to meet their obligations. Lend stability to any project or group. Thorough, painstaking, accurate. May need time to master technical subjects, as their interests are usually not technical. Patient with detail and routine. Loyal, considerate, concerned with how other people feel.

</td></tr>
</table>

INTROVERTS

ISTP
Cool onlookers—quiet, reserved, observing and analyzing life with detached curiosity and unexpected flashes of original humor. Usually interested in impersonal principles, cause and effect, how and why mechanical things work. Exert themselves no more than they think necessary, because any waste of energy would be inefficient.

ISFP
Retiring, quietly friendly, sensitive, kind, modest about their abilities. Shun disagreements, do not force their opinions or values on others. Usually do not care to lead but are often loyal followers. Often relaxed about getting things done, because they enjoy the present moment and do not want to spoil it by undue haste or exertion.

ESTP
Matter-of-fact, do not worry or hurry, enjoy whatever comes along. Tend to like mechanical things and sports, with friends on the side. May be a bit blunt or insensitive. Adaptable, tolerant, generally conservative in values. Dislike long explanations. Are best with real things that can be worked, handled, taken apart or put together.

ESFP
Outgoing, easygoing, accepting, friendly, enjoy everything and make things more fun for others by their enjoyment. Like sports and making things. Know what's going on and join in eagerly. Find remembering facts easier than mastering theories. Are best in situations that need sound common sense and practical ability with people as well as with things.

EXTRAVERTS

ESTJ
Practical, realistic, matter-of-fact, with a natural head for business or mechanics. Not interested in subjects they see no use for, but can apply themselves when necessary. Like to organize and run activities. May make good administrators, especially if they remember to consider others' feelings and points of view.

ESFJ
Warm-hearted, talkative, popular, conscientious, born cooperators, active committee members. Need harmony and may be good at creating it. Always doing something nice for someone. Work best with encouragement and praise. Little interest in abstract thinking or technical subjects. Main interest is in things that directly and visibly affect people's lives.

INFJ

Succeed by perseverance, originality and desire to do whatever is needed or wanted. Put their best efforts into their work. Quietly forceful, conscientious, concerned for others. Respected for their firm principles. Likely to be honored and followed for their clear convictions as to how best to serve the common good.

INTJ

Usually have original minds and great drive for their own ideas and purposes. In fields that appeal to them, they have a fine power to organize a job and carry it through with or without help. Skeptical, critical, independent, determined, often stubborn. Must learn to yield less important points in order to win the most important.

INFP

Full of enthusiasms and loyalties, but seldom talk of these until they know you well. Care about learning, ideas, language, and independent projects of their own. Tend to undertake too much, then somehow get it done. Friendly, but often too absorbed in what they are doing to be sociable. Little concerned with possessions or physical surroundings.

INTP

Quiet, reserved, impersonal. Enjoy especially theoretical or scientific subjects. Logical to the point of hair-splitting. Usually interested mainly in ideas, with little liking for parties or small talk. Tend to have sharply defined interests. Need careers where some strong interest can be used and useful.

ENFP

Warmly enthusiastic, high spirited, ingenious, imaginative. Able to do almost anything that interests them. Quick with a solution for any difficulty and ready to help anyone with a problem. Often rely on their ability to improvise instead of preparing in advance. Can usually find compelling reasons for whatever they want.

ENTP

Quick, ingenious, good at many things. Stimulating company, alert and outspoken. May argue for fun on either side of a question. Resourceful in solving new and challenging problems, but may neglect routine assignments. Apt to turn to one new interest after another. Skillful in finding logical reasons for what they want.

ENFJ

Responsive and responsible. Generally feel real concern for what others think or want, and try to handle things with due regard for other person's feelings. Can present a proposal or lead a group discussion with ease and tact. Sociable, popular, sympathetic. Responsive to praise and criticism.

ENTJ

Hearty, frank, decisive, leaders in activities. Usually good in anything that requires reasoning and intelligent talk, such as public speaking. Are usually well-informed and enjoy adding to their fund of knowledge. May sometimes be more positive and confident than their experience in an area warrants.

INTROVERTS

EXTRAVERTS

Read over the following list of life values (adapted from a self-awareness exercise used in the General Electric Corporation). Which ones mean the most to you? Check your top three or four or number them in order of priority. Remember that at certain times we opt for certain values; at other times our needs change and so do our values. So of course, you will have to make trade-offs as you choose among these values to pick your top ones.

_____ 1. Location: Being able to live where I want to live.

_____ 2. Enjoyment: Enjoying my work; having fun doing it.

_____ 3. Friendship: Working with people I like and being liked by them.

_____ 4. Loyalty: Being loyal to my boss and peers; having their loyalty in return.

_____ 5. Family: Having time with my family.

_____ 6. Leadership: Being truly influential.

_____ 7. Achievement: Accomplishing important things; being involved in significant undertakings.

_____ 8. Self-realization: Doing work that is personally challenging and that will allow me to realize the full potential of my talent.

_____ 9. Wealth: Making money and becoming financially independent to do what I want to do.

_____ 10. Expertise: Being a pro (skillful), an authority in what I do.

_____ 11. Service: Contributing to the satisfaction of others; helping people who need help.

_____ 12. Social Service: Contributing to my country, my community, or to the world at large.

_____ 13. Prestige: Being seen as successful; becoming well known, perhaps; obtaining recognition and status.

_____ 14. Security: Having a secure and stable position.

_____ 15. Power: Having the authority to approve or disapprove proposed courses of action; making assignments, initiating projects, and controlling allocation of resources.

_____ 16. Independence: Freedom of thought and action; being able to act in terms of my own time schedule, work style, and priorities.

_____ 17. Aesthetics: Contributing to the truth, beauty, and culture of life.

_____ 18. Morality: Performing by a standard of personal, professional, and social ethics

O **Personal Needs Questionnaire**

Fill out this questionnaire (developed by Ralph Minker, Washington, D.C.). Part 1 will help you assess your individual needs. Part 2 will help you determine which of your needs are most important.

O **Part 1 Needs Assessment**

Write the number 10 next to the question if the characteristic is _very important_ to you and you experience the feeling or need quite intensely and perhaps quite often.

Write the number 5 next to the question if you experience the characteristic _only occasionally_ and it is of only average concern to you.

Write 0 next to the question if you experience the characteristic _seldom or never_ and if is of almost no consequence to you as a feeling or need.

_____ 1. I strive for perfection and excellence.

_____ 2. I avoid unpleasant jobs.

_____ 3. I am eager to help others.

_____ 4. I like to be alone.

_____ 5. I want others to do things my way.

_____ 6. I follow the suggestions of others.

_____ 7. I am concerned about what others think of me.

_____ 8. I want to break out with new things.

_____ 9. Getting the job done is more important to me than the feelings of others.

_____ 10. I would rather not argue or debate.

_____ 11. I try to do things better than others.

_____ 12. I leave things unfinished.

_____ 13. I am loyal to friends and organization.

_____ 14. I would rather do things for myself than for others.

_____ 15. I get upset when others do not act the way I think they should.

_____ 16. I want someone else to be the leader.

_____ 17. I get the opinion of others.

_____ 18. I like to tell jokes and say things for the reaction of others.

_____ 19. I am jealous or envious.

_____ 20. I am easygoing.

_____ 21. I stick to a job until it is done.

_____ 22. I want more leisure time.

_____ 23. I show affection easily.

_____ 24. I don't like people to get too close to me.

_____ 25. I want to be in charge.

_____ 26. I am reluctant to do things on my own initiative.

_____ 27. I wait until new styles are well established before changing.

_____ 28. I do things just for the principle involved.

_____ 29. I get revenge for injustices or insults.

_____ 30. I am noncompetitive and will not try too hard to get ahead of others.

_____ 31. I want to write a great book, song, or play.

_____ 32. I put things off.

_____ 33. I give encouragement and praise to others.

_____ 34. I am more interested in things than in people.

_____ 35. I want to influence and persuade others.

_____ 36. It is easy for others to get me to do things.

_____ 37. I like to follow habit and tradition.

_____ 38. I want to look different from others.

_____ 39. I am critical of others.

_____ 40. I do not react too emotionally to things.

_____ 41. I like to accomplish difficult tasks.

_____ 42. I do not want to get involved.

_____ 43. I like to do things with others instead of alone.

_____ 44. I want to get away from it all.

_____ 45. I am willing to settle arguments.

_____ 46. I want the advice of others before making up my mind.

_____ 47. I like to talk about my personal viewpoints and achievements.

_____ 48. My opinions and viewpoints are different from those of other people.

_____ 49. I am interested in violence and tragedy.

_____ 50. I do not exert effort to meet new people.

_____ 51. I have a feeling there is work to do.

_____ 52. I would rather let others get the credit for doing things.

_____ 53. I go along with group decisions.

_____ 54. I like to do things by myself.

_____ 55. I look for books, ideas, and ways to influence and persuade others.

_____ 56. I am fearful of authority (police, boss, etc.).

_____ 57. I am eager for affection from others.

_____ 58. I do things my own way.

_____ 59. I make fun of others.

_____ 60. I try to avoid getting or giving personal criticism.

_____ 61. I like to keep busy.

_____ 62. I like to be entertained in my spare time (with TV, newspaper, games).

_____ 63. I seek suggestions and help from others.

_____ 64. I feel that small talk is a waste of time.

_____ 65. I make plans for the group.

_____ 66. My opinion is easily swayed by others.

_____ 67. I look for encouragement from others.

_____ 68. I like to be the center of attention.

_____ 69. I blame others when things go wrong.

_____ 70. I am reluctant to voice personal viewpoints.

_____ 71. My spare time is involved with creating, building, changing things.

_____ 72. I work no more than I have to.

○ Part 2 Personal Needs Analysis

The characteristics listed below are personal needs you have that strongly influence the direction of your life, your personality, and the way you relate to others.

To determine the intensity of each need, total your points for the question in Part 1 listed after each characteristic here. Record the score for each characteristic (total points) in the blanks.

NEED	RESPONSES	SCORE
1. ACHIEVEMENT	Questions 1, 11, 21, 31, 41, 51, 61, 71	_____
2. CONTENTMENT	Questions 2, 12, 22, 32, 42, 52, 62, 72	_____
3. BELONGING	Questions 3, 13, 23, 33, 43, 53, 63	_____
4. ISOLATION	Questions 4, 14, 24, 34, 44, 54, 64	_____

5. DOMINANCE	Questions 5, 15, 25, 35, 45, 55, 65	_____
6. SUBMISSIVENESS	Questions 6, 16, 26, 36, 46, 56, 66	_____
7. ACCEPTANCE	Questions 7, 17, 27, 37, 47, 57, 67	_____
8. INDIVIDUALISM	Questions 8, 18, 28, 38, 48, 58, 68	_____
9. AGGRESSION	Questions 9, 19, 29, 39, 49, 59, 69	_____
10. PASSIVITY	Questions 10, 20, 30, 40, 50, 60, 70	_____

○ Trait Checklist

Quickly go through the following list of traits (developed by Ralph Minker). Put a check (✔) beside those that fit your self-image. Use a cross (×) to mark those that do not fit. Use a question mark (?) when you are unsure.

_____ Like myself

_____ Afraid of or hurt by others

_____ People can trust me

_____ Put up a good front

_____ Usually say the right thing

_____ Feel bad about myself

_____ Fearful of the future

_____ Dependent on others for ideas

_____ Waste time

_____ Use my talents

_____ Discouraged about life

_____ Don't like to be around others

_____ Have not developed my talents

_____ Glad I'm the sex I am

_____ Often do the wrong thing

_____ Involved in solving community problems

_____ People like to be around me

_____ Competent on the job

_____ People avoid me

_____ Think for myself

_____ Know my feelings

_____ Don't understand myself

_____ Feel hemmed in

_____ Use time well

_____ Can't hold a job

_____ Trust myself

_____ Usually say the wrong thing

_____ Enjoy people

_____ Don't enjoy being the sex I am

_____ Disinterested in community problems

_____ Enjoy work

_____ Enjoy nature

_____ Don't enjoy work

_____ Control myself

_____ Enjoy life

_____ Trouble controlling myself

_____ Don't like myself

Now look at the traits you have marked. Is there a pattern? What do you see? Write your observations here or in your notebook.

_____

_____

_____

_____

_____

_____

_____

_____

_____

_____

_____

_____

_____

_____

_____

_____

_____

_____

_____

_____

_____

_____

_____

_____

_____

_____

228   What traits would you like to change? Write about them here or in your notebook.

The "executive quotient" (developed by Ralph Minker) is a tool to help you assess whether you have the ability to handle management jobs.

On a scale of 1 to 10, rate yourself on the following statements. Circle the best number value (10 is the highest).

I am profit-oriented.	1 2 3 4 5 6 7 8 9 10
I am results-oriented.	1 2 3 4 5 6 7 8 9 10
I have sales ability.	1 2 3 4 5 6 7 8 9 10
I understand cost effectiveness.	1 2 3 4 5 6 7 8 9 10
I can make decisions and stick to them.	1 2 3 4 5 6 7 8 9 10
I am skilled in human relations.	1 2 3 4 5 6 7 8 9 10
I am self-confident.	1 2 3 4 5 6 7 8 9 10
I am a believable person.	1 2 3 4 5 6 7 8 9 10
I can delegate authority.	1 2 3 4 5 6 7 8 9 10
I am honest.	1 2 3 4 5 6 7 8 9 10
I am willing to assume responsibility.	1 2 3 4 5 6 7 8 9 10
I know my field.	1 2 3 4 5 6 7 8 9 10
I can communicate effectively.	1 2 3 4 5 6 7 8 9 10
I am creative.	1 2 3 4 5 6 7 8 9 10
I can solve problems.	1 2 3 4 5 6 7 8 9 10

Therefore, based on the above

I am a capable manager.	1 2 3 4 5 6 7 8 9 10
I have the ability to add to my company's income.	1 2 3 4 5 6 7 8 9 10
I have the ability to reduce expenses for my company.	1 2 3 4 5 6 7 8 9 10

❧ **Encounter**

Finding Clues for Success in Your Past

○ **Looking at Your Achievements or Successes**

List your past successes—things you have accomplished that you're proud of, that make you feel real or energized as your recall them. Include your earliest memories of achievement. They can be anything from building a house with blocks or drawing a picture to running a race. They don't have to be things that other people recognized as significant. The standard to use in choosing items for this list is your own secret pride in the feeling "I did that myself!"

Put items down in the order that they occur to you, without prioritizing them. Try to come up with fifty items (or at least twenty).

My Successes

1. _____
2. _____
3. _____
4. _____
5. _____
6. _____
7. _____
8. _____
9. _____
10. _____
11. _____
12. _____

13. _____

14. _____

15. _____

16. _____

17. _____

18. _____

19. _____

20. _____

21. _____

22. _____

23. _____

24. _____

25. _____

26. _____

27. _____

28. _____

29. _____

30. _____

31. _____

32. _____

33. _____

34. _____

35. _____

36. _____

37. _____

38. _____

39. _____

40. _____

41. _____

42. _____

43. _____

44. _____

45. _____

46. _____

47. _____

48. _____

49. _____

50. _____

○ **Your Top Ten Successes**

Since one aspect of career development is the art of prioritizing, now choose from your previous list the top ten achievements according to your *pride* in them, *joy* in doing them, and level of *energy* in recalling them. List them below or in your notebook.

Top Ten Successes

1. _____

2. _____

3. _____

4. _____

5. _____

6. _____

7. _____

8. _____

9. _____

10. _____

○ **Ten Success Stories**

Write a story in your notebook about each of your top ten successes.

Relive the experience, giving sequences of events, your strategy, who helped you, what problems you solved, which aspects you are proudest of, and so forth.

If you like, write each story as though you were telling it to a five-year-old child. For instance, in telling the story of Goldilocks and the Three Bears, you would not leave out any details of the three bowls of porridge, the chairs, and the different beds. So don't leave out any details here. Use your personal career development notebook to complete each story. Review the success stories in Part Two; they will give you an idea of what I mean by "success."

❀ The Developing Self

Identifying Your Growth Potential

○ Success Factors List

Share your ten success stories with your career consultant if you have one. As you read your stories aloud, ask him or her to write down the key success factors (skills, strengths, characteristics, etc.) you exhibit in your success stories; they are your success factors list. If you are working alone and composing your list by yourself, read through your stories again. Look for the things that you did that made the experiences rewarding or satisfying. If you are having a problem figuring out what these success factors were, the following categories may help:

Creating, inventing, designing
Talking—on the phone, to groups, etc.
Listening
Showing others how to do things
Gardening
Cooking
Drawing and painting—all kinds of art
Writing—even lists, notes to yourself, letters, journals, reports
Working with your hands—carpentry, sewing, car repair, typing
Doing technical, mechanical, scientific work (including computers)
Supervising, training, teaching
Budgeting, saving money, or spending money wisely
Meeting and greeting people, communicating, interviewing
Shopping for business or pleasure
Organizing—closets or cupboards, civic groups, trips, office procedures

Decorating business settings or personal space
Negotiating, bargaining, persuading
Coming up with new ideas, solutions, etc.
Finding what you need to know—in the library, telephone
    directory, civic organizations, professional listings
Music—playing an instrument, collecting records, etc.
Social skills—entertaining
Record-keeping, bookkeeping, accounting

Don't forget to note factors such as ingenuity, drive, perseverance, and independence.

You are sure to have your own personal success factors, similar to these, but unique to *your* stories, *your* life. They could be anything—the possibilities are virtually unlimited. Use these as examples and add your own. List each of your own success factors here or in your notebook. You want as many words as possible so that you will have many options to choose from in discovering your top twenty factors to take into the future. From these you will do the prioritizing grid.

1. _____   17. _____

2. _____   18. _____

3. _____   19. _____

4. _____   20. _____

5. _____   21. _____

6. _____   22. _____

7. _____   23. _____

8. _____   24. _____

9. _____   25. _____

10. _____   26. _____

11. _____   27. _____

12. _____   28. _____

13. _____   29. _____

14. _____   30. _____

15. _____   31. _____

16. _____   32. _____

33. _____   42. _____

34. _____   43. _____

35. _____   44. _____

36. _____   45. _____

37. _____   46. _____

38. _____   47. _____

39. _____   48. _____

40. _____   49. _____

41. _____   50. _____

Now you are ready to look at each of the factors ten times.

List each factor on this chart (make extra copies of it first as necessary), without indicating which story it came from. Weigh each factor on a scale of 1 to 5 and indicate how much you used it in each of the ten stories. (See Don's chart on page 60.)

Total the numbers to find your winning cluster of success factors. Circle the top twenty.

STORIES

SUCCESS FACTORS	1	2	3	4	5	6	7	8	9	10	TOTAL

❀ **Experience**

Clarifying Your Career Goal

○ **Your Top Success Factor for the Future**

The previous page was based on your past successes. Now you are ready to indicate which factors you cherish most for use in the future.

Take the top twenty factors from your master list (prepared by you or by your consultant—see your Success Factors Chart in Step 4). Copy them here so that they are numbered from 1 to 20.

Use the Prioritizing Grid (page 239) to rank one factor over each other one. You will be comparing each factor twenty times.

First, compare number 1 with the others, numbers 2 to 20.

Circle the number of your choice each time.

A good way to make your choice is to ask: What would I hold on to the longest if I were on a desert island or in jail and forced to relinquish everything one by one? Or ask yourself: What factor would I feel most unhappy to stop using? Which would I rather die than give up?

Then compare number 2 to the remaining factors. Continue on down the grid.

Next add up the times each number or factor was circled. Put the number on the chart below. The factor circled the most times is your Top Success Factor for the Future. You will want to build your next career around it. (The top five factors are also very important, especially in combination with the top one.)

Top 20 Factors (from Success Factors Chart)	**Number of Times Circled on Prioritizing Grid** (Fill in after you have done grid on page 239.)
1. _____	
2. _____	
3. _____	
4. _____	
5. _____	
6. _____	
7. _____	
8. _____	
9. _____	
10. _____	
11. _____	
12. _____	
13. _____	
14. _____	
15. _____	
16. _____	
17. _____	
18. _____	
19. _____	
20. _____	

○ **Prioritizing Grid**

Follow the instructions given on page 237 to rank your success factors and find your Top Success Factor with this grid.

```
1   1   1   1   1   1   1   1   1   1   1   1   1   1   1   1   1   1   1
2   3   4   5   6   7   8   9  10  11  12  13  14  15  16  17  18  19  20

    2   2   2   2   2   2   2   2   2   2   2   2   2   2   2   2   2   2
    3   4   5   6   7   8   9  10  11  12  13  14  15  16  17  18  19  20

        3   3   3   3   3   3   3   3   3   3   3   3   3   3   3   3   3
        4   5   6   7   8   9  10  11  12  13  14  15  16  17  18  19  20

            4   4   4   4   4   4   4   4   4   4   4   4   4   4   4   4
            5   6   7   8   9  10  11  12  13  14  15  16  17  18  19  20

                5   5   5   5   5   5   5   5   5   5   5   5   5   5   5
                6   7   8   9  10  11  12  13  14  15  16  17  18  19  20

                    6   6   6   6   6   6   6   6   6   6   6   6   6   6
                    7   8   9  10  11  12  13  14  15  16  17  18  19  20

                        7   7   7   7   7   7   7   7   7   7   7   7   7
                        8   9  10  11  12  13  14  15  16  17  18  19  20

                            8   8   8   8   8   8   8   8   8   8   8   8
                            9  10  11  12  13  14  15  16  17  18  19  20

                                9   9   9   9   9   9   9   9   9   9   9
                               10  11  12  13  14  15  16  17  18  19  20

                                   10  10  10  10  10  10  10  10  10  10
                                   11  12  13  14  15  16  17  18  19  20

                                       11  11  11  11  11  11  11  11  11
                                       12  13  14  15  16  17  18  19  20

                                           12  12  12  12  12  12  12  12
                                           13  14  15  16  17  18  19  20

                                               13  13  13  13  13  13  13
                                               14  15  16  17  18  19  20

                                                   14  14  14  14  14  14
                                                   15  16  17  18  19  20

                                                       15  15  15  15  15
                                                       16  17  18  19  20

                                                           16  16  16  16
                                                           17  18  19  20

                                                               17  17  17
                                                               18  19  20

                                                                   18  18
                                                                   19  20

                                                                       19
                                                                       20
```

❀ **Imagination**

Defining and Projecting Your New Self-Image

○ **Highlights from Success Stories**

Look back over your success stories. What experiences or feelings would you like to have more of or have again? List them here or in your notebook in the form given below. Then go on to identify below the things that you can now stop doing because they stand in your way or because they are no longer important to you. Finally, list those things which you are now ready to start doing.

I would like to experience or reexperience the following things:

At work: _____

_____

At home: _____

_____

Other places: _____

_____

I can now stop doing the following things:

At work: _____

_____

At home: _____

_____

Other places: _____

_____

I can now start to do the following things:

At work: _____

_____

At home: _____

_____

Other places: _____

_____

○ **Aspirations**

Now complete the following sentences.

The thing I have done that I am proudest of is:

_____

_____

_____

_____

_____

_____

One thing I want to do that I have never yet done is:

_____

_____

_____

_____

_____

_____

242   *One thing I am currently doing this year that I haven't done before is:*

_____

_____

_____

_____

_____

_____

When I daydream, I wish:

_____

_____

_____

_____

_____

_____

❋ Symbol

Finding the Appropriate Symbol to Propel You

○ Symbol Exercise

At this stage you are ready to form images of who you are, what you would like to be, what hinders you, and what will overcome the obstacle. Review the symbols of my clients reproduced in this book—but don't think that your symbols have to resemble theirs in any way. Remember that you cannot make a mistake or do it "wrong." Anything that comes up is to be accepted. Don't try to make sense of it in a logical way. This exercise uses your intuitive self, not your rational mind. Trust the process. You will be excited about what comes up for you.

Preparation: Before each of the four steps described below, do the Awareness Exercise (page 245). This exercise is basically a process of relaxation in which you sit, with eyes closed, and focus attention on specific parts of the body, from toes to head, until they relax. When you are fully relaxed, with a clear, open mind, allow your symbols to come into your mind.

First Symbol: Who I Am. Do the Awareness Exercise and find your center. Allow an image of who you are to come into your consciousness. Hold the image in focus until it is completely formed, right in color and design. Your symbol can be anything. Mine was an apple tree, which suited my nature as a nurturer with a prominent "big mama" subpersonality.

Stay with the image until you have internalized its qualities. *Become* it. Then open your eyes and draw and color the symbol in the space provided or in a separate notebook with unlined paper. Next write down the qualities of what you saw. Describe it and begin to own those qualities for yourself until you can say "I am ——" (whatever the symbol is). When I did the exercise, I said, "I am colorful, strong, rooted in the earth, reaching out to others who come to get my fruit."

Second Symbol: What I'd Like to Be. Repeat the awareness exercise, locate your center, and form an image that represents what you would like to be. My symbol was a bushel basket running over with apples—a full harvest with enough to nurture everybody. Draw and color your own symbol, and write down its qualities.

Third Symbol: What Hinders Me. Do the Awareness Exercise again, locate your center, and now form an image of what hinders you. My third symbol was a hungry vulture who perched on the apple tree, which was now completely barren of leaves—the vulture had torn them off. I discovered that this hungry vulture was my destructive nature, which I experienced when my own need for nurturance was not met. So I put a bushel basket of apples in the orchard with a tag that read "Vulture." After I gave my vulture what it needed, it was no longer a threat to me. I realized that the same creator who brought me into existence also put the vulture here. I concentrated on the nature of the vulture and realized that the message it had for me was that I needed to feast off of others like a vulture. When I take care of myself, I can have the full harvest of apples, with my basket running over to nurture others.

Draw and color your symbol, and write about its qualities. Be sure to internalize all the qualities of your third symbol in such a way that it becomes a help instead of a hindrance. Notice how my vulture symbol alerted me that I also have needs. Because of its message, I was then able to turn that hungry vulture into a force that would help keep me replenished.

Fourth Symbol: What Will Overcome the Obstacle? Do the Awareness Exercise, locate your center, and form an image of the quality that will enable you to overcome what hinders you. My fourth symbol was a huge orange sun, representing light, illumination, ideas, and the ability to see my vulture in time to provide for its needs. Whenever I begin to get tired and depleted, I know that it's time to see the light and take care of myself. Draw and color your own symbol, and write about its qualities.

Note: It is important that you *draw* and *color* all your symbols, using crayons, colored pencils, markers, or other such media. Putting these inner images into concrete form helps you to use them for daily edification. Otherwise they tend to fade from consciousness. Many of my clients hang their drawings up at home so that they have a daily reminder of their insights.

This is a guided meditation exercise. Read the instructions onto a tape, or have a friend record them, and use the tape to guide you through the steps of the meditation. At the end of the meditation, jot down any ideas that come to you as you sit quietly in an altered state of consciousness. Put down just single words or flashes that occur to you. Do this each day over a period of two weeks. During that time you will see a pattern forming: certain ideas, images, and memories will keep coming back when you are not programming them. You will see clues to what is going on directly beneath your conscious mind. In particular, this exercise meditation is to be used in the Symbol Exercise described in Chapter 7. For the Symbol Exercise, follow the directions given in the preceding pages.

Get seated in a very comfortable position, on a chair with your feet firmly planted on the floor and your spine pressed against the back of the chair. Fold your hands in your lap and close your eyes. Or perhaps you would rather lie in a very quiet, relaxed position. The purpose, though, is to be relaxed but not to go to sleep.

Now focus on a particular spot in the big toe of your left foot. Focus all of your attention on that specific spot until you know exactly where it is. Hold it in your focus for a moment and then relax.

Now move up to the middle of your foot and find a specific spot in the middle of your foot. Hold . . . then relax.

Go to your ankle, find a specific spot . . . hold . . . and relax.

Now move up to the midcalf, where you locate a specific spot in the middle of your left calf . . . focus . . . and relax.

Move up to the left hip . . . find a specific spot . . . hold it . . . and relax.

Now move into the buttocks . . . focus on a specific spot in the left buttock . . . hold . . . and relax.

Now move up to the waist area. Find a specific spot in the left side of the waist . . . hold . . . and relax.

Now move up to the chest. Focus on a specific spot in the left side of the chest . . . and go around the back and focus on a specific spot there. . . . Hold . . . and relax.

Go up now to the shoulders. . . . Find a specific spot in the left shoulder . . . hold . . . and relax.

Now go up into the neck. . . . Find a specific spot in the left side of your neck . . . focus . . . and relax.

Go down into the left arm. Find a specific spot in your upper arm . . . focus . . . and relax.

Now find a specific spot in your left elbow. . . . Focus . . . and relax.

Move now to your lower left arm. Find a specific spot there. . . . Hold and relax.

Now to the wrist. Find a specific spot . . . hold . . . and relax.

And now to the hand. Find a specific spot in your left hand . . . focus . . . and relax.

Send your attention into your fingers of your left hand. Find a specific spot . . . focus . . . and relax.

Now return your attention all the way up from the tips of your fingers back to your neck. Find a specific spot around your left ear. Focus . . . and relax.

Move up to the back of your head . . . focus . . . and relax.

Now to the top of your head . . . focus . . . and relax.

Now to the left side of your face . . . focus . . . and relax.

Your eye . . . focus . . . and relax.

Your nose . . . focus . . . and relax.

Your left cheekbone . . . focus . . . and relax.

Your lips . . . focus on a specific spot . . . relax.

Now you move to the right side of your face. . . . Find a specific spot there . . . focus . . . and relax.

Up into the right eye . . . focus . . . and relax.

The right side of your forehead . . . focus . . . and relax.

Your right ear . . . focus . . . and relax.

Now to the right side of your neck . . . find a specific spot . . . focus . . . and relax.

Now go down into your right upper arm . . . focus . . . and relax.

Into your right elbow . . . focus . . . and relax.

Into your lower arm . . . focus . . . and relax.

Into your right wrist . . . focus . . . and relax.

Now find a specific spot in the middle of your hand . . . focus . . . and relax.

Now bring your attention to your fingers. . . . Find a specific spot . . . focus . . . and relax.

Now move up to your right shoulder . . . focus . . . and relax.

And down into the right side of your spine . . . focus . . . and
relax.

Now send your attention into the right side of your waist . . . focus . . . and relax.

Move on to your right hip . . . focus . . . and relax.

Into the pelvic area . . . focus . . . and relax.

Into your right thigh . . . focus . . . and relax.

Into your kneecap . . . focus . . . and relax.

Into your calf . . . focus . . . and relax.

Now down into your ankle . . . focus . . . and relax.

Your right foot . . . find a specific spot . . . focus . . . and relax.

The toes of your right foot . . . focus . . . and relax.

Now let your attention focus on the skin that covers your whole body. Starting with your right foot, move your focus over the entire body, retracing the steps that you've just taken.

Hold the consciousness of your body before you, and allow into your consciousness whatever symbols arise, whatever memories come, whatever desires you feel, whatever thoughts come to you, whatever images appear to your mind. Write them down when you open your eyes.

If you are doing the Symbols Exercise, hold the symbol of who you are in front of you. See it in all its richness, colors, and shapes, and begin to experience the reality of your symbol. When it is completely formed in your consciousness, you may open your eyes, take your pencils or crayons and paper, and re-create your symbol. Then write down the qualities of the symbol and how it is used, and begin to contemplate: "I am these qualities, and I am useful for these purposes."

When you are done with the symbol of what you are, repeat the Awareness Exercise to find the symbol of what you would like to be. Let it come into complete formation, with all its colors and richness, and experience it completely. Take whatever comes; don't try to force it. Don't try to make sense out of it from a rational, left-brain point of view: accept it. There is an orderliness about it that you can trust. Your subconscious never lies.

248   **First Symbol**
       Who I Am

250 **Second Symbol**
What I'd Like to Be

Third Symbol
What Hinders Me

Fourth Symbol
What Will Overcome the Obstacle

❈ **Form**

Planning the Strategy for Getting There

○ **The "I Am" Treatise**

Fill in the following statements based on all the work you've done
so far—with your images, success factors, etc.

I am: _____

_____

_____

_____

_____

_____

_____

_____

_____

_____

I need: _____

_____

_____

_____

_____

_____

_____

_____

_____

_____

_____

_____

_____

_____

_____

○ **The Game Plan**

Make out your life time line. Put a checkmark at the place where you think or feel you are now.

birth _____ *death*

If you prefer, draw in your notebook any other design that represents how you see your life unfolding, indicating where you have been and where you are going.

Now make your goals "game plan." Write here or in your notebook under the following headings:

Immediate steps toward career goal

_____

_____

_____

_____

_____

_____

Next steps (six months)

_____

_____

_____

_____

_____

_____

Five-year goal

_____

_____

_____

_____

_____

Ultimate goal

_____

_____

_____

_____

_____

_____

Get your resources together. Begin these processes: (1) define your long-range objectives in light of your feelings toward your career; (2) compile a resource file on your credentials; and (3) pull together a "pool" of qualifications to be drawn on later for information relating to a specific position.

Begin by gathering together, in one place, any *credentials* you may have. These may take the form of records, degrees, transcripts of grades, copies of honors, testimonials, patents, recommendations of previous employers, publications, evidence of membership in associations, additional training—anything that might enhance your potential value to an employer or be used in a marketing program if you go into business for yourself.

Then develop a *qualifications information pool* listing concrete accomplishments under broad areas of responsibility. These areas might include administration, planning, control, personnel, budget and finance, programming, marketing, sales, public relations, community relations, purchasing, training, and so forth.

Begin your descriptions of these accomplishments, whenever possible, with action verbs such as "developed . . .", "conceived . . .", "designed . . .", "started . . .", etc. Relate them to *measurable quantities* such as percentages or dollars. Do *not* refer to work with specific organizations, firms or to specific groups of people (e.g., "ABC Company," "Youth Groups").

EXAMPLES

Personnel: Reduced office personnel by one-fourth while maintaining office procedures at a high level of efficiency.
Sales: Increased sales from $250,000 to over $4,000,000 in three years as Director of Sales.
Attendance: Sparked 250% increase in attendance over a 12-month period (from 75 to 350 persons per session).
Finance and Budget: Reduced overall cost of operation by 150% in a 6-month period by redesigning the budget and eliminating duplication of effort within the total operation.

Study the examples of résumés in this book. They all went through this early stage before reaching their final form. After you have drafted your descriptions of accomplishments, arrange them in list form under similar categories. Put what you feel are your most notable accomplishments at the top of each category. Then, type them in *rough draft* form only.

This material then becomes a reservoir of experience. Use it to draw qualifications from for a specific position.

○ Organizing Your Basic Skills

The following list, developed by Ralph Minker, will help you see how many possible skills can appear under the three categories— People, Data, and Things.

PEOPLE

1. *Mentoring:*	Dealing with individuals to bring about in-depth personality changes in their lives.
2. *Counseling:*	Relating to individuals as an advisor or counselor on legal, clinical, personality, or spiritual matters.
3. *Consulting/ Teaching:*	Teaching subject matter to others or training others (including animals) through exploration, demonstration, and supervised practice; or making recommendations on the basis of technical discipline.
4. *Managing:*	Organizing, coordinating, and developing human and material resources to bring about greater productivity.
5. *Supervising:*	Determining and interpreting work procedures for a group of workers, assigning specific duties to them; maintaining harmonious relations among them, and promoting efficiency.
6. *Organizing:*	Bringing together individuals or groups that have not previously had an organic relationship; creating new groupings for the common purpose.
7. *Persuading/ Influencing:*	Influencing others in favor of a product, service, or point of view.
8. *Speaking:*	Talking with and/or signaling people to convey or exchange information, including giving assignments to helpers or assistants.
9. *Serving:*	Attending to the needs of people or animals. Immediate response is involved.

1. *Conceptualizing*:   Integrating analysis of data to discover facts
                          and/or develop knowledge concepts or
                          interpretations.
2. *Interpreting*:   Disseminating by written form the facts
                          and/or interpretation of the analysis of
                          researched data.
3. *Researching*:   Critically and exhaustively investigating or
                          experimenting with the aim of revising
                          accepted conclusions in the light of newly
                          discovered facts.
4. *Coordinating*:   Determining the time, place, and sequence
                          of operations or actions to be taken on the
                          basis of analysis of data; executing

5. *Analysis*:   Examining and evaluating data; presenting
                          alternative actions in relation to the evaluation
                          is frequently involved.
6. *Computing*:   Performing arithmetic operations and report-
                          ing on and/or carrying out a prescribed action
                          in relation to them. Does not include
                          counting.
7. *Collating*:   Gathering and classifying information about
                          data, people, and things; reporting and/or car-
                          rying out a prescribed action in relation to the
                          information is frequently involved.
8. *Comparing*:   Judging the readily observable functional,
                          structural, or compositional characteristics
                          (whether similar to or divergent from obvious
                          standards) of data, people, or things.
9. *Copying*:   Transcribing, entering, or posting.
10. *Observing*:   Learning as an adaptive function to the area of
                          data, people, or things.

THINGS

1. *Designing*:   Fashioning according to a plan; sketching as
                          a pattern or model; conceiving of or executing
                          a scheme or plan.

2. *Precision working*: Using body members and/or tools to guide objects or materials where responsibility for standards occurs.

3. *Building*: Setting up and/or adjusting machine/equipment by replacing/altering tools, jigs, fixture, or attachments.

4. *Operating*: Starting, stopping, and controlling the actions of machines.

5. *Manipulating*: Moving, guiding, or placing objects. Involves some judgment with regard to precision.

6. *Inspecting*: Observing functioning; adjusting materials or controls of machine. Involves little use of judgment.

7. *Repairing*: Restoring to sound condition after breakdown or injury.

8. *Collecting*: Assembling; accumulating in one place for future or anticipated use; also, gathering for study and appraisal.

9. *Maintaining*: Upkeep of property, equipment, tools. Also involves establishing schedule for regular maintenance of same to minimize production "downtime."

10. *Purchasing*: Obtaining goods, materials, equipment at most advantageous price; i.e., to keep costs at lowest possible levels.

Now write a rough draft of a new résumé, based on your new career objective.

Research is the persistent disciplined effort to make sense and order out of the phenomena of subjective experience.
—Carl Rogers, *On Becoming a Person*

Standard Industrial Classification (S.I.C.) Lists

Go to your local library. Start your research by using the list of references and resources that follows here, beginning with the *Standard Industrial Classification (S.I.C) Manual* published by the Bureau of the Budget.

Plan on spending a minimum of two sessions with the S.I.C. manual. It catalogs many major fields of endeavor and lists them in a four-digit "S.I.C. code number." Carefully look through the entire book listing. Note by S.I.C. number and name any field that has inherent interest to you.

Do not make choices on the basis of training or experience! We want gut-level decisions here!

You may come up with as many as twenty to sixty possibilities on your first run through the publication. When you are ready, pick out the top twelve fields that really interest you.

Then narrow your list down to a preferential list of six fields with your prime choice at the top. Once again, this list should reflect your inner desires, *not* your education and training!

Use the following forms (or your notebook) for the record of your research.

○ **First List**

S.I.C. #	Product or Service	S.I.C. #	Product or Service

_____   _____
_____   _____
_____   _____
_____   _____
_____   _____
_____   _____
_____   _____
_____   _____
_____   _____
_____   _____
_____   _____
_____   _____
_____   _____
_____   _____
_____   _____
_____   _____
_____   _____
_____   _____
_____   _____
_____   _____
_____   _____
_____   _____

○ **Intermediate List**

S.I.C. #   Product or Service   S.I.C. #   Product or Service

_____   _____
_____   _____
_____   _____
_____   _____
_____   _____
_____   _____

_____   _____

_____   _____

_____   _____

○ **Final List, in Order of Preference**

Prime area
of interest: _____

2nd choice: _____

3rd choice: _____

4th choice: _____

5th choice: _____

6th choice: _____

Library Resource Materials

Standard Industrial Classification Manual (S.I.C. Manual)
Classifies and assigns numerical code to industries and lists both
manufacturing and nonmanufacturing concerns by title, alphabetically, and numerically by S.I.C. numbers.

Dun and Bradstreet (D&B) Both middle and million markets
   Alphabetical—company names, addresses, phone numbers,
   annual sales, total employees, S.I.C. numbers, names, and func-
   tions of divisions, executive names.
   Geographically with S.I.C. numbers
   S.I.C. number listing
   By product classifications

*Standard and Poors Register of Corporations, Directors and
Executives*
   Lists companies by S.I.C. numbers and alphabetically with S.I.C.
   numbers
   Alphabetical corporation directory
   Register of Directors and Executives—includes names, business

and home addresses, school attended, graduation year, positions held
Geographical index

Thomas's Register
Volumes 1–6: Geographical listing of American manufacturers
Volume 7: Trademark listings
Location of a company's plants
Capital ratings of some companies
Company officers
Subsidiary companies

Klein's Directory of Directors
Directory of corporation directors and executives

Moody's Industrial Manual
Comprehensive source of information on industrial corpora-tions, with capital structure tables, financial statements on some companies, statistical record of selected companies

Local and State Manufacturers Registers Directories for:
Telephone companies
Chambers of Commerce
Boards of Trade
Trade Associations
Foundations
Environmental protection

Special Industry Reference Books
Some examples:
Who's Who in insurance
Directory of the forest products industry
World mines register
PR blue book
Gebbie house magazine directory
Who's Who in consulting
Shopping center directory
Who Makes Machinery

U.S. Department of Labor, *The Dictionary of Occupational Titles,*
2 vols. plus supplements. Invaluable aid to expand one's personal conception of careers available. Job descriptions and a tabular

listing of jobs are grouped by function. Trait categories that can cut across conventional job fields are discussed.

Vocational Pamphlets. These types of publications can give a good overview of a broad subject area (chemistry, mathematics, health occupations, etc.) and may include publications from professional organizations and periodicals in the specialized area of interest.

Periodical Indexes. These indexes are guides to current magazine materials that include the most recent articles on employment and the vocational field.

United States Employers.
Directory of Corporate Affiliations. A master list of corporations, their officials, and subsidiaries. Includes cross-index of subsidiaries, listing parent companies. Published annually.
Association of Commerce and Industry's Directory of Commerce and Industry. Lists Long Island companies engaged in Industry or services. More or less limited to larger companies. Arranged by product, community, and company name. A similar one may be available in your area—check with your local Chamber of Commerce or public library.
Specific Territories . . . Classified Business Directory. Includes information on companies in New York City, Long Island, Northern New Jersey, Westchester County and Southern Connecticut. Classified by product, the entries provide name, address, and phone number of companies. Annual. Check to see if a similar guide is available in your area.
State Industrial Directories. Companies all through the states, arranged by county. Particularly useful for its listing of companies in the New York metropolitan area. Annual.
Rand McNally International Bankers Directory. Lists banks of every type by state within the U.S. and by country throughout the world. Special section gives synopsis of banking and commercial laws of each state and Canadian province. Published twice a year.
MacRae's Blue Book. Similar to *Thomas's Register* (above) but lacks geographical location index. Also annual.

Overseas Employers.
(These are just a sample of available international guides. Check the reference shelves in the HF 3400 and 4000 catalog area for

other directories such as *Directory of Israel, Jaegar's Europa Register, Sell's Directory of Products and Services,* and the *Standard Trade Index of Japan.*)

Directory of American Firms Operating in Foreign Countries. Part 1 is an alphabetical list of American corporations, giving address, officers, line of business, and foreign countries where each one operates. Part 2 lists by country the American firms operating there, giving local name and address.

Dun and Bradstreet, Inc.'s Principal International Businesses. Section 1 lists business under country. Section 2 is a listing by product, subdivided by country. Section 3 is an alphabetical list by company name, giving address. Annual.

Jane's Major Companies of Europe. An informative annual guide to major European companies, similar in format to *Standard and Poor's Register of Corporations, Directors and Executives.*

Kelly's Directory of Manufacturers and Markets. A foreign counterpart to *Thomas's Register,* divided into two parts—one for the United Kingdom and the other international. Each has alphabetical lists (classified, exporters, importers) with a separate "Trades and Services" index.

Encyclopedia of Associations, Gale Research Co., Detroit, Michigan, 12th edition, 1978.

Occupational Outlook Handbook, U.S. Department of Labor, latest edition.

Local Newspapers, especially the Sunday classified ads and the Sunday business and finance sections; the Tuesday *Wall Street Journal* and the Sunday *New York Times.* (In the *Times,* jobs in finance, sales, market research, engineering, the sciences, computer technology, and profit oriented management are in the Business and Finance Section; jobs in health, education, social work, special types of counseling and the nonprofit area of management are in the Week in Review section.)

Area phone books. In the White Pages, check key words; in the Yellow Pages, check categories of interest. You can find telephone books for distant locations at phone company headquarters and some central libraries.

Trade papers and magazines.

The Federal Telephone Directory, the *Federal Employment Directory* (personnel officers for vacancy announcements), the *Congressional Directory* and the *Congressional Staff Directory.* Check these and other publications of the U.S. Printing Office, Washington, D.C.

Professional Organizations

Association membership lists of countless professional organizations will enable you to get in touch with people in the field you want to explore. Here are some examples of the types of organizations that are available as networks and resource centers in many fields. Look over this partial list and use it as a guide when compiling your own. Then research the organizations in your field or fields.

Advertising
   American Advertising Federation
   American Association of Advertising Agencies

Accounting
   American Institute of Certified Public Accountants
   National Association of Accountants

Banking
   American Bankers Association
   American Institute of Banking

Broadcasting
   National Association of Broadcasters

Information/Data Processing
   American Federation of Information Processing Societies, Inc.
   Data Processing Management Associations

Insurance
   American Mutual Insurance Alliance
   Institute of Life Insurance
   Insurance Information Institute
   Life Insurance Marketing and Research Association

Special Libraries Association

Marketing
American Marketing Association

Personnel
American Society for Personnel Administration

Planning
American Institute of Planners

Psychology
American Psychological Association

Public Relations
Public Relations Society of America, Inc.

Publishing
American Newspaper Guild
Association of American Publishers, Inc.

Purchasing
National Association of Purchasing Management, Inc.

Research
Research and Information Department
The Newspaper Guild

Realty
National Association of Realtors

Retail
National Retail Merchants Association
National Association for Female Executives
Chamber of Commerce for the U.S.

Now make your own lists from your research, in your notebook.

○ **Resource Centers**

There are many different local resource centers to help you today with your career development and job search. Check with your Y's, local colleges, state and county governments, public library, etc.

One resource center you may want to contact is Catalyst, 250
Park Avenue South, New York, NY 10003, (212) 777-8900. Catalyst
is an information clearinghouse specializing in careers and career
planning. Write or call them for a list of local resources centers in
the Catalyst national network of career centers for women (some
also serve men), and for a list of their publications.

List your own local resource centers in your notebook.

❀ Communication

What Happens between You and Others

○ **Interview Questions**

Questions You Must Be Ready to Answer

First think about your answers. Then write them out. Finally, role-play an interview with your consultant or a competent peer. What is the question *really* asking? Take time to think before your answer. There are no pat answers. If you are unsure, ask for clarification from the interviewer. During your interview, answer the question directly and to the point. Give *only* the facts needed to satisfy the questioner. Be truthful, but do not offer unsolicited information that could detract from your potential. Focus and refocus attention on your skills, strengths, and related accomplishments as you respond.

1. Tell me about yourself.
2. What are your greatest strengths and skills?
3. What are some of your weaknesses or failures?
4. Is this a career switch?
5. Do you think that your education qualifies you for this position?
6. Actually, this position is below your ability level, isn't it?
7. How much money do you want?
8. You are too old (or too young). We were thinking of a person about——.
9. Why do you want to work here?
10. Why did you leave your last job?
11. Why did you leave the ones prior to the last one?
12. How long have you been out of work?
13. What have you been doing all this time?

14. What did you like best and least in your last job?
15. Tell me about the best boss you ever had. The worst!
16. Tell me about the hardest job you've ever performed.
17. If you had your choice of jobs, what would you like to do most?
18. Tell me about your health.
19. How do you spend your spare time?
20. Have you done anything to improve yourself during the last year? What?
21. What do you think management can do to help you function at your best?
22. If you were choosing a person for this job, what kind of an individual would you select?
23. What does your spouse (or significant other person) think about your work?
24. Assuming we hire you, what do you see as your future?
25. Everybody has pet peeves. What are yours?
26. What does success mean to you? How do you measure success?
27. What do people criticize about you, and what do you criticize in other people?
28. If you feel any weakness pertaining to the job, what would it be?
29. Are you considering other positions at this time?
30. If you could relive your life, what changes would you make?
31. What else do you think I should know about you?

○ **Pre-Interview Information**

Duplicate this information form for each company you contact. It will be a valuable record to refer to during your job search.

Company or organization: _____

_____

_____

_____

Address and phone: _____

Contact and title: _____

Type of organization: _____

Products or services: _____

Private: _____ Public: _____

Parent Company: _____ Year of origin: _____

Source of contact: _____
                   (NEWSPAPER, OTHER PERSON, RESEARCH SOURCE, ETC.)

Telephone contacts: _____
                   (INCLUDE DATES, NAMES, ETC.; ATTACH QUESTIONS)

_____

_____

_____

_____

_____

_____

_____

Questions: (List on a separate sheet.)

Research completed: (Include information from basic research, annual report, visits, newspaper articles, trade publications, company newsletter, library, etc. Record on a separate sheet for future reference.)

Use your notebook for recording post-interview information.

○ Post-Interview Information

Duplicate this information form. Use it to record information obtained during and after the interview.

Company or organization: _____

Address and phone: _____

Date of interview: _____ Time: _____

Interviewer: _____ Title: _____

Points discussed: _____

_____

_____

_____

Positions discussed? Offered? Yes ___ ___ No _____

Describe functions: _____

_____

_____

_____

Pay offered: $ _____ base $ or % (circle)

Commissions: _____   Bonus: _____

Pension: _____   Relocation pay: _____

Vacation/other leave: _____

Medical plan: _____   Retirement: _____

Other perks: _____
(INCLUDE INFORMATION ON USE OF COMPANY CAR, OWN OFFICE, CLERICAL HELP, ETC.)

Action: _____

_____

_____

Date/time of next interview: _____

Comments: _____

_____

Referrals: _____

Use your notebook to critique each interview.

Interview Critique Form

Duplicate this form and use it for each interview you attend.

Interview with: _____

_____

_____

Date/time: _____

Length of interview: _____

Interviewer talked _____% of the time.

I talked _____% of the time.

Questions I wrote out to prepare for this interview were in number.
(Attach list of your questions to this sheet.)

Problems I experienced in interview: _____

_____

_____

Way I feel interviewer perceived me: _____

_____

_____

My style during interview could be described as: _____

_____

Follow-up letter sent on: _____
(See guidelines on the following page.)

Called consultant to review progress on: _____

Additional comments: _____

_____

_____

_____

_____

_____

After networking interviews
1. Thank interviewer for her or his time.
2. If possible, mention a new idea that was stimulated by your conversation.
3. Express appreciation for any additional suggestions for action that you received.

After interviews with officials of corporations or organizations when you are exploring career opportunities
1. Thank interviewer for her or his time. (Sometimes the person who says "thank you" gets the job!)
2. Include a new idea that came to you after you left.
3. Recap highlights of interview.
4. Express enthusiasm about the position or possible ones.
5. Restate time for next appointment (if applicable).
6. Thank official for any additional introductions or leads.

○ People Resource List

People you meet or already know can be one of your best sources of information and help, no matter what their actual positions may be. Keep lists of people you know and meet, and use them frequently. Go through your company phone book, alumni newsletter, holiday card list, church friends, personal phone book, professional or other club membership list, etc. to build a complete list of "people" resources.

Remember: Almost anyone can be a good resource for referrals. Don't overlook *anyone*—your child's teacher, long-lost relatives, grocer, dry-cleaner clerk, tennis partner, dentist, people you meet on the plane, subway, or bus or in the parking lot. Include the following categories and add as many others as you can.

People I work with now
People I have worked with previously
Former teachers or professors
Club members, fraternity brothers or sorority sisters, etc.
Other professional connections
Relatives
Neighbors
Friends—present and past
Friends of friends

○ **Professional Networks**

List appropriate networks—formal and informal professional groups under this heading. Use this list as your guide when contacting them. (Also see the examples of professional organizations given in Step 8.)

_____

_____

_____

_____

_____

_____

_____

_____

_____

_____

_____

_____

_____

_____

_____

_____

_____

_____

_____

_____

_____

_____

_____

_____

○ **An Ad for Yourself**

After you have done all the things suggested up to this point, read back over the materials in your notebook and your worksheets. Consider your career goals again. Think about who you are, what you know about yourself. Then write an ad for yourself.

Include in your ad all your attributes and characteristics that are pertinent to the career you seek. Describe your qualifications for the job. Think of yourself as a "product." What would a Madison Avenue copywriter say about your skills, your experience, and your potential in a newspaper ad or television commercial?

Make your ad for yourself as interesting and yet complete as possible. *Remember*: you are competing with lots of other products in the marketplace—both different and similar. What makes you special? Try to capture it in your ad.

❧ Eternity

Assimilating the New Form into Your Life

_____

○ Your Obituary Column

Write a news story that you would like published in your local paper when you die. Include as many elements of a good story as you can. Don't be afraid to use your imagination and be as "far out" as you want!

When will you "go"?
Where will you be?
How will you "go"?
Who will you be remembered as?
What will you have accomplished? (Include positions held, publications, honors, children and grandchildren, etc.)
Why should anyone remember you?

_____

_____

_____

_____

_____

_____

_____

_____

_____

You will want to continue to form images to help you as you develop in your career and your life. Creativity is part of you, an essential part of your life.

One way to use your creativity is through imagining your concept of paradise. It can be an ideal place you create for yourself in your mind. It can be the place you see as your ultimate goal—where you want to "live" forever in your next cycle.

Imagine the perfect resting place or mental workshop, free of all the stress of modern life. What does it look like? How would you describe it?

Let your image of paradise be a place that gives you a peaceful, calm, relaxed feeling. Go there in your mind when you need rejuvenation. It can be a good source of mental and spiritual energy at times when you find that your career or job search demands more than you think you can give.

Now draw a picture of your idea of paradise here or in your notebook. Then describe it in words. Begin to envision yourself living there "forever."

❀ Notes

Preface

1. James Joyce, *Ulysses* (New York: Modern Library, 1946), pp. 184, 210.

2. The dictionary gives two ways of spelling this word—*wholistic* and *holistic*. I have chosen to use *holistic* since the myths have close identification with the religious context and root word *holy*.

3. This project, under my direction, resulted in a book, *A Job at the End: Guidelines for Teen Counseling Training and Career Development*, published by National Board, YWCA, 135 West 50 St., New York, NY 10020.

4. Carl Jung, *Memories, Dreams, Reflections* (London: Collins & Routledge & Kegan Paul, 1963), p. 35.

Part One. Basic Assumptions

1. David Maclagan, *Creation Myths* (London: Thames & Hudson, 1977), pp. 5, 6, 8.

2. Sir Arthur Eddington, *Nature of the Physical World* (Ann Arbor: University of Michigan Press, 1958).

3. Archibald Macleish, *J.B.* (Boston: Houghton Mifflin, 1957), pp. 152–153.

4. Paul Tillich, *Systematic Theology* (Chicago: University of Chicago Press, 1957), p. 34.

5. Ibid.

6. Martin Buber, *I-Thou* (New York: Scribners, 1958).

7. H. Westman, *The Springs of Creativity* (New York: Atheneum, 1961), p. 83.

8. Ibid.

9. Rollo May, *Courage to Create* (New York: Norton, 1975), p. 27.

10. Maclagan, p. 16.

11. From Gary Snyder, *Turtle Island*, cited in Maclagan, p. 23.

12. Rollo May, *Man's Search for Himself*, (New York: Norton, 1951), p.136.

13. Heinrich Zimmer, *Philosophies of India*, Bollingen Series XXVI (New York: Pantheon, 1951), p. 300.

14. Translation by Tagore in *Personality* (London: Macmillan, 1959), pp. 25–27.   *285*

15. Maclagan, p. 25.

16. Maclagan, p. 8.

17. Maclagan, p.24.

18. I am aware of the sexist implications (God is male, and man is dominant, made prior to the creation of woman) in certain variations of the creation myths. The Genesis account has two versions. I choose to accept the one that is nonsexist. The ancient Lillith myth has the female as the dominant sex. Many prefer this account.

Part Two. Introduction

1. Nicholas Berdyaev, *The Divine and the Human* (London: Blis, 1949), chap. 13.

2. In the course of my work, I recognize that the creative character of career development is at the point where personal mythology connects with universal mythology. I am able to activate the client's creativity through an approach derived from the creation myths. The subsection titled "Recalling the Creation Myths" delineates this connection.

3. I learned this concept from a Psychosynthesis workshop conducted in New York by Harry Sloan, of the faculty of the Synthesis Institute for Study of Man in San Francisco.

Chapter 1

1. The phrase "success factors" was first coined by Bernard Haldane, a pioneer in career development.

Chapter 2

1. Mary Caroline Richards, *Centering in Pottery, Poetry, and the Person* (Middletown, Conn.: Wesleyan University Press, 1964), p. 23.

2. Rainer Maria Rilke, *Letters to a Young Poet*, transl. M. D. Herter Norton (New York: Norton, 1934), pp. 18–21.

3. Edmund Fuller, *Man in Modern Fiction* (New York: Random House, 1949), pp. 163–164.

4. Adapted from an exercise I did during the est training.

Chapter 3

1. Sigmund Freud, *On Creativity and the Unconscious: Papers on the Psychology of Art, Literature, Love, Religion* (New York: Harper Colophon, 1958).

2. Archibald MacLeish, *Poetry and Experience* (Boston: Houghton Mifflin, 1961),
p.8.

3. Ideas in this section are based on theories developed in *Alternate States of Consciousness* (New York: Wiley, 1969) and *Language of the Brain* (New York: Free Press, 1977).

Chapter 4

1. Lewis J. Sherrill, *The Struggle of the Soul* (New York: Macmillan, 1952), p. 10.

Chapter 5

1. Donald W. MacKinnon in *Saturday Review*, February 10, 1962.

Chapter 6

1. William Wordsworth, "Preface to Second Edition of Lyrical Ballads," from "Preface," in *Lyrical Ballads and Other Poems* (London: Methuen, 1965).

2. Quotations in this section are from Stephen Spender's "The Making of a Poem," in *The Creative Process*, ed. Brewster Ghiselin (New York: New American Library, 1952).

3. Paul Valéry, "The Course of Poetics: First Lesson," in *The Creative Process*.

4. Ideas in this section have been drawn from Silvano Arietti's *Creativity: The Magic Synthesis*, chap. 3, "Imagery" (New York: Basic Books, 1976), pp. 37–52.

5. Finley Eversole, *The Politics of Creativity*, quoted by Elizabeth O'Connor, *Eighth Day of Creation, Gifts and Creativity*, (Waco, Tex.: Word Books, 1971), p. 59.

6. Hermann Hesse, *Demian* (New York: Harper & Row, 1965), p. 80.

7. This is Paul Tillich's phrase.

Chapter 7

1. Lewis J. Sherrill, *The Gift of Power* (New York: Macmillan, 1959).

2. See Erich Fromm's *The Forgotten Language* (New York: Grove, 1956) for a fuller description.

3. Spender, op cit., pp. 112–122.

4. For a description of this struggle, read "Imagination and Experience," in *The Writer's Book*, ed. Helen Hull (New York: Barnes & Noble, 1959), pp. 42–54.

5. Edward Sapir, *Language* (New York: Harcourt Brace, 1949), p. 221.

6. Joyce, op cit., p. 184.

7. Martin Buber, *Between Man and Man* (Boston: Beacon, 1955).

8. Abraham Maslow, *Toward a Psychology of Being* (New York: Van Nostrand, 1962), p. 191.

9. Marie-Louise von Franz, *Interpretation of Fairy Tales* (New York: Spring, 1970), chap. 6, p. 12).

10. Sherrill, *The Gift of Power*, pp. 124–125.

Chapter 8

1. Rabindranath Tagore, "Vision," *Hungry Stones and Other Stories* (New York: Macmillan, 1916), p. 151.

2. J. Krishnamurti, *Think on These Things* (New York: Harper & Row, 1964), pp. 40, 47, 52–53, 155.

3. Taken from a tape of Lyall Watson, author of *Super Nature*, *The Romeo Error*, and *Gifts of Unknown Things*. I heard him tell this story at the New Dimensions Conference.

Chapter 9

1. See Sheldon Kopp, *If You Meet the Buddha on the Road, Kill Him* (Lomod, Calif.: Science and Behavior Books, 1972).

2. *The Complete Short Stories of Mark Twain* (Garden City, N.Y.: Hanover House, 1957), pp. 272–294.

3. Paul Tillich's words, op. cit.

4. David Spangler in a speech at the New Dimensions Conference.

5. Ibid.

Chapter 10

1. Nicholas Berdyaev, *The Destiny of Man* (London: Blis, Centenary Press, 1937).

2. Somerset Maugham, *Cakes and Ale* (New York: Penguin, 1977).

3. High Prather, *Notes to Myself* (Lafayette, Calif.: Real People Press, 1979)

4. Maslow, *Toward a Psychology of Being* pp. 201, 204.

5. Muses, *New Dimensions of Consciousness*.

🌿 Bibliography

*When you dream alone, it is but a dream. But when we
dream together, it is but the beginning of reality.*
—Brazilian proverb

○ Recommended Career Guides

These books will help you get started in your actual job search—
after you know *who* you are and *what* you have to offer. (The books
listed in the Bibliography that follows are for more leisurely reading. They include works of psychology and philosophy as well as
more practical guides to career and personal development; they also
include the works that form the basis of my research into creativity.)

Bird, Caroline. *Everything a Woman Needs to Know to Get Paid
    What She's Worth*, edited by Helene Mandelbaum. New York:
    David McKay, 1973 (updated annually).
Bolls, Richard N. *What Color is Your Parachute?* Berkeley: Ten Speed
    Press (updated annually).
Catalyst Staff. *What to Do with the Rest of Your Life*. New York:
    Simon & Schuster, 1980.
Catalyst. *Marketing Yourself*. New York: Bantam Books, 1980.
———. *Making the Most of Your First Job*. New York: Ballantine
    Books, 1981.
———. *Upward Mobility*. New York: Warner Books, 1983.
———. *When Can You Start?* New York: Macmillan, 1981.
———. *It's Your Future*. Princeton, N.J.: Peterson's Guides.
Figler, Howard. *The Complete Job-Search Handbook*. New York:
    Holt, Rinehart & Winston, 1979.
Josefowitz, Natasha. *Paths to Power*, Reading, Massachusetts:
    Addison-Wesley, 1980.

○ References and Other Recommended Books

Adler, Alfred. *Understanding Human Nature*, translated by W. Biran
    Wolfe. Greenwich, Connecticut: Fawcett World, 1968.
Alexander, Shana. *Women's Legal Rights (Marriage, Divorce,*

290   *Children, Work, Abortion, Rape, Death and Taxes).* Los Angeles: Wollstonecraft, 1975.

Arietti, Silvano. *Creativity, The Magic Synthesis.* New York: Basic Books, 1976.

Assagioli, Roberto. *Psychosynthesis.* New York: Viking, 1975.

———. *The Act of Will.* Baltimore: Penguin, 1974.

Bach, Richard. *Illusions.* New York: Dell, 1977.

Barr, Beryl. *Wonders, Warriors and Beasts Abounding.* Garden City, N.Y.: Doubleday, 1967.

Bartley, III, W. W. *Werner Erhard.* New York: Clarkson N. Potter, 1978.

Berdyaev, Nicholas. *The Destiny of Man.* London: Centenary, 1937.

———.*The Divine and the Human.* London: Centenary, 1949.

Berne, Eric. *Transactional Analysis in Psychology.* New York: Grove, 1961.

———. *What Do You Do after You Say Hello?* New York: Grove, 1972.

Billings, Victoria. *The Womansbook.* Los Angeles: Wollstonecraft,1974.

Bloom, Lynn; Coburn, Karen; and Pearlman, Joan. *The New Assertive Woman.* New York: Dell, 1975.

Bodkin, Maude. *The Quest for Salvation in Ancient and Modern Play.* Oxford: Oxford University Press, 1941.

Bostwick, Burdette E. *Resume Writing.* New York: John Wiley and Sons, 1980.

Bonhoeffer, Dietrich. *Life Together.* New York: Harper and Row, 1954.

Buber, Martin. *Between Man and Man.* Boston: Beacon Press, 1955.

———. *I-Thou.* New York: Scribners, 1958.

Butler, Pamela. *Self-Assertion for Women.* San Francisco: Harper & Row, 1976.

Campbell, Joseph. *The Flight of the Wild Gander.* New York: Viking, 1951.

———. *Myths to Live By.* New York: Bantam, 1972.

———. (with Bill Moyers). *The Power of the Myth.* New York: Doubleday, 1988.

Cane, Florence. *The Artist in Each of Us.* New York: Pantheon, 1951.

Castillejo, Irene Claremont de. *Knowing Woman: A Feminine Psychology.* New York: Pantheon, 1973.

Chrenzweig, Anton. *The Hidden Order of Art.* Berkeley: University of California Press, 1972.

Coffin, William Sloan. *Once to Every Man.* New York: Atheneum, 1977.

Corriera, Richard, and Hart, Joseph. *The Dream Makers*. New York:
Bantam, 1977.

Curran, Charles. *Religious Values in Counseling and Psychotherapy*.
New York: Sheed and Ward, 1969.

Curtis, Jean. *A Guide for Working Mothers*. New York: Simon &
Schuster, 1975.

Daly, Mary. *Beyond God the Father*. Boston: Beacon Press, 1973.

Davy, Charles. *Toward a Third Culture*. London: Faber & Faber, 1961.

Dible, Donald M. *Up Your Own Organization: A Handbook for the
Employed, the Unemployed, and the Self-Employed on How to
Start and Finance a New Business*. Santa Clara, Calif.:
Entrepreneur Press, 1972.

Driver, Tom F. *Patterns of Grace*. San Francisco: Harper & Row, 1977.

Drucker, Peter. *Management: Tasks, Responsibilities, Practices*. New
York: Harper & Row, 1973.

Eddington, Sir Arthur. *Nature of the Physical World*. Ann Arbor:
University of Michigan Press, 1958.

Ellis, John. *A Financial Guide for the Self-Employed: Taxes,
Employees, Accountants, Insurance, Bill Collecting, Loans, Time
Management, Retirement, Paperwork*. Chicago: Henry Regnery,
1972.

Erickson, Eric. *Childhood and Society*. New York: Norton, 1963.

Eversole, Finley. "The Politics of Creativity," quoted by O'Connor,
Elizabeth, *Eighth Day of Creation, Gifts and Creativity*. Waco,
Tex.: Word Books, 1971.

Fagan, Joan, and Shepherd, Urma Lee (eds.). *Gestalt Therapy Now*.
New York: Harper & Row, 1970.

Fasteau, Marc. *The Male Machine*. New York: McGraw-Hill, 1974.

Fensterheim, Herbert, and Baer, Jean. *Don't Say Yes When You Want
to Say No*. New York: Dell, 1975.

Freud, Sigmund. *On Creativity and the Unconsciousness: Papers on
the Psychology of Art, Literature, Love, Religion*. New York: Harper & Row, 1958.

Friday, Nancy. *My Mother/My Self: The Daughter's Search for Identity*. New York: Delacourt, 1977.

Friedman, Martha. *Overcoming the Fear of Success*. New York: Warren Books, 1980.

Friedman, Sande, and Schwarz, Lois C. *No Experience Necessary: A
Guide to Employment for the Female Liberal Arts Graduate*. New
York: Dell, 1971.

Fromm, Erich. *The Forgotten Language*. New York: Grove, 1956.

Fuller, Edmund. *Man in Modern Fiction*. New York: Random House, 1949.

Garfield, Patricia. *Creative Dreaming*. New York: Ballantine, 1974.

Geri, Georgine. *Man and His Images*. New York: Viking, 1968.

Ghiselin, Brewster (ed.). *The Creative Process*. New York: New American Library, 1952.

Goldenthal, Allan B. *The Teenage Employment Guide*. New York: Simon & Schuster, 1969.

Goodman, Joseph. *How to Publish, Promote and Sell Your Book*. Chicago: Adams, 1970.

Gornick, Vivian, and Moran, Barbara K. *Women in Sexist Society*. New York: Basic Books, 1971.

Greene & Lattimore (eds.). *The Complete Greek Drama*. Chicago: University of Chicago Press, 1959.

Hall, Calvin. *A Primer of Freudian Psychology*. New York: Mentor, 1954.

Hall, Calvin, and Nordly, Vernon J. *A Primer of Jungian Psychology*. New York: Mentor, 1974.

Hamilton, Edith. *Mythology*. Boston: Little Brown, 1942.

Handel, Lawrence. *The Job Handbook for Postcollege Cop-outs*. New York: Pocket Books, 1973.

Harding, M. Esther. *The Way of All Women*. New York: Harper Colophon, 1970.

Harvey, Joan C., with Katz, Cynthia. *If I'm So Successful, Why Do I Feel Like a Fake?* New York: St. Martin's Press, 1985.

Harragan, Betty. *Games Mother Never Taught You*. New York: Warner, 1977.

Henderson, Bill. *The Publish It Yourself Handbook: Literary Tradition and How To*. Yonkers, N.Y.: Pushcart, 1973.

Hennig, Margaret, and Jardim, Anne. *The Managerial Woman*. New York: Simon and Schuster, 1978.

Henry, Leon, Jr. *The Home Office Guide: How to Work at Home and Like It*. New York: Arco, 1977.

Hesse, Hermann. *Demian*. New York: Harper & Row, 1965.

Hill, Napoleon. *Think and Grow Rich*. New York: Fawcett Crest, 1985.

Hole, Judith, and Levine, Ellen. *Rebirth of Feminism*. New York: Quadrangle, 1971.

Horney, Karen. *Feminine Psychology*. New York: Norton, 1967.

Hull, Helen (ed.). "Imagination and Experience," in *The Writer's Book*. New York: Barnes and Noble, 1956.

Hyatt, Carole. *The Woman's Setting Game*. New York: Warner Books, 1979.

Janeway, Elizabeth. *Between Myth and Morning*. New York: William Morrow, 1974.

Jessup, Claudia, and Chipps, Genie. *The Woman's Guide to Starting a Business*. New York: Holt, Rinehart & Winston, 1976.

Johnson, Willis (ed.). *Directory of Special Programs for Minority Group Members: Career Information Services, Employment Skills Banks, Financial Aid*. Garrett Park, Md.: Garrett Park Press, 1978.

Joward, Sidney. *The Transparent Self*. New York: Van Nostrand, 1971.

Joyce, James. *Ulysses*. New York: Modern Library, 1946.

Jung, Carl. *Man and His Symbols*. New York: Doubleday, 1964.

———. *Four Archetypes, Mother/Rebirth/Spirit/Trickster*. Princeton: Princeton University Press, Bollingen Series, 1959.

———*Memories, Dreams, Reflections*. London: Collins & Routledge & Kegan Paul, 1963.

———. *Symbols of Transformation*. Princeton: Princeton University Press, Bollingen Series, 1956.

———. *Mandala Symbolism*. Princeton: Princeton University Press, Bollingen Series, 1959.

———. *Collected Works*, 20 vols. 3rd ed. Princeton: Princeton University Press, 1968.

———. *Dreams*. Princeton: Princeton University Press, Bollingen Series, 1974.

Kalins, Dorothy. *Cutting Loose: A Civilized Guide for Getting Out of the System*. New York: Saturday Review, 1973.

Klein, Melanie. *Our Adult World and Its Roots in Infancy*. London: Tavistock, 1960.

Kopp, Sheldon. *If you Meet the Buddha on the Road, Kill Him.*. Lomond, Calif.: Science and Behavior Books, 1972.

Krishnamurti, J. *Think on These Things*. New York: Harper & Row, 1964.

Landau, Ellen. *Woman, Woman!* New York: Julian Messner, 1974.

Latner, Joel. *The Gestalt Therapy Book*. New York: Bantam, 1973.

Lederman, Janet. *Anger and the Rocking Chair*. New York: Viking, 1969.

Leith, Mysena A. *Summer Employment Directory of the United States*. 23rd ed. Washington: National Directive Service, 1974.

Lembeck, Ruth. *Job Ideas for Today's Woman for Profit, for Pleasure, for Personal Growth, for Self Esteem, Ways to Work Part-Time, Full-Time, Free-Lance at Home and in the Office and as an Entrepreneur*. Englewood Cliffs, N.J.: Prentice-Hall, 1974.

Leonard, George. *The Silent Pulse: A Search for the Perfect Rhythm That Exists in Each of Us*. New York: Bantam Books, 1981.

LeShane, Lawrence. *How to Meditate*. Boston: Bantam, 1974.

Lips, Hilary M. *Women, Men and the Psychology of Power*. Englewood Cliffs, N.J.: Prentice Hall, 1981.

Lowen, Alexander. *The Betrayal of the Body*. New York: Collier, 1967.

Lundberg, Ferdinand, and Farnjam, Marynia. *Modern Woman, The Lost Sex*. New York: Grosset & Dunlap, 1947.

Maclagan, David. *Creation Myths*. London: Thames & Hudson, 1977.

MacLeish, Archibald. *J.B.* Boston: Houghton Mifflin, 1957

———. *Poetry and Experience*. Boston: Houghton Mifflin, 1961.

Marine, Gene. *A Male Guide to Women's Liberation*. New York: Holt, Rinehart & Winston, 1972.

Maslow, Abraham. *Religious Values and Peak Experience*. New York: Penguin, 1976.

———. *Toward a Psychology of Being*. New York: Van Nostrand-Rinehold, 1962.

Maugham, Somerset. *Cakes and Ale*. New York: Arno, 1977.

May, Rollo. *Man's Search for Himself*. New York: Norton, 1951.

———. *Courage to Create*. New York: Norton, 1975.

McClure, Larry, and Buan, Carolyn (eds.). *Essays on Career Education*, Portland Ore.: N.W. Regional Educational Laboratory, 1973.

Meher Baba. *Discourses*. Rev. ed. Myrtle Beach, S.C.: Sheriar Press, 1987.

Miller, Jean Baker. *Toward a New Psychology of Women*, Boston: Beacon Press, 1977.

Millett, Kate. *Sexual Politics*. Garden City, N.Y.: Doubleday, 1970.

Mitchell, Joyce Slayton. *I Can Be Anything*. New York: College Entrance Examination Board, 1975.

Montans, Patrick J., and Higginson, Margaret V. *Career Life Planning for Americans*. New York: American Management Association, 1978.

Neugarten, Bernice. *Personality in Middle and Late Years*. New York: Atherton, 1964.

Nicholas, Ted. *How to Form Your Own Corporation without a Lawyer for under $50*. Wilmington, Delaware: Enterprise, 1973.

O'Connor, Elizabeth. *Eighth Day of Creation, Gifts and Creativity*. Waco, Tex.: Word Books, 1971.

O'Neil, Nena. *Shifting Gears*. New York: Avon, 1975.

Perls, Frederick S. *Gestalt Therapy Verbatim*. Lafayette, Calif.: Real People Press, 1974.

Pogrebin, Letty Cottin. *Getting Yours*. New York: Avon, 1975.

Polster, Ervine and Miriam. *Gestalt Therapy Integrated*. New York: Brunner/Mazel, 1973.

Prather, Hugh. *Notes to Myself*. Lafayette, Calif.: Real People Press, 1979.

Prentice, Barbara. *The Back to Work Handbook for Housewives: 500 Job and Career Ideas*. New York: Collier, 1971.

Pribram, Karl. *Alternate States of Consciousness and Language of the Brain*. New York: Free Press, 1977.

Progroff, Ira. *The Death and Rebirth of Psychology*. New York: McGraw-Hill, 1956.

———. *The Symbolic and the Real*. New York: McGraw-Hill, 1963.

Reed, Ann, and Pfaltz, Marilyn. *Stop the World We Want to Get On*. New York: Scribners, 1974.

Reik, Theodore. *The Creation of Woman*. New York: McGraw-Hill, 1960.

Richards, Mary Caroline. *Centering in Pottery, Poetry, and the Person*. Middleton, Conn.: Wesleyan University Press, 1964.

———. *The Crossing Point*. Middleton, Conn.: Wesleyan University Press, 1966.

Rilke, Rainer Maria. *Letters to a Young Poet*. New York: Norton, 1934.

Ringer, Robert. *Looking Out for Number One*. New York: Fawcett Crest, 1977.

Rogers, Natalie. *Emerging Woman*. Point Reyes, Calif.: Personal Press, 1980.

Rolf, Ida P. *Structural Integration*. Boulder, Colo.: Rolf Institute of Structural Integration, 1963.

Rubin, David M. *The Independent Teen-ager: 350 Summer Jobs for High School Students*. New York: Collier, 1971.

Sapir, Edward. *Language*. New York: Harcourt Brace, 1949.

Schaef, Ann Wilson. *Women's Reality*. New York: Harper and Row, 1985.

Scobey, Joan, and McGrath, Lee Parr. *Creative Careers for Woman: A Handbook of Sources and Ideas for Part-Time Jobs*. New York: Simon & Schuster, 1968.

Scott, Miki. *The Working Woman: A Handbook*. Kansas City: Universal Press Syndicate, 1977.

Sheehy, Gail. *Passages: Predictable Crises for Adult Life*. New York: Dutton, 1974.

———. *Pathfinders*. New York: Morrow, 1981.

Sherrill, Lewis. *The Struggle of the Soul*. New York: Macmillan, 1952.

————. *The Gift of Power.* New York: Macmillan, 1959.

Sinetar, Marsha. *Do What You Love, the Money Will Follow.* New York: Panhit Press, 1987.

Smith, Manual J. *When I Say No I Feel Guilty.* New York: Bantam Books, 1975.

Snelling, Robert, Sr. *The Opportunity Explosion.* New York: New American Library, 1969.

Splaver, Sarah. *Non-Traditional Careers for Women.* New York: Julian Messner, 1973.

Steiner, Rudolph. *The Education of the Child.* London: Rudolph Steiner Press, 1965.

Stevens, Barry. *Don't Push the River.* Moab, Utah: Real People Press, 1970.

Tagore, Rabindranath. *Hungry Stones and Other Stories.* New York: Macmillan, 1916.

————. *Personality.* London: Macmillan, 1959.

Tillich, Paul. *Systematic Theology.* Vol 2. Chicago: University of Chicago Press, 1959.

Twain, Mark. "The Diary of Adam and Eve," from *The Complete Short Stories of Mark Twain.* Garden City, N.Y.: Hanover House, 1957.

Ullman, Liv. *Changing.* New York: Bantam, 1976.

von Franz, Marie-Louise. *Interpretation of Fairy Tales.* New York: Spring Publications, 1970.

Waisor, Charlotte (ed.). *The Creative Process.* New York: Bank Street College of Education, 1976.

Watters, Pat. *The Angry Middle-Aged Man.* New York: Viking, 1976.

Weaver, Peter. *You, Inc.* Garden City, N.Y.: Doubleday, 1973.

Westman, H. *The Springs of Creativity.* New York: Atheneum, 1961.

Wood, Jane. *Selling What You Make.* Baltimore: Penguin, 1973.

Wordsworth, William. *Lyrical Ballads.* London: Metheun, 1965.

Young, Jean and Jim. *Garage Sale Manual.* New York: Praeger, 1973.

Zimmer, Heinrich. *Philosophies of India.* Bollingen Series XXVI. New York: Pantheon, 1951.

Zinker, Joseph. *Creative Process in Gestalt Therapy.* New York: Random House, 1977.

About the Author

Hilda Lee Dail, Ph.D., is an international human resources consultant, a psychotherapist, and a career counselor who specializes in creativity and problem solving. She works with corporations, institutions, governmental agencies, professional groups, and individuals. She is an adjunct professor at Coastal Carolina College, University of South Carolina, and Webster University at Myrtle Beach (S.C.) Air Force Base. Dr. Dail has traveled throughout the world as a lecturer, educator, and consultant. Before opening her own business, she served on the executive staffs of four international organizations. An experiential psychotherapist certified by the American Expressive Association, she is also a member of the American Society for Training and Development and the American Association for Counseling and Development. She is the author of four previous books and has written hundreds of articles, including regular columns in Myrtle Beach newspapers. Currently she is president of the Mental Health Association in Horry County, South Carolina.